It Was Like a Fever

It Was Like a Fever

Storytelling in Protest and Politics

FRANCESCA POLLETTA

The University of Chicago Press   Chicago and London

FRANCESCA POLLETTA is associate professor of sociology at
Columbia University and the University of California, Irvine. She is
the author of *Freedom Is an Endless Meeting: Democracy in American
Social Movements* and coeditor of *Passionate Politics: Emotions and
Social Movements*, both published by the University of Chicago Press.

The University of Chicago Press, Chicago 60637
The University of Chicago Press, Ltd., London
© 2006 by The University of Chicago
All rights reserved. Published 2006
Printed in the United States of America

15 14 13 12 11   3 4 5

ISBN: 0-226-67375-8 (cloth)
ISBN: 0-226-67376-6 (paper)

Library of Congress Cataloging-in-Publication Data

Polletta, Francesca.
  It was like a fever : storytelling in protest and politics / Francesca Polletta.
    p. cm.
  Includes bibliographical references and index.
  ISBN 0-226-67375-8 (cloth : alk. paper) — ISBN 0-226-67376-6 (pbk. :
  alk. paper)
    1. Storytelling—Political aspects. 2. Communication—Political aspects.
  3. Politics and culture. 4. Communication in folklore. 5. Social movements. 6. Protest movements. I. Title.
    GR72.3.P65 2006
    808.5'43—dc22

                                                              2005027015

⊗ The paper used in this publication meets the minimum requirements of the American National Standard for Information Sciences—
Permanence of Paper for Printed Library Materials, ANSI Z39.48–1992.

Contents

Preface

In the grim dawn after the 2004 presidential election, Democratic Party strategists tried to figure out what had gone wrong. For much of the campaign, they thought they would win back the White House. President George W. Bush had led Americans into a war in Iraq with mounting casualties and no exit plan. Polls showed deep public concern about Bush's leadership and pessimism about the economy. The Democrats, for their part, had in John Kerry a respected Congressman and Vietnam War hero, and, for the first time in a long time, they had almost matched the Republicans in campaign fund-raising—spending $1.08 billion to the Republicans' $1.14 billion.[1]

What they did not have, Democratic strategists agreed in retrospect, was a good story. "A narrative is the key to everything," pollster Stanley Greenberg told reporters in an election postmortem. The Republicans "had a much more coherent attack and narrative that motivated their voters." James Carville, famous for engineering Bill Clinton's presidential victory in 1992, agreed: "I think we could elect somebody from the Hollywood Hills if they had a narrative to tell people about what the country is and where they see it." A few days later on *Meet the Press,* Carville again took up the narrative theme. "They produce a narrative, we produce a litany. They say, 'I'm going to protect you from the terrorists in Tehran and the homos in Hollywood.' We say, 'We're for clean air, better schools, more health care.' And so there's a Republican narrative, a story, and there's a Democratic litany." Close readers will note that "I'm going to protect you from the terrorists in Tehran and the homos in

Hollywood" are not narratives either. But Carville's listeners surely understood the difference. The Republicans gave voters villains and heroes; new characters in age-old dramas of threat, vengeance, and salvation. The Democrats ticked off a dry list of familiar issues.[2]

I mention Greenberg's and Carville's comments partly because I agree with them. I too believe that stories can win and lose elections, that they strengthen bonds of political belonging and clarify the stakes in issues in ways that compel people to take a stand. But I believe that stories do those things for reasons that have not been fully recognized. Good stories are not necessarily simple ones, with unambiguous moral punch lines. Rather, narrative's power stems from its complexity, indeed, its ambiguity. More than other discursive forms, narrative demands an effort of interpretation. Following a story means more than listening: it means filling in the blanks, both between unfolding events and between events and the larger point they add up to. When listeners or readers reach the story's end, they have the experience of loose ends being tied up. But the closure is never complete. The possibility remains that the same events told differently would have yielded a different normative point. Of course, all discursive forms are interpretable—formal arguments and commands as much as stories. But we *expect* to have to interpret stories. We expect their meaning to be both larger than the events they relate and allusive.

Take a story that, some say, won George Bush the 2004 election: a thirty-second television spot titled "Ashley's Story." The spot was produced by a conservative group, and it aired in nine contested states in the month before the election. It recounted sixteen-year-old Ashley Faulkner's meeting with the candidate at a campaign rally in Lebanon, Ohio. Ashley had lost her mother in the 2001 World Trade Center attack, and after that, the spot's narrator reported, she had "closed up emotionally." The narrator continued, "But when President George W. Bush came to Lebanon, Ohio, she went to see him, as she had with her mother four years before." As Bush made his way through the crowd of well-wishers, a friend of the Faulkners told him that Ashley's mother had been killed in the 9/11 attack. Bush turned and spontaneously embraced the girl, saying that he knew it was hard and asking if she was all right. "And it was at that moment," the family friend recounted, "that we saw Ashley's eyes fill up with tears." Ashley herself explained, "He's the most powerful man in the world and all he wants to do is make sure I'm safe, that I'm okay." The spot concluded with Ashley's father saying, "What I saw was what I want to see in the heart and soul of the man who sits in the highest elected office in our country."[3]

Of the spot's role in the election, *Advertising Age* later wrote, "We said, 'It might come down to one commercial,' and it may well have." Other publications also attested to the ad's success in swaying voters in battleground states. It is easy to see why. The spot showed a commander in chief who was deeply in touch with the human costs of terrorism. It showed a presidential candidate who was willing to go off-schedule and off-script to comfort a young girl in pain. It represented the 9/11 attack as something that was experienced by those in America's heartland, and represented its victims as Bush supporters.[4]

Especially interesting, though, is how the story turned on the ambiguity of the word *safe*. Ashley Faulkner said, "He's the most powerful man in the world and all he wants to do is make sure I'm safe, that I'm okay." Safe from what? The word means free from danger or injury, which we usually think of as physical. But safe also has a therapeutic meaning: safe in the sense of emotionally secure. One can read Ashley's comment as eliding the two. If she answered Bush's solicitous question—"Are you all right?"—in the affirmative, she would be attesting to her physical safety as well as her emotional recovery. Indeed, as the family friend recounted, the solicitous question *enabled* Ashley's emotional recovery: before it, she was emotionally closed; after it, she began to cry ("and it was at that moment that we saw Ashley's eyes fill up with tears"). The spot also turned the terrorist threat into something that had taken place in the past. Making Ashley safe meant easing the emotional aftereffects of a terrorist attack, not protecting her from future attack.

Ashley's story may have been powerful, then, not because of its simple message but because of its complex one: the president would make people safe by helping them to recover emotionally from a danger that the story—not events themselves—put in the past. In this book, I describe narratives that are even more ambiguous, and ambiguous in different ways. Although narrative's ambiguity, or, as I prefer to say, its openness to interpretation, can make for confusion, it can also generate political resources. In the following chapters, I show that stories in which words or images are oddly juxtaposed have helped disadvantaged groups to chip away at the conceptual oppositions responsible for the uneven benefits of social policies. Citizens have used stories with seemingly contradictory normative points in deliberative forums to arrive at unanticipated areas of agreement. In fledgling movements, stories that have obscured more than explained people's motivations for participation have served to mobilize others. On the floor of the United States Congress, stories with shifting points of view have created new bases for political authority.

This is not to say that, for disadvantaged groups, narrative creates only resources. To the contrary, most of the time, familiar stories reproduce the status quo. They make the conceptual oppositions behind social policies seem as if they capture reality: that, for example, people are either independent or dependent on others, not both, and that women who have been abused are either victimized or rational, not both. When groups challenge the status quo, the familiar stories they tell themselves as they strategize sometimes make it difficult for them to come up with tactics that are truly new. Alternatives to the familiar are never unthinkable. But they are unappealingly abstract in the first case and seem inappropriate in the second.

One of the things I try to do in this book is to shed light on the specific discursive mechanisms by which the canonical stories that make up a political common sense operate. But I also believe that for disadvantaged groups, the problem is not only popular stories but popular beliefs *about* storytelling. To explain, let me return to the 2004 presidential election. Veteran journalist William Safire too was struck by Carville's and Greenberg's comments about the electoral power of storytelling and devoted his weekly *New York Times Magazine* column that Sunday to what he said had become a "hot word," the "favorite son of the politerati": narrative. Safire quoted a series of academics attesting to the political importance of a good story—in the 2004 presidential campaign as well as in the notorious Starr Report on the Clinton-Lewinsky affair (which reported its findings in a section titled "Narrative") and in the 9/11 Commission Report (which became a bestseller). But Safire was actually skeptical of the power of stories. After rehearsing a narrative theorist's less than profound insight that the Democrats' main postelection narrative was about their lack of a coherent narrative, Safire quoted the same theorist acknowledging that if Americans had voted for Kerry instead of Bush, "the Democrats would probably be congratulating the Kerry campaign for having constructed a coherent narrative."[5]

Safire was on to more than he recognized. He was right to draw attention to a contemporary self-consciousness about narrative, one that extends beyond academics to political strategists, businesspeople, therapists, journalists, physicians, and others. Narrative has indeed become a hot topic. But Safire also captured, without reflecting upon, contemporary Americans' *mixed* views of narrative. Stories are commonly seen as normatively compelling (so a coherent narrative would virtually require that one vote Democrat or Republican). But they are also seen as simply rhetoric, with all the triviality the word implies. There are other tensions in popular views of storytelling. Stories are commonly thought of both as authentic and as deceptive ("telling my story" versus "telling stories"). They are seen as universal in their implications and as dangerously particularistic—idiosyncratic, even. Storytelling is appreciated, enjoyed, and distrusted.

This ambivalence is important, I believe, because it is rare that people hold negative and positive views of narrative at the same time. Instead, worries about the particularity, subjectivity, or deceptiveness of narrative are more likely to surface in some settings than in others and when stories are told by some people rather than others. To give just one example, in the 2000 election, George Bush's Democratic challenger the first time around told just the kind of stories that James Carville wanted to hear. Far from a litany of "clean air, better schools, more health care," Al Gore poignantly described a seventy-nine-year-old Iowa woman who was scavenging redeemable cans to pay for her prescription drugs, a Florida high school student forced to stand in her classroom without a desk because of budget cuts, and other Americans struggling to get by. But Gore was widely attacked for exaggerations when it emerged that the Iowa woman had an affluent son whose largesse she chose not to accept, and the student had had to stand for only one day. "You just knew that Al Gore couldn't make it through a 90-minute presidential debate—heck, probably couldn't even make it through a nine-minute debate—without telling some tall tale," one columnist wrote, and the Bush campaign managed to erase Gore's lead in the polls by attacking his alleged "problem" with the truth. Gore would say anything to get himself elected, critics charged. Bush, for his part, created nothing like the same storm of recrimination when it was revealed that he was promising twice as much in spending programs as his own budget allowed for and misrepresenting his tax plan as benefiting primarily the poor.[6]

It may have been that Gore lacked a knack for persuasive storytelling. But it also may have been that he was widely seen as an intellectual, a policy wonk. Since narrative is popularly thought of as the opposite of intellectual and is thought to persuade through its appeal to emotion rather than reason, Gore's use of the form may have triggered concerns both about the form's openness to manipulation and about Gore's manipulative intent. By extension, as long as Democrats are seen as the party of East Coast eggheads, their efforts to style themselves folksy raconteurs may be more difficult than Carville and Greenberg imagine. The bar for telling a credible story may be higher for Democrats than for Republicans.

To put it another way, some stories are more potent than others not because of their content or the skill with which they are told but because of assumptions made about their tellers. Likewise, if stories are seen as both normatively powerful and politically unserious, then their credibility or relevance may be questioned when they are told in discursive contexts that are considered technical, policy-oriented, information-driven, or otherwise politically serious. Unsurprisingly, people may avoid telling stories on such occasions or may tell them in ways that undercut their impact. I describe just these things happening in Congress, in court, and in citizens' deliberative forums. In each setting, I show how popular beliefs about the epistemological status of narrative have diminished the practical benefits of telling stories for disadvantaged groups.

The book's conclusion in this respect is that culture may curb challenge less through the canonical limits on what kinds of stories can be imagined than through the social conventions regarding when and how stories should be told. That conclusion has implications for scholars of culture as well as for scholars of political contention. It encourages us to pay attention not just to meaning but also to the social organization of the capacity to mean effectively—and it suggests how we might do so. It also has implications for those who engage in political contention, but not necessarily dispiriting ones. Rather, it suggests that change may come as much from challenging the norms of culture's use and evaluation as from challenging those of its content.

When I was a little girl, my sisters and I had such fine and easily tangled hair that having it combed out by our parents after our baths was painful. The ordeal was made bearable only by the stories my father recounted of an extraordinary girl named Snarly. Her exploits ran to rescuing fleets of storm-tossed ships and rounding up herds of errant cattle—always, of course, with her tangled hair. That was one of my first reckonings with the power of stories. Later, my father introduced me to the peculiar satisfactions of textual interpretation, and later still, to those of literary theory. One of the great pleasures in writing this book has been the long conversations we have had about narrative along the way. I thank Gregory Polletta for his keen insights, for the grace with which he listened to my fumbling attempts to parse ideas that surely seemed obvious to him, and for the sheer enthusiasm with which he tackled questions sociological as well as literary.

John Lee worked with me on all phases of the research described in chapter 4, and I thank him for his sharp insights and hard work. I am grateful too to Christopher Anderson, Neal Caren, Caroline Carr, M. Kai Ho, and Joshua Karp, who also helped with coding and analysis for that chapter. Linda Catalano did painstaking work in locating the sit-in accounts that are described in chapter 2. And I thank the many librarians and archivists who helped me locate references for that chapter and others.

Funding for the research described in chapter 4 was provided by the National Science Foundation Grant #IIS 0306868. Support from the ASA/NSF Fund for the Advancement of the Discipline, Harvard University's Hauser Center, and MIT's Sociology and Anthropology Department made it possible for Marshall Ganz, Susan Silbey, and me to gather an eclectic group of sociologists for two workshops on narrative in 2002. The discussions we had there proved critical to my own thinking about the topic. Revisions to the manuscript were made while I was a visiting scholar at the Russell Sage Foundation in 2004–5. Fellow scholars with a truly remarkable range of interests and a staff as intellectually engaged as it was supportive made the foundation an ideal environment in which to think and write.

Parts of chapter 2 appeared previously in "'It Was Like a Fever . . . ': Narrative and Identity in Social Protest," *Social Problems* 45 (May 1998): 137–59; © 1998 by The Society for the Study of Social Problems. Parts of chapter 3 appeared in "How Participatory Democracy Became White: Culture and Organizational Choice," *Mobilization* 10, no. 2 (June 2005). Parts of chapter 6 appeared in "Legacies and Liabilities of an Insurgent Past: Remembering Martin Luther King, Jr., on the House and Senate Floor," *Social Science History* 22, no. 4 (1998): 479–512. I thank the editors and publishers of those journals for permission to reuse the material.

Edwin Amenta, James Jasper, Robert Zussman, and an anonymous reviewer for the University of Chicago Press read the entire manuscript. Their suggestions were invariably on the mark, and I wish I had had the time and talent to follow all of them. Many other friends and colleagues either read portions of the manuscript or fed me ideas for it. Both proved enormously valuable. I offer warm thanks to Jeffrey Alexander, Peter Bearman, Kim Blanton, Vince Boudreau, Lynn Chancer, Patty Ewick, Gary Alan Fine, Bill Gamson, Marshall Ganz, Jeff Goodwin, Jennifer Gordon, Jed Miller, Ann Mische, Kelly Moore, Calvin Morrill, Frank Munger, Charlotte Ryan, Susan Silbey, David Snow, David Stark, Charles Tilly, Marc Weiss, Rhys Williams, and Elisabeth Wood. My thanks also to participants in colloquia at Yale University, the University of California–Irvine, SUNY–Stony Brook, the University of Arizona, and New York Law

School; to members of Columbia's Contentious Politics workshop; and to audiences at the 2002 meetings of the American Sociological Association and the 2005 Digital Governance Conference.

I have had the good fortune to have Doug Mitchell as both friend and editor. Doug gets me thinking in new ways no matter what we talk about, but his deep knowledge of rhetoric has made working with him on this project especially rewarding. Tim McGovern, Nicholas Murray, and Christine Schwab, wise in their advice and always good-humored, made the final stages of writing a pleasure.

Authors often thank their children for their patience while their parents toiled on "The Book." I had no such luck. Instead, I thank Lynn James for making it possible for me to work for uninterrupted stretches by taking such marvelous care of my children, as well as for being a good friend to me.

My sisters, Gabriella and Maddalena Polletta, have always been supremely confident in my abilities, evidence to the contrary notwithstanding, and they are very precious to me. So are my brother-in-law and nephew, Pedro and Dante Diez. The Amentas delighted me from the beginning with their zest for telling family stories; they have touched me since with their warmth. Edwin Amenta gives the lie to the commonplace that people are either literary or logical. I have shamelessly exploited his ability to sharpen any argument, to coax sense out of muddled prose, and to offer seemingly endless encouragement. Finally, I thank my children, Gregory and Luisa Amenta, not for their willingness to let me work but for their determined insistence that I work much less. I have been so much the happier for it.

ONE

Why Stories Matter

Modern Americans are ambivalent about stories. On one hand, we celebrate storytelling, and especially personal storytelling, for its authenticity, its passion, and its capacity to inspire not just empathy but action. Everyone has a story, we often say, and that makes for a discourse with uniquely democratic possibilities. In recent years, storytelling has been promoted in surprising places. Managers are now urged to tell stories to motivate workers and doctors are trained to listen to the stories their patients tell. Reporters have rallied around a movement for narrative journalism and psychologists around a movement for narrative therapy. Every year, tens of thousands of people visit the International Storytelling Center in Jonesborough, Tennessee, join the National Storytelling Network, or flock to one of the more than two hundred storytelling festivals held around the country. And a quick scan of any bookstore reveals scores of popular books on the art of storytelling as a route to spirituality, a strategy for grant seekers, a mode of conflict resolution, and a weight-loss plan.[1]

To be sure, we battle over storytelling as well as celebrating it. Museum curators, history textbook writers, and holiday parade organizers have all been the targets of groups vociferously insisting that their story be told the right way. For the beleaguered organizers of a Smithsonian exhibit on the Enola Gay and the planners of sesquicentennial commemorations of Christopher Columbus, the public's investment in storytelling has been a mixed blessing but an undeniable fact. Getting the story right, we feel, is of real political consequence.[2]

Alongside testimonials to the power of stories, however, run deep anxieties. We worry that stories are easily manipulable, that the line between art and artifice too often blurs. The emotional identification that stories produce may compel moral action but may also undermine rational action. And perhaps stories are simply too variable to serve as the basis for social policy. After all, if everyone has her own story, then whose story should be privileged when it comes to making policy for everyone? Finally, we worry that, in the end, stories may be just stories. They may be untrue: fiction masquerading as fact. Or they may be true, but fleeting in their impact, with their normative force easily trumped by considerations of economic efficiency or political expediency. As a New Yorker deliberating with his fellow citizens about a memorial to the victims of the 2001 attack on the World Trade Center put it, "Yes, we could float bonds, but is the legacy we want to leave to our children an inspiring story, a fine view, and a pile of debt?"[3]

What accounts for this ambivalence? Postmodernists argue that the grand narratives of progress, faith, and rationality that once held the status of common sense have lost their force, replaced by a babble of competing moral values and authorities. If that is true, our testimonials to the power of narrative may be wishful and wistful, and set against nagging doubts about the actual reach of any moral discourse. Alternatively, with the old master narratives now suspect, *stories*—particular, local, claiming only verisimilitude, never absolute truth—may be all that we trust. Whether or not either of those explanations is right, I begin with them because, for all scholars' attention to narrative in recent years, there has been little discussion of how people commonly view narrative as a discursive form. We have rich analyses of the broad cultural preoccupations that popular narratives reflect and careful examinations of how storytelling in small groups sustains relations of solidarity and deference. By contrast, we know relatively little about what narrative is popularly seen as good for. Outside a limited range of settings, such as courtrooms and medical diagnostic interviews, we do not know when narrative is considered an appropriate form of discourse, how people are expected to respond to stories, and what kinds of stories and storytellers are thought to be credible.[4]

Yet grasping the prevailing common sense about storytelling is important to understanding not only how narrative figures in everyday life but also how it figures in efforts to bring about social change. In this book, I stake two claims that go against the grain of current scholarship. Most recent theorizing about narrative has attested to its value for disadvantaged groups. Personal stories chip away at the wall of public indifference, scholars argue. Stories elicit sympathy on the part of the powerful and sometimes mobilize official action against social wrongs. Where authorities are unyielding, storytelling sustains groups as they fight for reform, helping them build new collective identities, link current actions to heroic pasts and glorious futures, and restyle setbacks as way stations to victory. Even before movements emerge, the stories that circulate within subaltern communities provide a counterpoint to the myths promoted by the powerful.[5]

Without denying narrative's political potency, I argue that for disadvantaged groups, narrative comes with risks as well as benefits. The story lines available to modern American activists make it more difficult to tell a story of long-term endurance than one of short-term triumph and more difficult to argue that to "keep on keeping on" is success. When people recount their experiences of inequality or injustice in court, they may simultaneously win legal victories for the cause and alienate potential recruits who are unwilling to see themselves as passive victims. And if those challenging the system can tell stories that elicit sympathy, so can their opponents. But the risks in storytelling, I argue, come as much from the norms of narrative's use and interpretation as they do from the norms of its content. This is the second claim I want to stake. Stories are differently intelligible, useful, and authoritative depending on who tells them, when, for what purpose, and in what setting. When telling your own story in a loan office, you will probably say very different things than when telling it in a church confessional or a courtroom. If you are a woman, you will be expected to tell certain kinds of stories. If you are a professional, your story will carry a certain kind of weight. If your story is true, people will expect it to be the same in each retelling.

Those who want to effect social change understandably try to capitalize on familiar conventions of storytelling. After all, they want to frame their message in ways that will rally support. But playing by the rules may be difficult. If the fact that everyone can tell his own story makes it easier for people to challenge the assurances of the powerful that certain policies are to everyone's advantage, the fact that narrative is seen as less authoritative than other discursive forms may weaken that challenge. Encouraging disadvantaged groups to tell their stories may give others a new appreciation for their plight. But the limited range of responses to stories that are popularly considered appropriate may prevent people from doing much more than expressing appreciation. Political officials struggle to assert the contemporary relevance of a past movement, but the occasions on which they are permitted to do so may communicate the movement's pastness, and present irrelevance, no matter what they say. Popular beliefs about storytelling—about how authoritative it is, when it is appropriate, and how it is properly responded to—may curb the impact of otherwise compelling stories.

Toward a Sociology of Storytelling

This is not to say that people fighting for social change should stop telling stories. To the contrary, I believe that in some respects, narrative's political potency has been underemphasized. But I do want to press for a better understanding of how narrative works politically. To advance such an understanding, I treat storytelling in diverse political arenas. I analyze how black congressional representatives tell stories of Martin Luther King, Jr., on the House and Senate floor and the difficulties they face in using such stories to argue for more generous social policies. I study citizens deliberating in a public forum to determine whether people with unpopular views are better served by making arguments or telling stories. Conventions of news reporting and television talk show production shed light on why some victims of social injustice are appealing and others simply pathetic.

Given my interest in narrative's capacity to bring about social change, however, I focus on storytelling by organized collective actors. The movements I study are diverse, ranging from sixteenth-century French tax disputes to the twentieth-century American civil rights movement and from nineteenth-century abolitionism to 1970s advocacy on behalf of battered women. Movements by adult survivors of child abuse, Mexican farm workers, abortion reformers, Nicaraguan Sandinistas, and people with AIDS all make appearances in the following chapters. Throughout, I am interested in how activists have used stories strategically. I try to identify what it is about stories, as opposed to arguments or analyses, that equips them to forge mobilizing identities, and why some stories bridge differences while others harden them. I ask whether compelling stories have simple moral messages or complex, even ambiguous, ones. I compare the stories of victimization told by activists now with those told by activists two hundred years ago to figure out why victims today have a harder sell.

But I also want to show how stories set the very terms of strategic action. Familiar stories make some courses of action seem reasonable, fitting, even possible, and others seem ineffectual, ill-considered, or impossible. Familiar stories shape the interests and identities on behalf of which people take strategic action in the first place. These are processes that remain poorly understood by sociologists of social movements, for reasons that I explain below. But the questions they raise about the relations between culture, power, and practical action extend well beyond social movements. In short, we know that people in all settings use culture practically and creatively to pursue their interests. But culture also defines what counts as practical and what counts as an interest. And most of the time it does so in ways that, willy-nilly, reproduce existing arrangements of power and privilege. For analysts, this presents a conundrum—actually, two conundrums. To talk about culture as constituting people's interests seems to suggest that culture is all-powerful. Surely, my interests are shaped as much by my structural position, that is, the fact that I am a woman, a citizen of the United States, and an employee of a university, as by my left-liberal political beliefs or my atheism. If, along with many other left-wing atheists, I were to develop an interest in banning the teaching of evolution in public schools and sociologists wanted to explain that peculiar development, they might well cite the new popularity of Christian fundamentalism among university professors. But they would then want to account for that popularity, which they would do by identifying structural trends such as, hypothetically, the growth of a grassroots fundamentalist mobilizing network or generational rebellion among left-wing academics. Claiming that culture is constitutive of people's interests seems to confine analysts to simply describing current ideas. To talk about culture constraining people's practical options, for its part, seems to suggest that people are practical dopes or ideological dupes, somehow unable to imagine courses of action that would better serve their purposes. Surely, people's imaginations are unlimited, or at least no more limited than those of the analysts who study them.[6]

The task, then, is to grasp not only how culture shapes interests and identities but the structural conditions in which it has more or less independent force in doing so. We should also be able to identify the typical features of ideas that gain political purchase even in circumstances that do not seem auspicious for cultural innovation. Finally, we should flesh out the discursive and organizational mechanisms by which culture defines the bounds of strategic choice, rather than locating those mechanisms in people's heads. The field of social movements should be an especially useful place in which to do those things. Although some social movements simply escalate routine contention, many involve new issues and new contenders. The mix of structural and cultural processes that produce new identities and interests should be thrown into sharp relief. Too, we should be able to identify rhetorical patterns in the kinds of challenges that succeed in unsettling familiar calculi of interest and risk. Once movements are underway, activists have a real stake in using culture strategically, embracing dominant beliefs and conventions of representation where it serves them and refusing them where it does not. It is at the point where they reproduce such conventions in spite of their strategic liabilities that we should be able to see culture operating to constrain activists' options.

Studying movements should therefore provide insight into much broader dynamics of cultural innovation and constraint. Surprisingly, sociologists of social movements have not capitalized on that opportunity. To be sure, in recent years, they have made cultural processes central to their models of mobilization. Movement scholars now recognize that it is through the lens of shared values and understandings that people perceive opportunities for effective collective action and come to feel a moral obligation to act. As normative commitments—to nonviolence, say, or radical democracy—cultural factors shape groups' tactical choices. And whether or not groups seek mainly to change laws and policies, the outcomes of movements are often most visible in the arenas of culture and everyday life rather than in institutional politics. Yet, for all the attention to culture, movement scholars have still tended to conceptualize culture narrowly: more as furthering people's interests than as constituting them; more as people's explicit normative commitments than as their practical assumptions; and more as a resource than as a constraint. The focus is understandable. Movement scholars too have been wary of the kind of cultural fundamentalism that makes obdurate structures such as laws and political party systems simply epiphenomenal to hegemonic ideas. And they too have been wary of false consciousness arguments. But the result has been to foreclose important questions about protest and its effects. For example, we now know a great deal about the conditions in which people mobilize on behalf of long-standing interests, but we still know relatively little about why certain areas of social life—race relations, say, or nuclear policy, or university curricula—suddenly generate new or newly conflicting interests. We know something about how activists juggle instrumental commitments with ideological ones as they choose among tactical options, striving to stay true to their normative beliefs as they aim for concrete victories. But we know very little about where activists' beliefs about what is instrumental come from and how those beliefs eliminate options as well as opening them up.[7]

Studying the stories people tell can help to answer those questions. Certainly, scholars already have an arsenal of concepts for studying culture in movements: *ideology, frame,* and *discourse,* as well as older terms like *rhetoric* and *belief*. Why not simply talk about the structural conditions in which particular frames gain force, or draw on Marxist notions of ideology to show how a cultural common sense reproduces existing economic arrangements? The reason is that narrative has several features that make it worth studying in its own right. Methodologically, it is fairly easy to identify a narrative in a chunk of discourse. Narratives have beginnings, middles, and ends, as well as features that set them off from other forms of discourse. By contrast, it is difficult to say where a frame begins and ends, or what is *not* ideology. The fact that we can isolate narratives in discourse and can isolate different versions of the same narrative makes it possible to trace the careers of particular stories, exposing not only the political processes by which they come to be tellable or authoritative but also the dynamics by which newly legitimated stories produce new modes of action and new terrains of contention. This should help to identify the structural conditions in which culture has independent force in defining new interests and identities. We can also trace the processes by which stories become canonical *within* movements and what effect that has on groups' tactical choices. Comparing personal accounts of mobilization in different historical periods can shed light on how logics of agency have changed over time.[8]

Thanks to a substantial literature on narrative in diverse fields, we also know a good deal about how narrative operates rhetorically: for example, how shifting the point of view establishes and conceals authority and how plot structures causality. This makes it possible to work in from the other side of the structure/culture mix: along with identifying the structural conditions in which new ideas and identities are likely to have political force, we can determine why particular cultural narratives gain currency even in structural conditions that are not primed for cultural innovation. But narrative's value in this respect goes further. Research in cognitive and social psychology has documented how storytelling helps to make sense of the anomalous, how it elicits and channels emotions, and how it sustains individual and group identities. These processes are all critical to collective action, and we can draw on them to develop the microfoundations of collective action that we still lack.

Finally, and, again, unlike frames, ideologies, and discourses, all of whose referents are defined by analysts rather than the people who produce or act on them, most people know when they are telling a story. They know how to construct a story, and when and why they should tell stories, as well as how to respond to a story. In some settings, such as a courtroom, conventions of storytelling are formalized and recorded. Even where that is not the case, we can extrapolate narrative conventions from stories' distribution across settings, speakers, and topics of discussion. People often reflect openly on what they see storytelling as good for and where they see its limitations. From there, we can begin to determine the work that such epistemologies do in legitimating institutions and in shaping strategies for transforming them. Of course, people operate with different ideas of how stories work. But I argue that those ideas are socially patterned. Concerns about stories' credibility and authority are more likely to be engaged in some settings than others and with respect to some storytellers rather than others. That has implications for people's ability to use otherwise persuasive stories effectively.

So I study storytelling especially in movements because movements have been such important forces for social change and because they illuminate cultural processes that operate much more broadly. I draw ideas and methodological tools from literary theory, psychology, anthropology, legal theory, and sociolinguistics. But I also want to demonstrate the yields of a fully sociological approach to narrative, one that focuses on story*telling* as much as on stories, and, in particular, on the social organization of storytelling authority. Such an approach may be used with other cultural objects: we can study the ways in which concerns about statistics' manipulability or bureaucracy's inefficiency are more likely to be engaged when some people use the form than when others do. I will have more to say about all this. But let me turn now to narrative: to its distinctive formal features and the ways in which it is conventionally used and then to its role in dynamics of contention that remain poorly understood.

What Makes a Story? Conventions of Narrative's Form

What makes a story a story? The lines that rhetorical scholars once drew between prose and poetic discourse and between epideictic, deliberative, and forensic forms of persuasive rhetoric are now recognized as not so neat. People tell stories when making speeches and logical arguments, when deliberating, and when interpreting scientific phenomena. Still, narrative has features that distinguish it from other discursive forms— for example, arguments, descriptions, explanations, and reports—as well as from concepts such as frame and ideology that have been used to analyze political discourse (note that here and throughout the book, I use the words *narrative* and *story* interchangeably).[9]

Like a speech or a song, but unlike a chronicle, a frame, or an ideology, a story has an identifiable beginning, middle, and end. "When we 'tell a story,'" writes literary theorist Peter Brooks, "there tends to be a shift in the register of our voices, enclosing and setting off the narrative almost in the manner of the traditional 'once upon a time' and 'they lived happily ever after.'" Stories are bracketed in a flow of discourse; they call the listener's attention to the reality they reveal. Stories usually begin by establishing a setting, a time and place where events will unfold: "Once upon a time, in a land far, far away . . ."; or, "Well, we were having our dinner once at me Mum's . . ."[10]

All stories have characters and a point of view or points of view from which the events in the story are experienced. Characters need not be human or even living. But we expect to experience the moral of the story through characters' fates. The person who tells us his story expects to gain our empathy, and we judge him by assessing his actions in the light of the character they reveal. The story's point of view may be that of the narrator, as is often the case in first-person narratives. But many stories, including those we tell in conversation as well as those we read in novels, shift perspectives. We see war from the point of view of Prince Bolkonsky and Pierre Besuhov in *War and Peace*. When we recount the story of a conflict among friends, we shift from one friend's perception of what was going on to another's. In thus alternating points of view, storytellers make it possible for listeners to identify with different perspectives and, at the same time, to recognize each one as incomplete. Storytellers may selectively erase point of view, giving listeners the characters' thoughts and feelings as if unmediated. Even first-person stories may draw attention to a gap between the narrator and the story's point of view—for example, between me as I am now and me at the time I experienced the events that I am recounting. As I show later, that gap can serve to create a special kind of authority.[11]

Events in a story are usually recounted in the order in which they occurred. But what links them is more than chronology. Events are configured by plot, the logic that makes recounted events meaningful. Plot is the structure of the story. Without it, events would be mere occurrences, discontinuous and separate moments. They would simply follow each other rather than unfold. "The king died and then the queen died" is not a narrative. The events are chronological but not causally linked. "The king died and then the queen died of grief" is a story because "of grief" connects the events. Plot involves a reversal: at the beginning of the story, there was a living queen and king; at its end, they are both dead.[12]

What makes the example about the grieving queen barely a story is that the reversal does not make much of a point. In most stories events drive toward a normative conclusion. They project a desirable or undesirable future. Stories, says historian Hayden White, are "chronicles invested with moral meaning through emplotment." Some stories moralize more explicitly than others, but all have what linguists William Labov and Joshua Waletsky call an *evaluative* component indicating why the story is important to tell. Storytellers rarely say explicitly to their audiences, "And the moral of the story is . . ." Rather, the story's larger meaning seems to arise from the events themselves. The final events in the story resolve the problems raised by earlier events in a way that tenders a more general normative point.[13]

Narrative theorists differ on how many possible narrative plots there are and how universal they are. Moreover, the relation between the particulars of a story and a cultural stock of plots is complicated. As sociologists Patricia Ewick and Susan Silbey observe, "Narratives are fluid, continuous, dynamic, and always constructed interactively—with an audience and within a context—out of the stuff of other narratives." Still, most theorists agree that there is a cultural stock of plots. Stories that draw on plots outside that stock or that are incompatible with the "stuff" of other narratives are seen either as bad stories or as not stories at all. We believe a story because it is familiar. Indeed, we find a story coherent because it resonates with stories we have heard before. A character's actions seem to reflect his character; the reversal in the story makes sense; the story's end seems, in retrospect, to have a certain inevitability.[14]

However, if stories must hew to familiar plotlines, a story that was so familiar as to be entirely predictable would be no story at all. It would be the moral without the story. Literary theorist Wolfgang Iser writes, "It is only through inevitable omissions that a story will gain its dynamism." Stories require our interpretive participation. They require that we work to resolve ambiguities as events unfold, to anticipate the normative conclusion to which the story is driving. Indeed, the closure stories promise may never be fully realized. A story's meaning may remain elusive. Stories are thus distinctive in their openness to interpretation. This is not to say that other forms of discourse are not interpretable. To the contrary, analyses as much as narratives can be plumbed for multiple meanings. So can arguments, descriptions, and formal mathematical proofs. But we *expect* to have to interpret stories, while we tend to see ambiguity in logical arguments as imprecision or error, and we are less likely to do the work necessary to make sense of an allusive passage or what appear to be contradictory developments. When we hear a story, we are often comfortable thinking about our interpretation as provisional and open to revision.[15]

Unlike a description, then, a narrative provides an explanation for the events it describes. Unlike an explanation, a narrative represents cause and effect relations through its sequencing of events rather than by appeal to standards of logic and proof. Reports also explain through their representation of events, but they do not organize events as carefully—nor, in particular, do they rely on suspense—to make a normative point. An argument makes a normative point, but the point is not, as it is in a story, integrated into the account of events and revealed by the story's dénouement. Narratives are forms of discourse, vehicles of ideology, and elements of collective action frames. But grasping how narratives operate should lead us to modify our theories of how discourse, ideology, and frames operate.[16]

We tell stories for many, perhaps innumerable, reasons: to entertain, to illustrate, to instruct, to envision alternatives, to comfort, to dramatize, to help us live with the contradictions that are an unavoidable feature of existence, to grasp temporality, to feel—the list goes on. I want to focus, first, on narrative's configurational, sense-making, functions, next on how stories help to sustain existing inequalities, and then on how they may threaten such inequalities. The term *narrative* comes from the Latin words both for "knowing" ("gnarus") and "telling" ("narro"). The etymology is instructive. For psychologist Jerome Bruner, narrative is a distinctive way not just of representing reality but also of apprehending it. Where the *paradigmatic* mode of cognition that is characteristic of formal logic and science adjudicates between truth claims on the basis of empirical evidence and formal logic, a narrative mode instead seeks time- and place-specific connections between events. Think about how we understand a story. We move back and forth between the events narrated and the gradually revealed plot, with each making sense of the other. Narrative understanding proceeds by tacking from the raw datum —the occurrence or behavior—to the developing whole of which it is part. Of course, we should be wary of suggesting that logicians and scientists do not tell stories. They do tell stories, and they do so to arrive at their findings as well as communicate them. To talk about two ideal types of cognition is just the first step in studying how they, along with other types of cognition, intermingle in concrete instances of meaning-making. But the contrast does suggest that stories organize experience in a distinctive way.[17]

We may be especially likely to turn to narrative when we encounter phenomena that depart from our usual categories and experiences. Psychologist A. E. Michotte found that when presented with small colored rectangles moving on a screen, viewers constructed elaborate narrative plots such as these: "It is as if A's approach frightened B and B ran away." "It is as if A, in touching B induced an electric current which set B going." "The arrival of A by the side of B acts as a sort of signal to B . . ." "It is as if A touched off a mechanism inside B and thus set it going." Observers often laughed at the rectangles' movements. Like Michotte's subjects, we rely on narrative to make strange phenomena intelligible, to reduce the anxiety produced by the unfamiliar. We turn to narrative, say analysts of divorce and serious illness, to comprehend changes that shatter our routines and threaten our sense of self. When I wrote the first draft of this chapter the week after the 2001 terrorist attack on the World Trade Center in New York, I was struck by people's compulsion to tell their stories, myself included—to recount where we were when we saw or heard about the attack, how we struggled to grasp what was happening, and what we did next. Our stories had a broken-off quality, though, something that psychologists say is characteristic of people who have undergone more serious traumas. We had not yet narrativized our experiences, not yet found the moral in them that would give them the coherence, but also the distance, of a story. Perhaps we told our stories in the hope that our interlocutors would supply the moral we could not yet find. Now, four years later, my story does have coherence, centering on my and others' strange determination to remain in line at the hospital to give blood even after we had been told that the supplies were full and that we should go home. Our seemingly irrational behavior becomes, in my story, an expression both of our need to do something to help the victims of the tragedy and of the fact that there was nothing we could do.[18]

The relation between narrative and self operates also in everyday contexts. We act, say narrative psychologists, not on the basis of identities defined in categorical terms but by locating events within an unfolding life-story. We fit events in our lives into incipient stories of tragedy or triumph, redemption or self-discovery. We usually rely on several stories simultaneously and sometimes they are inconsistent. Still, the stories that we tell ourselves align our actions with our identities, often subtly altering both. This is true of collective identities as well as individual ones. In telling the story of our becoming, as an individual, a nation, a people, we define who we are. Narratives may be employed strategically to strengthen a collective identity, but they also may precede and make possible the development of a coherent community or collective actor.[19]

The dynamic at work here is an emotional one. Stories of exodus, revolution, foes vanquished, and threats averted strengthen national identities by stimulating emotions of fear, pride, longing replaced by determination, and grief replaced by joy. Indeed, a notion of narrative as sense-making may underestimate the extent to which the coherence that stories provide is emotional. Again, think about how we understand a story. We identify with the story's protagonist, loathe the villain, experience a frisson of fear as the hero strides into danger and relief when he returns unscathed. Depending on how dramatic the story is, we experience the events' resolution as a veritable release of psychic energy; we talk about a story's "climax." Probably because we tend to think of emotions as located inside us, we often talk about stories as providing a *deeper* understanding than logical explanations or non-narrative accounts.[20]

Scholars have written a great deal about how stories sustain individual selves and how they sustain nations. But stories figure in many institutions that we encounter in our daily lives. For example, the copier technicians observed by anthropologist Julian Orr told endless stories to each other about puzzling problems, recalcitrant machines, and shrewd diagnoses. Those stories enabled copier technicians to do their work by relaying experiential knowledge. They also communicated how copier technicians were expected to relate to customers, suppliers, and each other. In similar fashion, the stories that insurance agents tell about a firm's history specify the normative obligations of being an employee of that firm; the stories that families tell define what it is to be a family member; and the stories that American fathers tell indicate what it is be a (patriarchal) father—all settings in which ethnographers have observed everyday conversation.[21]

In this sense, stories make explicit the cultural *schemas* that underpin institutional practices. Schemas are logics or models of action and interaction. They are enacted in formal rules, rituals, and routines as well as in stories, but we probably turn to stories to communicate them for several reasons. A story captures the particularity of a unique set of events while conveying the general point or pattern of which those events are an instance. When you tell a story about your firm, or a particular repair job, or your recently married friends, your audience hears the story as having larger implications—about the culture of this firm, or what it is to be a copier repairperson, or the trials facing the newly married. Stories also integrate description and evaluation. The story of how a particular marriage went wrong is implicitly a story of how a marriage should work. And stories integrate cause and consequence in a way that foregrounds the contingency of human action. The element of suspense in the story of the marriage that went wrong, that is, the uncertainty about why the relationship is failing and whether it will survive after all, allows us to glimpse alternative possibilities and their likely consequences. Stories allow us to think in the subjunctive mode, as sociologist Robin Wagner-Pacifici puts it.[22]

Of course, people do many things aside from telling stories. They decide between courses of action by compiling lists of pros and cons; they experience the bonds of nationhood in holiday parades; they reinforce the corporate chain of command every time they address the CEO as Mr. Smith and an assistant as Jennifer; they define the institution of marriage by applying for a marriage license. Again, institutional schemas are reproduced through rituals, routines, and formal rules as well as stories. And people *do* things with stories. They entertain and persuade, build social bonds and break them, make sense of their worlds and, in the process, create those worlds. Although they occasionally do so in ways that are socially transformative, much of the time, the stories that people tell discourage overt challenge.

How does that happen? Narrative's canonical quality is surely important. Stories make sense in terms of already familiar stories. Each time such stories are told, one might argue, their normative message is reinforced. Stories outside the canon should be difficult to tell. But the stories that are familiar to us are diverse. For every story that enjoins us to turn the other cheek when insulted, another instructs us to let no assault on our dignity go unavenged. Stories attesting to the virtue of the unencumbered individual are countered by stories about the virtue of loyalty to the group. Perhaps, then, their power comes less from the explicit moral instruction they provide than from the normative possibilities that are excluded from the pattern of their interrelationship. This is the conclusion one can draw from a line of structuralist and poststructuralist theorizing. In his famous analysis of primitive myths, anthropologist Claude Lévi-Strauss argued that myths do not provide logical answers to existential questions such as the origins of human beings and whether individuals are fundamentally alike or different. Rather, they provide a way to think about the relation between possible answers. For example, the Oedipus myth resolves the conflict between the belief that humans are autochthonous and the belief that they are born from the union of man and woman by comparing that conflict to the one between overvaluing and undervaluing blood relations. Both are demonstrated to be inescapable: "[T]he overrating of blood relations is to the underrating of blood relations as the attempt to escape autochthony is to the impossibility to succeed in it." Today, one could say, we grasp what reason is by telling stories that thematize not only reason's difference from passion but its similarity to men's difference from women, culture's difference from nature, and so on. Myths make reality intelligible, but they do so governed by a logic of symbolic relations rather than by reality's inherent meaningfulness.[23]

What poststructuralist theorists add is the insight that alternative relations are actively ruled out. They are suppressed. As philosopher

Jacques Derrida describes it, the culturally privileged pole of supposedly fundamental oppositions can always be shown to be dependent on the denigrated pole. It therefore takes *work* to preserve any stability of meaning. To return to my example, our conception of reason requires that people make emotional performances of reason, that they demonstrate in their speech, tone, and gesture the seeming lack of affect that passes for reason—while at the same time maintaining that emotion and reason are mutually exclusive. Derrida himself focused on the instability of the foundational oppositions of Western philosophical texts (for example, oppositions of speech and writing, and nature and culture). But scholars taking his lead have turned to more overtly political discourses, probing the ways in which binary oppositions in legal and political discourse operate to exclude aspects of reality. For example, as I discuss in chapter 5, judges trying cases of sex discrimination have been receptive to stories of women as being just like men (and therefore entitled to similar jobs) or as being different from men (and therefore uninterested in such jobs), but they have been much less receptive to stories of women who are different from men and entitled to similar jobs. The effect has been to limit the legal options available to women.[24]

The relationship between culture, structure, and story is thus complex and, I would argue, variable. Much of the time, structures are reproduced through stories that thematize familiar oppositions. Sometimes, stories undermine those oppositions in ways that mobilize overt challenge. In their role as preservers of the status quo, stories are influential not because they are told over and over again in identical form but rather because they mesh with other familiar stories that navigate similarly between the culturally privileged and denigrated poles of well-known oppositions. Stories of women having different job aspirations than men make sense because they are heard against the backdrop of stories of women having different biologies than men and stories of little girls being different from little boys and stories of people having different tastes from each other and stories of people sacrificing personal ambitions for the good of their families, and so on. Such stories appear in many versions and in many media: in holiday cards and State of the Union addresses, advertisements and scientific articles, video games and school textbooks. In each setting, semiotic structures combine with distinctive institutional dynamics to marginalize alternative stories. In making this claim, I depart from the structuralist and poststructuralist line of thought I have just described. Network television's practice of avoiding financial risk by "recombining" successful story lines rather than producing new ones has the effect of limiting the kinds of stories it

15

is possible to air just as much as do deep structures of American culture. The adversarial system of American law narrows the range of stories told by dichotomizing arguments, sides, and verdicts. Narrative's role in social life cannot be understood outside the institutional conventions of its interpretation and use, to which I will turn shortly.[25]

People can and do tell stories that refuse the standard cultural oppositions, and sometimes these have powerful effects. But more often, such stories are discredited, ignored, or assimilated to one or the other side of the oppositions they are intended to challenge. For example, in her study of the 1989 Central Park jogger rape case, in which a young white woman was allegedly raped and left for dead by a marauding group of young black men, sociologist Lynn Chancer reports that several feminists refused the racial framing of the case that dominated the news. Feminist writers pointed out that more than one woman of color had been raped in New York the same night as the white jogger. The story feminists told was about violence against women. But, despite their best efforts, these writers were placed on the "side of the victim" and ranged with people like real-estate magnate Donald Trump, who was demanding the death penalty for out-of-control "wolf packs." So alternative stories were not unthinkable. Indeed, they appeared in the media. But they were responded to in ways that recast them in terms of the dominant narrative of a victimized white woman and victimizing black men. Note, too, that routine practices of news reporting contributed to pushing the alternative stories out of bounds. Presenting both sides of the news story is intended to guarantee objectivity by avoiding any semblance of partisanship. But the practice makes it difficult to present a third view on an issue or a critical interpretation of one of the opposing views. Specifically institutional conventions of narration thus operated alongside cultural conventions of emplotment to limit the kinds of stories that had clout.[26]

Stories as Challenge

As I just noted, however, sometimes stories unsettle the status quo. A familiar story that has a surprise ending makes the conventionality of our expectations suddenly obvious. A popular political leader who is reimagined as an emperor without clothes begins to lose support. A new telling of a group's glorious past and the indignities it has recently suffered moves its members from their usual state of resignation into active opposition. People can put stories to transgressive effect. But stories may also redefine people's interests and identities in ways that create entirely new lines of contention. Theorists of movements have seldom addressed the question of why issues come to be politicized when they do. They have tended rather to treat groups' interests as long-standing and have focused accordingly on the political shifts that open up opportunities for groups to act collectively on their interests. But in many cases, groups' interests are *not* long-standing. The theoretical task, then, is to account for the emergence of lines of contention without simply relying on idiosyncratic historical developments or describing broad cultural shifts that are completely unconnected to political and organizational conditions. An analysis of stories can help us to do that.

Consider several scenarios by which practices that were settled become contested. In one, the story or stories that define an institution lose credibility. Any institution has multiple accounts of itself: stories of its origins, stories of the typical career of an institutional member, and so on. None of them may describe actual practices very well. But in certain circumstances, the gap between story and reality is likely to be perceived as grounds for mobilization. This may happen when people transpose a story from one institution to another, using it as a kind of standard with which to attack institutional practices to which people were previously indifferent. External developments may discredit a dominant institutional story. Or external developments may heighten the tension between two institutional stories that once coexisted harmoniously. In any of these ways, a story's loss of institutional purchase—or better, the institution's loss of a credible story—gives some a stake in mobilization.

Just this seems to have happened to physicians who were performing abortions routinely in the early 1960s. As Kristin Luker shows in her history of the abortion reform movement, physicians at the time operated on the basis of two very different but rarely discussed moral stories. One was what Luker calls a strict constructionist account, in which the fetus was a full person, albeit unborn, whose abortion was justified only when its survival jeopardized the life of the mother. In the other, broad constructionist account, the fetus was only a potential person and was appropriately aborted if indications were strong that it would be abnormal. Some physicians subscribed to one story; some to the other. By the early 1960s, however, medical advances had made abortions to save the life of the mother an increasing rarity. The potential for outright tension between the two narratives increased. The conflict broke open in 1962 after the story was publicized of an Arizona woman who planned to terminate her pregnancy when she discovered that the Thalidomide she was taking would probably cause birth defects in her unborn child. The story spurred criticism, and the hospital reviewing the woman's case refused to

17

grant her request for an abortion. In the ensuing controversy, physicians subscribing to the broad constructionist narrative began to worry about not having legal protection for the therapeutic abortions they were performing routinely. They found themselves with a new stake in an emerging abortion reform movement.[27]

Now, consider a different dynamic, in which the institutionalization of a story rather than its loss of institutional authority creates new lines of contention. Past movements have defined the stakes for later ones through the stories they tell. This is true not only in the sense, for example, that the women's movement made it possible to tell rape stories and the gay and lesbian movement made it possible to tell coming-out stories. The stories told by those movements contributed to the very claims that activists made in subsequent movements. This is clear in the case of mobilization by adult survivors of child abuse in the 1970s. The stories told by survivors hewed to a story line established earlier by antirape activists, as sociologist Joseph Davis explains. Before the antirape movement, child sexual abuse was largely viewed through the lens of family systems and psychoanalytic therapies. Harm to the victim was not considered inevitable and was rarely thought to be long-lasting. Family members, and even the victim, were often seen as collusive with the abuser in tolerating the abuse. That story changed in the 1970s, when antirape and child protection movements converged on the issue of child sexual abuse. The rape experience was transposed to the experience of sexually abused children. In the new story, abuse was widespread but unrecognized, even by victims themselves, victimization was clearcut, and harm was profound and long-lasting. The proper response to such abuse was also defined by the antirape movement. It "emphasized believing victims, affirming inner strength, rejecting guilt, expressing anger, and claiming rights," Davis writes. Along the way, family systems and psychoanalytic accounts of child sexual abuse and its variable consequences were excised from the tellable story.[28]

I want to talk briefly about a third dynamic by which new stakes in contention have emerged because it highlights a feature of narrative that I see as critical to the form: its openness to interpretation. Most of us are familiar with a scenario in which reports of a shocking crime galvanize people to take action. Often, new legislation is speedily enacted in response. For example, New Jersey's Megan's Law, mandating that communities be notified when a convicted sex offender moves into the area, was passed less than three months after seven-year-old Megan Kanka was raped and murdered by a convicted sex offender. A federal version of the law was passed a year and a half after that. New York State's Kendra's Law, requiring outpatient treatment in certain cases of mental illness, was passed less than a year after Kendra Webdale was fatally pushed into the path of an oncoming subway by a schizophrenic man. Again, episodes of mobilization like these fit poorly into our standard models of movement emergence, which view challengers and their interests as long-standing. To the contrary, in these cases, people's stakes in collective action seem to have been generated by what sociologist James Jasper calls the "moral shock" of the event, which drove people to act even in the absence of organizations devoted to the cause. The force of stories of a child abused or a community endangered seems to come from the clarity of their normative conclusions. Events demand concerted action.[29]

However, a closer analysis raises the possibility that such stories may be influential precisely insofar as they are open to multiple interpretations, which enables activist groups to redefine the issues at stake in a way that accords with their existing agendas. I mentioned the newspaper story of the woman whose Thalidomide use led her to seek an abortion in 1962. The story created a political furor about the morality of therapeutic abortions and spurred an abortion reform movement. But the story is actually open to various interpretations. It could be read as the story of a mother of four and her husband who were subjected to the whim of a hospital board (and therefore as an argument for abortions on demand); or as about the clear need for therapeutic abortions (and therefore as an argument for clearer rules); or as about the dangers of Thalidomide (as the reporter actually intended the story).[30]

Far from discouraging concerted action, the story's ambiguity may have enabled groups with very different agendas to come together in a common stance of indignation. The groups that rallied to support a legislative bill that would relax restrictive abortion rules included public health officials concerned about the incidence of criminal abortions, medical professionals who wanted legal protection for the therapeutic abortions they were already performing, activists who wanted the repeal of all abortion laws, liberal religious groups, and civic groups such as the Jaycees and chambers of commerce—the latter comprising mainly family men who disliked granting professionals the right to make family decisions. These groups did not form a natural coalition of interests. The story's openness to interpretation probably did not *create* interests in contention, but it may have allowed diverse groups to see their interests as alike enough to act collectively.

In the episodes I have described, narrative's normative character, its canonicity, and its openness to interpretation account for its role in turning previously settled issues into disputed ones. But in each case, too, those features of narrative only mattered in certain conditions, namely, when new information that was recognized as authoritative rendered existing institutional stories problematic; when past movements were successful enough to have gained credibility for the moral stories they produced; and when organizations existed with interests in an issue that were, if not obviously congruent, then also not obviously conflicting. To put it in the language I used earlier, particular configurations of power (structure) opened the space for stories (culture) to shape new interests in contention. Studying the stories people tell can make plain that process both because we know something about how stories operate rhetorically and because, by tracing variation in the stories told across groups, institutional settings, and time periods, we can zero in on the conditions in which stories gain and lose influence.

Note, finally, that the stories I have just described operated at different levels of explicitness. The stories of Megan Kanka and Kendra Webdale appeared in the news in full-blown narrative form with beginnings, middles, and ends, with characters, suspense, and horrific dénouements. Later, they circulated as *kernel* stories: one could talk in shorthand about "the Megan Kanka case," or the "Kendra Webdale episode." The moral accounts of mothers and fetuses on which physicians operated were not often made explicit, although they would have been articulated in an interview or where a physician felt called upon to justify his or her practices. Finally, the rape stories served as a kind of background for the stories of child sexual abuse, a template or paradigm in terms of which the abuse stories made sense. Analysts have captured some of these differences by referring to *narratives* and *master-narratives, narratives* and *paradigmatic narratives,* or *stories* and *narratives,* with the first of each pair referring to the story that is told and the second referring to the background story.[31]

Many of the stories that orient action are these kinds of background stories, simply referred to or even assumed rather than told explicitly. But getting at those kinds of narratives poses a real methodological challenge. I try to do so in two chapters. In chapter 3, I argue that the literary trope of *metonymy* provides the causal thread of a story that is assumed to be familiar. By studying the emergence of new metonymies in the tactical deliberations of movement groups, we can trace the process by which one version of the past becomes standard and also trace the effects of that process on groups' tactical choices. In chapter 6, I argue that to make sense of congressional speakers' references to Martin Luther King, Jr., requires that one hear them in the context of very different versions of the civil rights past. White congressional representatives, black congressional representatives, and black activists referred to a past with different protagonists and antagonists, a different arc of events, and a different meaning for the present. What makes it possible for me in both chapters to tell stories that were never told explicitly by the people I study is that my aim is not to reconstruct a particular story in all its detail but to identify differences in the stories that were referred to; differences over time, in the first case, and between speakers, in the second.

In these two cases, and in the rest of book, I argue that narrative analysis can help to explain not only the emergence of contentious issues but other processes that are central to politics and protest: mobilization in fledgling movements, tactical choice in movement groups, the legal adjudication of equal rights claims, compromise in public deliberation, and competition between activist elites and electoral ones. Features of narrative that I have already described, notably, its integration of explanation and evaluation, its dependence on a common stock of plots, and its openness to interpretation, are all important to narrative's role in those processes. Equally important, however, are the conventions of narrative's use and interpretation, to which I turn now.

When Is a Story Appropriate? Conventions of Narrative's Use

Most scholars agree that we develop the capacity to tell stories early in life and that storytelling serves sense-making functions in all cultures. But narrative's use is also governed by conventions that are not universal. As folklorists and historians have shown, stories are seen in different places and periods as fitting on some occasions, capable of eliciting some responses, and properly told about certain topics and in certain ways. When middle-class American families sit down to dinner, talk usually focuses on the stories told by the children at the table. Storytelling at the middle-class Israeli dinner table tends to be shared. In a working-class black community in the American south in the 1970s, parents encouraged their children to tell tall tales as a display of linguistic competence. In a nearby working-class white community, parents encouraged more factual stories with clear moral conclusions. Unlike us moderns, antebellum Americans familiar with Christian conversion narratives did not worry about stories' tendency to manipulate their audience's emotions. Rather, in the narrative epistemology that dominated at the time, readers' identification with the story's protagonist was thought to lead to spiritual enlightenment.[32]

Where does our twenty-first-century common sense about storytelling come from? How do we know how to tell stories, who should tell them and on what occasions, how we should respond to stories, and what effects they are likely to have? We do not always know perfectly, of course. Nor do we know in the same ways. But to the extent that there is commonsense knowledge about storytelling, which I believe there is, it comes from the rules that structure storytelling in different institutions and from symbolic associations that reach across institutional settings. First, the institutional conventions. A judge can tell a story if she wants to, but a defendant may be penalized for doing so. The rules governing storytelling as testimony are formal; others are less so. Judges instruct litigants in small claims court that they can tell their stories any way they want to. But when they tell the kinds of stories that are familiar in everyday conversations, in which an event is made sense of in terms of the social relationship of which it was a breach, they generally lose their cases. Stories like these are simply too unlike the rule-oriented accounts that judges are used to hearing in higher courts, in which agency and responsibility are represented in straightforward chains of causality. Callers to emergency response (911) operators are discouraged from telling stories at all as operators struggle to elicit the information they need to complete their electronic dispatch forms. Ministers in liberal Protestant churches tell stories that encourage much more interpretation on the part of listeners than do their fundamentalist counterparts.[33]

Some conventions of institutional storytelling reflect bureaucratic needs for the swift and uniform processing of information, as with 911 calls. Storytelling conventions also reflect institutions' need to distinguish their domain from those of proximate institutions. The line that is drawn between appropriate and inappropriate occasions for telling stories aids in that task. When scientific journals frown on scientists who report their results as a personal narrative of discovery, they legitimate science as a form of knowledge that is removed from everyday modes of cognition and representation. When jurists counterpose law and story, even though much of what happens in court is storytelling, they demarcate law's realm from that of extralegal systems of moral sanction. As I suggest later, governments have an interest in recounting stories of the nation's past, but they also have an interest in defining some arenas and occasions as inappropriate for commemorative storytelling. In other words, there are real stakes in enforcing boundaries between narrative and non-narrative forms.[34]

How people tell stories in court, in hospitals, at family dinners, and in Congress is also shaped by epistemologies of storytelling that reach across institutions. By an epistemology of storytelling, I mean a set of popular assumptions about how stories work: how audiences respond emotionally to stories, how stories convey or circumvent the truth, and so on. Scholars have paid relatively little attention to this source of influence on storytelling performances. They have tended to work from concrete storytelling exchanges to the social and institutional functions that different kinds of storytelling performance presumably serve. While valuable, that perspective leaves unexamined popular beliefs about story's operation and value as a discursive form. Such beliefs shape people's use and interpretation of stories where those things are not formally prescribed, and even, sometimes, where they are prescribed.

To begin to get a handle on our contemporary epistemology of storytelling, I turn to an odd place: an article that ran in a London newspaper in 2001 about a new boutique called "Story." The article is revealing, I believe, for what it says about how a shop owner and a reporter, who presumably assumed a community of interpretation with consumers and newspaper readers respectively, saw narrative operating. The story begins by describing Story, the boutique, as being like an "Aladdin's cave," with "diaphanous textiles, vintage bags, Modern Movement chairs, and a toddler ([the owner's] eleven-month-old son) playing inside a French antique bedstead which doubles as his playpen." The reporter quotes the shop owner's retail philosophy: "Everything I do is about story. I'll find a little flower in the garden and instantly start looking for the right vase. Then I'll place different objects, like a silk dress, a handbag, or a string of crystal beads, to complete the composition." Note here an echo of the theory of narrative cognition that I described earlier. To make sense of events (or here, objects), we tack between them and an unfolding plot, with each one giving meaning to the other.[35]

Other familiar views of narrative appear in the newspaper account. Story—the store and, implicitly, the discursive form—is idiosyncratic and emotional ("It's all very personal and self-indulgent," the shop owner explains. "It was important that the place have heart and soul"). Story is the opposite of utilitarian (the reporter: "It's not just about selling product—it could never be a cynical exercise," and she describes Story as the "ultimate anti-shop"). Story is accessible to all; it is socially equalizing ("There is no design snobbery here"). Finally, Story is both authentic and carefully crafted ("It looks artless, but in among the bric-a-brac you'll find volumes of poetry, antiquarian prints and a recent copy of *Vogue Italia*"). In its incarnation as a clothing boutique, storytelling is personal rather than public, expressive rather than instrumental, populist rather than elitist, relational rather than categorical, and artfully uncontrived.

Like the shop owner and reporter, I believe, we moderns tend to see stories as better able to capture particularity than universality and concreteness rather than abstraction. We associate stories with emotions rather than logic and see them as typical of informal and personal relations more than formal and public ones. As a corollary, we associate narrative with groups, settings, and ways of knowing that are also associated with the particular, the emotional, the personal, the concrete, and the informal. So, we think of storytelling as characteristic of women and nonprofessionals, common in private settings rather than public ones, good for expressing moral concerns rather than strategic ones, the hallmark of folklore rather than science, and of custom rather than rules.

This suggests misleadingly that we have a single and consistent view of storytelling. In fact, as I show in several chapters, storytelling is seen in contrary ways. One tension is between stories as unique, that is, told by special people or ordinary people in extraordinary circumstances, and stories as commonplace and told by everyone. This tension was evident in an online search I conducted of all newspaper articles that used some version of the phrase "tell a story" ("told a story," "told their stories," "telling stories," and so on) in a single week in 2002. "Telling one's story" often meant recounting a life that was characterized by high drama and stunning turnarounds. So, in a common formulation, one story was headlined, "John Walker Lindh tells his story," referring to the ordinary young man who became a traitor to his country. Yet, far from unique and dramatic, stories were also represented as things to which everyone has access. There were frequent references to people telling "the old story," meaning the story that everyone knows. In fact, not one but several tensions seem to be bound up in a popular view of stories' simultaneous ordinariness and extraordinariness. Storytelling is represented as a special talent that only some people possess *and* as a form of communication that comes naturally to everyone. One's own story is unique, and therefore special, or idiosyncratic, and therefore unrepresentative. Or one's story is commonplace, and therefore uninteresting, or universal, and therefore of interest to all.[36]

Another kind of tension is between the authentic and deceptive character of stories. Frequently, personal stories in the newspaper accounts demanded not just a change of opinion but action. Some version of "policymakers must hear this story" often followed profiles of heroic or wronged individuals. Phrases such as "the statistics tell the story," or "now the story can be told," were also common, all pointing to the authority of narrative. But "telling a story" colloquially means telling a lie. This view of stories was evident in statements such as "but the stories are true" in the newspaper accounts, formulations that make the credibility of the story seem counterintuitive. It is evident, too, in reporters' complaints to each other about the competing demands of telling a story and telling the truth. Even as they have called for more "narrative journalism" in recent years and for giving readers a sense of what it is actually like to experience the events they report, journalists worry that such stories may embellish reality in the interests of more evocatively conveying it.[37]

Finally, along with views of stories as both idiosyncratic and democratizing, and as authentic and manipulable, views of stories as potent and powerless coexist in the popular imagination. In public deliberations about a planned memorial for the site of the former World Trade Center, which I discuss in chapter 4, participants often talked about how survivors' stories had moved them emotionally and helped them comprehend the ramifications of the attack. They agreed that making the stories of the disaster's victims part of a memorial would ensure that they were remembered in their full humanity and even that such a disaster never happened again. But while attesting to storytelling's emotional, moral, and political power, speakers worried about the opposite: that stories' capacity to inspire was time-bound, fleeting. "You may remember what happened for the rest of your life, but future generations will not know the magnitude of what happened," one said. "They will only have a story in a history book."[38]

That we have contradictory ideas about storytelling's social value is not surprising. We have contradictory ideas about technology, sociologist William Gamson has observed, seeing it as both progressive and dangerous. We have contradictory ideas about love, Ann Swidler argues, thinking of it at times as an experience that is passionate, all-or-nothing, and once and for all, and at other times as a commitment that demands sacrifice, compromise, and hard work. Following Swidler, we can see these divergent perceptions as resources. Without the first image of love, few people might marry in the first place; without the second, few marriages would survive. But we can also see the ambivalent social valuation of cultural forms like love, technology, and storytelling as creating more resources for some groups than for others. When disadvantaged groups or people challenging the status quo tell stories, they may be especially vulnerable to skepticism about the authority, generalizability, or authenticity of the form. Advantaged groups, by contrast, may be less likely even to be seen as telling stories.[39]

If my hunch is right, groups and activities with higher social status should both gain from norms of storytelling and be able to breach them with fewer ramifications. Recall the stories that people told in small claims court that I referred to a moment ago: successful litigants told non-storylike stories in which rules were divorced from their social context, and unsuccessful litigants told stories that emphasized the obligations inhering in social relationships. The possibility I am raising here is not only that women are more likely to give the kind of relational accounts in which legal responsibility is poorly specified, but that they are more likely to be heard as doing so, no matter what their accounts actually sound like.[40]

My argument in this respect is in some ways similar to one advanced by sociologist Pierre Bourdieu. Bourdieu argues that people's ordinary use of language ends up reproducing existing inequalities. His explanation centers on the relationship between the linguistic competence with which speakers are socially endowed and the demands of the speaking situation. People with upper-class backgrounds have the training to adapt easily to the linguistic demands of most formal occasions. They also have more latitude in how they speak since, once their class background is communicated by way of dress, gesture, or title, their competence is assumed. As a result, if they breach the formal linguistic requirements of the situation, it may well be interpreted as deliberate rather than as a faux-pas. My argument centers rather on popular views of particular *discursive forms:* here, storytelling, but, more generally, interviews, statistics, arguments, apologies, and so on. I hypothesize that the ability to use such forms effectively is stratified not only because people have different levels of competence but also because doubts about the form's credibility and value are more likely to be triggered by some users and on some occasions rather than others.[41]

Along with conventions of narrative's content, then, conventions of narrative's use and interpretation thus delimit what people can do strategically with stories. Far from being attributable to false consciousness or people's inability to perceive alternatives, such cultural constraints are practical. They reflect the institutional rules of the game that those who want to effect change must play. But it is hardly surprising that challengers often fail to anticipate the costs of playing by the rules, especially since the risks of breaking them are substantial. For example, the animal rights activists whom sociologist Julian Groves studied discouraged women from serving in leadership positions because they believed that ordinary people saw women as prone to emotional stories about cruelty to animals. That emotionalism would cost the movement credibility. However, activists spent little time debating whether women were in fact prone to telling emotional stories or whether such stories rather than rational arguments were actually bad for the movement. So their calculations were strategic but were based on gendered assumptions about reason and emotion.[42]

In the following chapters, I describe citizens and elected officials as well as activists bumping up against popular beliefs about how stories work and when they are appropriate. African American members of Congress recounted the life of Martin Luther King, Jr., and his struggle to insist that his dream of racial equality remained unfulfilled. But the occasions on which they did so led them to call for commemoration rather than policy reform. Participants in a citizen's deliberative forum who described their personal experiences made it possible for fellow citizens to grasp and appreciate different priorities. But they generally refrained from describing personal experiences when discussions turned to areas of established policy. Women fighting for equality in court have been hurt not only by canonical story lines that misrepresent their experiences but by popular beliefs about what constitutes a true story that have discredited their accounts with judges and juries. In these and other cases, dominant epistemologies of narrative have imposed constraints on how effectively people can use stories to press for change.

The silver lining is that such epistemologies also provide persuasive resources. We are ambivalent about storytelling, not dismissive of it. There is a strong vein of skepticism toward professional expertise in American culture. Against that skepticism, the authenticity of personal storytelling makes the form trustworthy—sometimes more trustworthy than the complex facts and figures offered by certified experts. This probably accounts for the surprisingly high profile of ordinary people and grassroots groups in the mainstream American press. Moreover, insofar as current conventions of storytelling do fail to serve the powerless, activists can make them the targets of challenge. They can turn a congressional hearing into a speak-out or a courtroom appearance into a seminar. Indeed, one of the ways in which movements may have an impact is by gaining institutional purchase for new distributions of storytelling authority. For example, in the 1980s, AIDS activists succeeded in gaining formal representation on federal research review committees. But they also gained recognition for AIDS patients' personal accounts of their illnesses as authoritative knowledge in drug research. Refusing the institutional rules of storytelling can have powerful effects.[43]

At the beginning of this chapter, I argued that studying how storytelling figures in protest and politics would get us out of two analytical jams. It would help us to identify the ways in which culture interacts with structure in shaping the interests on behalf of which people mobilize and thus to avoid the shoals of both a structural fundamentalism and a cultural fundamentalism. It would also help us to identify the mechanisms by which culture sets the terms of strategic action, but without treating actors as strategic dupes. With respect to the conditions for cultural autonomy, I identified several circumstances in which particular narratives have had the capacity to define new stakes in contention. With respect to culture's role in shaping horizons of strategic possibility, I argued that although canonical stories may limit imaginable scenarios and, therefore, strategic options, just as high a hurdle for movement groups lies in the conventions and social valuations of storytelling. Narrative occupies a peculiar place in our cultural life: it is simultaneously ubiquitous and restricted to certain spheres of social life, trusted and denigrated. It is a legitimate form of political claimsmaking but also always at risk of being defined as personal rather than political and evocative rather than authoritative. These and other assumptions about narrative's uses—some enacted in formal policy, others in social etiquette—shape how challengers use culture and with what effects.

Outline of the Book

I pursue these hunches in chapters on mobilization in fledgling movements (chapter 2), movement strategizing (chapter 3), public deliberation by citizens (chapter 4), the legal adjudication and media coverage of political challenges (chapter 5), and congressional debate (chapter 6). In each chapter I take up a question that has puzzled scholars of protest and politics and show how an analysis of storytelling can improve on existing answers to it.

We still know relatively little about what persuades people to participate in collective action before movement organizations with strategic recruiting pitches have been established. To understand mobilization processes in those early phases, I analyze in chapter 2 the accounts that protesters gave of the 1960 student lunch counter sit-ins as they were occurring. What I find runs contrary to what movement scholars have identified as the ingredients of persuasive appeals. It was the stories' denial of individual intention, their vagueness about antagonists, and their ambiguity about the springs of collective action that made them so mobilizing. Students often described the sit-ins as "spontaneous" despite clear evidence of planning. But spontaneous meant local, moral, and urgent more than it meant unplanned. At the same time, the ambiguity of the term was important. Spontaneity figured in the sit-in narratives as a kind of ellipsis: it was the unspecifiable point at which individual action became collective and resistance became opposition. Students' stories may have engaged and mobilized their audiences partly through their promise to explain and their failure to do so. I show how the sit-in stories produced a new conception, and practice, of protest: as both moral and political, planned and expressive. Then I show how more conventional meanings eclipsed the earlier ones as the sit-in stories circulated over the next few years.

Why do movement groups choose the strategies, tactics, targets, and organizational forms that they do? Movement scholars have tended to picture activists juggling commitments to ideological consistency and strategic effectiveness, thus missing the role that ideology plays in activists' very definitions of what counts as strategic. In chapter 3, I argue that the emergence of metonymic structures in groups' deliberations can alert us to connections that have been drawn between a group, a strategic option, and a set of liabilities or strengths—often in the absence of any proof. This is what I find in tracing the rise and fall of participatory democracy in the radical wing of the southern civil rights movement. Contrary to standard explanations for activists' abandonment of participatory democracy in the mid-1960s, I show that a form that earlier had been seen as practical, political, and black was rejected when it came to be seen as ideological, self-indulgent, and white. Those symbolic associations made it easier to move toward an all-black movement, but they also surrendered the earlier practical benefits of participatory democratic decision making. And once established, the associations stuck, shaping later activists' views of the form. Tracing the establishment of metonymic structures in tactical debates can thus help us to understand how a tactical common sense is created and how it then shuts down possibilities as well as opening them up.

In chapter 4, I turn from storytelling by activists in movement strategy sessions to storytelling by ordinary citizens in deliberative forums. As democratic theorists have touted the potential of public deliberation to produce better policy and better citizens, critics have worried that the coolly logical and universalistic discourse that passes for deliberation further disadvantages already disadvantaged groups. Some critics have argued that encouraging personal storytelling in deliberation can make it more genuinely egalitarian, not only by enabling advantaged groups to identify emotionally with the experiences of others, but also by exposing the narrowness of supposedly universal standards. Deliberative democrats in the classical mold counter that stories are too personal, emotional, and ambiguous in their policy implications to foster good deliberation. My analysis of storytelling and classical reason-giving in a series of online public dialogue groups suggests that both sides are wrong. In the forum convened in the wake of the 2001 attack on the World Trade Center, stories were effective in fostering agreement across difference, not in spite of their normative ambiguity but because of it. Narrative's openness to interpretation allowed deliberators both to disagree with previous claims and to suggest compromises, all in the guise of telling similar stories. People did not always take advantage of that capacity, however. They tended not to tell stories in discussions of established policy, effectively treating those arenas as properly the purview of experts. Popular ideas about what stories are good for, rather than anything intrinsic to the form itself, thus limited storytelling's value in deliberation.

Does this mean that personal storytelling in general is ineffective for disadvantaged groups or that it inevitably reproduces rather than undermines the status quo? In chapter 5, I ask whether disadvantaged groups, especially women, are hurt by styling themselves as victims. Critics have argued that victim stories cast challengers as passive, helpless, and in need of protection rather than power. This cannot but repel potential recruits to the cause. However, to proclaim oneself a victim has not always been to trade agency for passivity. At times when different canonical story lines and narrative epistemologies have prevailed, the victims of social injustice have been seen as tutors in moral uplift rather than objects of pity, as experts rather than supplicants, and as capable of reforming audiences' rational faculties as much as their emotional sensibilities. On the other hand, given the story lines and narrative epistemologies that are institutionalized in American legal settings today, even critics may underestimate the political risks of telling victim stories. Focusing on women seeking gender equality in court, I show how canonical story lines have limited the legal remedies available to women. Then I suggest how women, and disadvantaged groups generally, might gain a hearing for non-canonical stories.

In chapter 6, I turn from the stories that activists and citizens tell to the stories that public officials tell. Scholars have devoted little attention to the competitive relations between those who represent disadvantaged groups within electoral institutions and those who do so outside mainstream politics. Through an analysis of storytelling on the House and Senate floor, I show that the stories black congressional representatives told about Martin Luther King, Jr., represented volunteers and institutional politicians like themselves as the proper heirs of King's legacy and as the best spokespeople for black people's interests—pointedly, *not* extra-institutional black protest leaders. Black protest leaders predictably told a different story about King. In this respect, the history of the civil rights movement was flexible enough to permit of competing uses. However, black congressional representatives also sought to persuade their white congressional colleagues to pass more redistributive social policies. Here, King's memory served them less well. The narrative conventions that restricted stories of King to purely ceremonial occasions made it difficult for speakers to do more on those occasions than call for more storytelling.

In chapter 7, I reprise the main arguments of the book and wrestle with a final question: Should students of political contention be telling stories as well as studying them? They should. Yet, champions of narrative—I focus on those in historical sociology—have missed some of the ways in which conventions of storytelling may compromise historical explanation. This is true even as they have sought to differentiate their conception of narrative from a literary one. The solution, I suggest, is to tell stories of past contention both in less literary ways and in more literary ways. Then I build on the sociology of narrative that I have developed in previous chapters in order to outline a much broader sociology of discursive forms.

TWO

"It was like a fever . . .":
Why People Protest

On February 1, 1960, four black students from North Carolina Agricultural and Technical College in Greensboro purchased a few items in the downtown Woolworth's and then sat down at its whites-only lunch counter. Told that they would not be served, they remained seated until the store closed. "Four guys met, planned, and went into action. It's just that simple," Franklin McCain explained later to those who wondered who had planned the demonstrations. The Greensboro Four came back the next day, and the next, now joined by students from surrounding colleges. Students in other cities began to sit in. Within a month, the sit-ins had spread to thirty cities in seven states. Within two months, they had spread to fifty-four cities in nine states. By mid-April, fifty thousand people had taken part in the protests.[1]

Students described the sit-ins as unplanned, impulsive, and, over and over again, as spontaneous. "It was like a fever," students told *Dissent* writer Michael Walzer. "Everyone wanted to go." Forty years later, we know, as did the students themselves, that there was a good deal of strategic planning behind the sit-ins. The Greensboro Four were members of an NAACP Youth Council and were in touch with activists who had led sit-ins in Durham in the late 1950s. When the protest began, a network of ministers, NAACP officials, and other adult activists contacted colleagues to spread the news, trained students in sit-in techniques, and persuaded other adults to support the cause.

This was far from the "grass fire" that protesters and observers described.[2]

Narrative reconstruction of this kind is not unique to the 1960 sit-ins. Consider the story of Rosa Parks. In 1955, this seamstress from Montgomery, Alabama, refused to yield her seat when a white passenger boarded the bus she was riding. She was tired, she explained later. In response to her arrest, Montgomery's black citizens vowed to stay off the buses. For over a year, they walked and carpooled until the boycott drove the bus company out of business and the Supreme Court ruled Montgomery's segregated busing illegal. That familiar story omits the fact that Rosa Parks was a longtime activist and Alabama state NAACP secretary, not just an ordinary woman whose fatigue inadvertently made her the hero of a movement. A cadre of black activists in Montgomery had been planning to challenge the city's bus ordinance for some time. They had considered a boycott after fifteen year-old Claudette Colvin was arrested but abandoned the idea when the unmarried Colvin became pregnant. Parks, who was married, middle-aged, and a churchgoer, better fit the bill as a test case. After her arrest, activists worked quickly to organize the boycott. No one knew it would prove so successful, that so many people would participate for so long, but the groundwork had been laid long before Parks boarded the bus.[3]

Groundwork of a different sort had been laid for Betty Friedan's *The Feminine Mystique.* A scathing exposé of the postwar ideology that chained women to home and hearth, the book was an immediate bestseller when it was published in 1963. It is widely credited with helping to launch a nationwide movement for women's equality. In it, Friedan described herself as until recently an apolitical suburban housewife, captive of the forces of domesticity. She was not "even conscious of the woman problem," she wrote later. We know now, however, that Friedan was a longtime labor writer and activist with special expertise in discrimination against women. Her journalism in the 1940s and 1950s was marked by sharp insight into the economics of feminine domesticity and a keen sense of the "woman problem."[4]

Why do activists so often describe protest as sprung from the head of Zeus, ignoring or downright denying the planning that preceded it? Why do they cast themselves not as strategic actors but as swept up by forces over which they have no control? Activists tell stories for strategic reasons, and the stories I just recounted are no exception. For American activists during much of the last century, one of the thorniest challenges was to avoid charges of communist influence. Representing protest as homegrown and spur-of-the-moment was a way to deflect claims that it was controlled by "outsiders," which meant Communists. In the Talla-hassee, Florida, sit-in campaign, adult leaders who helped plan the sit-ins denied their own involvement for that very reason. Rosa Parks's activism before the Montgomery bus boycott included a stint at the Highlander Folk School, a radical education center in Tennessee that was branded a "communist training school" soon after Parks's visit. This was reason enough for Montgomery activists to cast her as a political neophyte. Betty Friedan had also spent time at the Highlander Center. In addition to fearing redbaiting, she presumably wanted to appeal to women who had not been exposed to radical ideas and settings. Movement stories, in this view, are strategic bids for public support.[5]

But there is more to it than that. Student protesters in 1960 told the story of the sit-ins not only to reporters and the public but also to each other in letters to campus newspapers, editorials, handbills, flyers, and personal correspondence. In these less public venues, one might have ex-pected that people trying to convince others to participate would attest to the power of individual will and collective agency, and would argue that with adequate planning and determination, anyone could launch a sit-in. Instead, students represented the sit-ins as spontaneous and im-pulsive. "*No one* started it," one insisted.[6]

Why deny the intentionality that might have served to persuade other people of the ease of mobilization? Because stories are more than strate-gic devices. As I noted in chapter 1, we tell stories to persuade but also to make sense of the unfamiliar. Stories assimilate confusing events into fa-miliar frameworks while recognizing that things are no longer as they were and we are no longer who we were. Hence, we hear stories of being born during moments of rebellion, or having been blind and coming to see—formulations that both integrate novelty into narratives of birth and healing and recognize a generative breach. Movement stories turn the strange into the new. This does not mean, however, that they fully *ex-plain* the new. As I argue in this chapter, stories contain rather than re-solve ambiguity. This is part of what makes them so engaging and com-pels their retelling. When students described the sit-ins as "spontaneous," and as "exploding," "welling up," and "like a fever," they captured the indefinable moment when a group of separate individuals became a col-lective actor. The stories' ambiguity, their failure to explain a shift that seemed impossible to explain but could only be retold again and again, may have galvanized other students.[7]

This argument departs from current thinking about how people are persuaded to mobilize. Ever since economist Mancur Olson argued that it was irrational to participate in collective action, scholars have sought to explain why rational people nevertheless often do. Olson's argument was that, since one will enjoy the benefits of collective action whether one participates or not, it makes sense to free ride on the efforts of others—unless one is offered personal incentives to participate or is coerced into doing so. But movement scholars have identified other reasons that people join time-consuming and even risky movements: because it is fun; because their sense of solidarity with people they know who are already in the movement demands it; because if they don't do it, no one else will; because they are morally shocked and compelled by an injustice; because it is who they *are*.[8]

People also participate because movement activists *frame* protest in such a way as to make it seem a necessary solution to an obvious injustice. As framing theorists see it, if activists are shrewd, they make it obvious that people rather than impersonal forces are responsible for the injustice. They draw a sharp distinction between "we" and "they." And along with the injustice of the situation and the identity of those affected by it, they assert potential participants' efficacy, their capacity to bring about the changes they seek. Activists do not, in this view, deny their own agency by saying that "no one started it." They do not represent their struggle as against so vague an opponent as "apathy." They do not deny their own role in launching the struggle. At least, they do not do these things if they have any hope of mobilizing people.[9]

And yet students in the sit-ins did just those things and mobilized tens of thousands of people in the process. The key to this puzzle may lie in the fact that movement scholars have devoted very little attention to the kinds of discursive processes that characterize fledgling movements, before formal organizations with carefully crafted recruitment pitches even exist. In that context, I argue, narratives told by numerous actors more to make sense of surprising developments than to recruit participants may nevertheless endow events with the moral purpose, emotional telos, and engaging ambiguity that persuade others to participate. I advance this argument, first by discussing how sociologists have accounted for participation in the 1960 sit-ins, a protest that inspired important theorizing about participation generally. Then I draw on students' stories about the sit-ins to flesh out a different explanation, one in which ambiguity rather than clarity about the wellsprings of action spurs mobilization. What I am after is a discursive mechanism that operates in the fledgling stages of mobilization more generally, and I turn to several other movements to show the same mechanism at work.

Solidarity and Identity in the 1960 Student Sit-Ins

In his compelling analysis, sociologist Aldon Morris decisively rejected characterizations of the student sit-ins as spontaneous and as orchestrated by students. To the contrary, he showed that ministers, NAACP officials, and other adult activists mobilized to spread the word of the sit-ins, trained students in nonviolent tactics, and helped raise community support for them. "The sit-ins spread across the South in a short period because [adult] activists, working through local movement centers, planned, coordinated, and sustained them," Morris argued. But even if adult activists did play important roles in the sit-in movement, that alone does not explain why and how tens of thousands of students were persuaded to participate. Twenty or thirty activist ministers, even working overtime, could hardly have persuaded fifty thousand people to join the sit-ins.[10]

Sociologists Debra Friedman and Doug McAdam add a piece to the puzzle. For thousands of black southern students, Friedman and McAdam argue, protest became a normative expectation of being a student. In the early part of the civil rights movement, southern blacks had come to see activism as part of their role as churchgoers. In 1960, the same thing happened to students, as "activist" became what the authors call a "prized social identity." Such an identity supplied incentives to participate. Supporting Friedman and McAdam's explanation, eyewitness accounts suggest that in 1960 activism did indeed become normative for southern black college students. As Tallahassee sit-in leader Charles Smith put it, "a spirit of competition has found its way into the civil rights arena, and no college or university wants to be left behind or be found wanting in this kind of courage or conviction." In his survey of participants on eight college campuses shortly after the wave of sit-ins began, sociologist Paul Wehr found that "one common response to the question 'Why did the movement start at your school?' was '[W]e wanted to jump into the movement before [another school].'" Sociologist James Laue also observed that "the response of Negro students to Greensboro was almost always phrased in terms of 'keeping up' with the other students." Tuskegee Dean Charles Gomillion told Laue: "When students came to me to talk about their protest plans, I asked them, 'Where are you going to sit-in here?'—since Tuskegee was in a rural area. 'We *have* to go,' they said. 'What will other colleges think of us if we don't?'"[11]

Friedman and McAdam's claim that student and activist identities had become normatively fused is persuasive, but their explanation for it is incomplete. "In the first stage, the emerging movement grows out of but remains dependent upon preexisting institutions and organizations . . . *established groups* redefine group membership to include commitment to the movement as one of its obligations." In the case of the southern sit-ins, which established groups are they referring to? Southern college officials certainly did not promote an activist identity. Most student participants experienced their college administrations and faculties as unsupportive of the sit-ins. According to one survey, only 15 percent of the sit-in participants from public colleges reported that their administrations had been supportive. By the end of the 1960 spring term, more than a hundred students had been expelled from their colleges for their participation. My examination of campus newspapers showed that many made no mention of sit-ins in which their own students were participating. Some of the librarians I spoke to had been on staff at the time of the sit-ins, and they attributed this silence to the conservatism of campus administrations.[12]

If Friedman and McAdam mean instead that the equation of student and activist was effected by students themselves, then we need a better understanding of how that happened. To account for the emergence of a mobilizing identity on black college campuses and the development of such identities more broadly, we need to examine not only the instrumental framing efforts of established groups and movement organizations but also the larger cultural context in which an idiom of student activism made sense. Then we need to capture the diffuse, non-institutionalized discursive processes through which a rationale for protest, or a set of rationales, gained currency.

With respect to the context of student protest, black students in 1960 were exposed to student activism on a world-historical stage. "There was a feeling that it was the 'dawn of a new era,'" longtime activist Ella Baker recalled, "that something new and great was happening and that only [students] could chart the course of history." The sit-ins came at a time when students were playing visible and dramatic roles in regime changes around the world. Students had toppled military regimes in Turkey and South Korea and their representatives met with American students at the 1960 National Student Association conference. Some of the most momentous changes had been wrought by *black* student activists, and that was inspiring. "Sure we identified with the blacks in Africa," Nashville sit-in leader John Lewis said later, "and we were thrilled by what was going on. Here were black people, talking of freedom and liberation and independence, thousands of miles away. We could hardly miss the lesson for ourselves." Representatives of the Republic of Cameroon, Kenya, Nigeria, and other nations visited black college campuses in 1959 and 1960, and black campus newspapers devoted considerable coverage to events in Africa. "Today, the dark people on the other side of the earth are protesting and dying for their freedom," a Howard University editorialist noted in calling for student activism in early 1960. "All over the world a new generation of leadership is emerging," wrote a Fisk student. And another, "We realize that students can play an important role in the development and redevelopment of society."[13]

Black collegians were thus exposed to students as change-makers through their direct contacts with international student activists and through newspaper stories on protest abroad. At the same time, campus newspapers in 1959 and early 1960 referred frequently to the problems of student "apathy." Editorials chastised students for their lack of political and intellectual engagement: "The majority of our students are now apathetic toward student government"; "General student apathy towards affairs pertaining to them—political, social or otherwise—is a 'campus disease' badly in need of therapy"; "Throughout American education there is a growing concern for what has been labeled by some 'student apathy.'" Several editorials discussed the "beatniks" critically, attributing their rejection of middle-class conventionality to a pervasive normlessness.[14]

The cultural media to which students had direct access thus offered and evaluated two modes of being a student, praising the revolutionary aspirations of the international students and condemning the deviance of the beats. The dynamic involved in the fusion of prized role and activism that Friedman and McAdam describe was less engineered by established organizations than perceived by students on a world-historical stage. But how did the collective identity of student activist come to be associated with a particular set of expected behaviors? Even after news spread of the Greensboro protest, one could imagine that student activism might mean rallying financial and moral support for those taking part in the sit-ins, or organizing campus discussions about race relations or the upcoming presidential election. How and why did *student activist* come to mean putting one's body on the line and participating directly in nonviolent desegregation efforts? To begin to answer that question, I turn to what students themselves said to each other about their participation in the sit-ins.

Spontaneity in the Sit-In Narratives

The very first accounts of the Greensboro sit-in were not narrative in form. An editorial in the North Carolina Agricultural and Technical College *Register* used an explicitly persuasive mode: "You as students can believe me when I tell you this will benefit every one of us who sit at the Woolworth counter." The piece emphasized not the transformation that is characteristic of narrative, but continuity. "The waitress ignored us and kept serving the white customers. However, this is no great surprise to me because I have been exposed to segregation at lunch counters for 15 years and the situation is predominately unchanged." In the next days and weeks, however, as students from surrounding colleges joined the Greensboro protest and then launched their own sit-ins, narrative accounts began to appear. They circulated in flyers and handbills, campus newspaper articles and letters to the editor, and they figured in participants' speeches to student groups. After the Student Nonviolent Coordinating Committee (SNCC; commonly pronounced "Snick") was formed at a sit-in conference in April, stories submitted by sit-in groups appeared in its publication, *The Student Voice*.[15]

Students' accounts of the sit-ins took a similar form. They described events occurring on their campus in chronological order, with a beginning, middle, and end. They detailed a key transformation and its larger meaning. We might expect that student newspaper accounts would be more likely than speeches or personal letters to recount events in narrative form, and I cite more of the former than the latter. But newspaper stories typically do not display the degree of suspense that the sit-in narratives did. They usually place the important information at the beginning and then provide increasing detail as the story goes on. Narrativity—an elliptical quality that engages readers—is not prominent. Nor do newspaper stories usually foreground a moral transformation in the way that the sit-in stories did.

Framing theorists might expect student writers to emphasize the injustice of their situation, define themselves against clearly specified antagonists, and assert their capacity to bring about the changes they sought. In fact, the injustices student writers described were often vague: denial of "the humane aspects of the American dream," and "shackles of immorality, archaic traditions, and complacency." Students conducting the sit-ins pitted themselves against apathy, a condition that does not seem clearly situational rather than individual and political rather than personal. Students in the sit-in stories acted powerfully, transgressively, with immediate, real consequence. Yet they were simply the carriers of a force beyond them, they said. When one group of students launched a demonstration, they felt that "[t]his was a surprise (and shock) not only to the whole town but to themselves as well." Students attributed the sit-ins not to a newfound sense of collective efficacy but to forces over which they had no control. Would not this kind of framing discourage student participation rather than mobilize it?[16]

Consider the students whose flyer described their sit-in as "the result of spontaneous combustion," then chronicled the planning that had preceded it. They emphasized, however, that, "there was no organizational tie-in of any kind, either local or national." This seems to be the point of using the phrase "spontaneous combustion." But the students also acknowledged, "in order to make the story complete," that members of the sit-in organizing group had previously received a "Letter to Christian Students" from the National Student Christian Federation urging them to seek ways to participate. Students' characterization of the sit-ins as spontaneous even as they described planning them suggests that spontaneity meant something other than unplanned. In fact, closer examination of the sit-in stories indicates that it meant several things. Spontaneity denoted the sheer power of moral protest. Sitting in was motivated by an imperative to act now that brooked no compromise. One simply put one's body on the line, without debating its ideological potential or waiting for instruction from higher-ups. "The fact that the protest broke out overnight and spread with fantastic speed said simply this: the Negro, despite the thoughts of too many whites, is NOT content. . . . And *nobody* could escape this." A piece in the *Student Voice* opened with a story of one student's effort to launch a sit-in: "It is really strange—to do things alone. Sometimes we have no alternative." Descriptions of protest "burst[ing]," "breaking," "exploding," "sweeping," "surging," "rip[ping] through the city like an epidemic," of students "fired" by the "spark of the sit-ins," of a "chain reaction" all suggested an unstoppable moral impetus. "The spirit reached the boiling point at 11:00 a.m., March 10, 1960," wrote Philander Smith College students in Little Rock, Arkansas. For Vanderbilt students, the "current wave of demonstrations is the spontaneous ground swell of the profound determination of young Negroes to be first-class citizens."[17]

Spontaneity also connoted a sharp break with adult forms of protest. "Our impatience with the token efforts of responsible leaders was manifest in the spontaneous demonstrations which, after February 1, spread rapidly across the entire South," said Nashville participant Marion Barry.

"Spontaneous" meant free of the caution, slow-moving consultation, and sheer timidity that students saw in adult protest. Commending the formation of a new black periodical, SNCC wrote to its editors, "There is no longer a way to rationalize gradualism. It did die on February 1, 1960, in Woolworth's of Greensboro. It will die again and again when every individual rises to his responsibility."[18]

Spontaneity described the emotional experience of the sit-ins as well as their political message. Students applauded their comrades' discipline, calm, courage, and determination. Their "only prayer" was to "have the strength, knowledge, and fortitude that these students exhibited." They described the "spirit of love" with which participants had confronted their enraged white antagonists. But their accounts of the sit-ins also conveyed a sense of *fun*. They emphasized not the sober religiosity and seriousness characteristic of pacifist and Quaker nonviolent witness, but rather humor and a giddy sense of excitement. Editors of a college newspaper wrote, "Here were two harmless young people sauntering through a store . . . stalking them in true dragnetness were no less than half a dozen police officers, while customers and managers hovered in corners as if the invasion from Mars had come!" (ellipsis in original). A Knoxville College writer composed a poem entitled "Ode to a Lunch Counter": "Little lunch counter with your many stools / And your nervous pacing manager fools / How do you feel amid this confusion and strife? / Do you object to a change inevitable in life?" None of the stories represented participants as enraged or calculating.[19]

Protesters did frequently describe themselves as tired. They were tired "of waiting for the American dream to materialize"; "tired of un-American discrimination"; "tired of moving at an ox-cart pace"; tired of "wait[ing] for the course of time to supply us those rights we as first class citizens of this *our* America deserve." They had "'taken it' since the day [they] were born," and the sit-ins were the result of their impatience. "After 95 years of discussions, delays, postponements, procrastination, denials, and second-class citizenship, the Negro of today wants his full citizenship in his day." After "hundreds of years" of living "without pride and honor," the sit-ins "serve[d] notice that the Negro, particularly of the South, no longer accepts second class citizenship." These formulations are interesting. They merge the individual with the collective: *I* protest because *we* have waited for generations to be treated with dignity. "Our biggest influence has been inside—all those years of second-class citizenship," one protester wrote. The motivation in these formulations was a simple one. You did not have to have a sophisticated agenda or ideology in order to protest; you just had to be impatient, unwilling to "stifle" your "feelings any longer." Impatience was familiar to most adolescents.[20]

The "tired" formulation is interesting for another reason. It was often paired with a characterization of students before the sit-ins as apathetic. The sit-ins had destroyed "the myth of student apathy," had dealt "a death blow to apathy," to students' "false robe of sophistication and unconcern." "No longer may students be called the 'Silent Generation.'" Being tired and being apathetic both suggested passivity and inaction. Yet being tired of waiting issued in radical action. The narrative thus reconfigured apathy *as* being tired of waiting. Only one thing distinguished those who were laying their bodies on the line from those who were lying around in their dorm rooms: the first group recognized that their apathy was the repression of a desire for full political citizenship. It wasn't that they were apathetic; it was that they were "weary with waiting." In that sense, said students, "we had been ready to do something like this for a long time." Indeed, "we have been planning it all our lives." The story did not exhort students to shake off their apathy, an injunction that most students probably associated with the familiar calls to vote for student council, come to the debate club, or volunteer. Instead, it endowed apathy with a transformative telos:

Time was when our elders, those who in their school days dreamed radical dreams, wondered what disease was responsible for the apathy that was apparent among today's college students. Three months ago, they ceased from wondering about the apathy and began marveling over the radicalism . . . the students say—and it is reasonable to believe them—that they are tired of waiting for the humane aspects of the American dream to materialize.[21]

Other emotional transformations figured in the sit-in narratives. The "butterflies" of apprehension ceded to "joy" in demonstrating. Students in North Carolina, said *Dissent* writer Michael Walzer, "told one story after another about . . . minor but to them terribly important incidents in the buses, in stores, on the job. The stories usually ended with some version of 'I ran out of that store. I almost cried. . . .'" The sit-in narrative transformed a too-common story of humiliation into one of triumph.[22]

Narratives of the sit-ins, in which spontaneity denoted a break with adult gradualism, a moral rather than political strategy, a joy in action, and an unstoppable force, may have motivated students to engage in time-consuming and dangerous activism. Students narrativized what was happening in order to make sense of it and to signal its significance, "The sit-ins," SNCC Chairman Charles McDew said in October 1960, "have inspired us to build a new image of ourselves in our own mind." Along with that image came new behavioral expectations.[23]

Spontaneity as Ellipsis

The sit-in accounts may also have motivated action by their *failure* to account for mobilization. Their ambiguity about agents and agency, not their clarity, may have engaged their audiences. I have argued that the elliptical character of storytelling is necessary to stories' suspensefulness. But literary critic J. Hillis Miller takes the argument further. The impossibility of logically explaining events compels us to tell stories, which in turn preserve the ambiguity that compels us to tell more stories. All narratives are characterized by the repetition of what Miller calls a complex word, one with multiple, even incongruous, meanings, as we use "right" in the phrases "to have the right," "to be right," or "to go right." Each of those meanings may or may not be simultaneously operative in the same story. This indeterminacy is both what rivets our attention and invites more stories. "[W]e always need more stories because in some way they do not satisfy," Miller observes. The dynamic is clearest in stories of humankind's origins. The point at which humans separate themselves from beasts is unknowable, since "whatever is chosen as the moment of origination always presupposes some earlier moment when man first appeared." The question cannot be answered logically, and the alternative is a mythical narrative whose illogical premises will nevertheless require that it be retold.[24]

As a poststructuralist, Miller believes that meaning is not only polyvalent but indeterminate. This is true in all discursive forms. Logical arguments are just as dependent on a complex word whose meaning is undecidable as is a work of literary fiction. However, one need not endorse Miller's argument in its entirety to accept the possibility that in accounting for *origins,* in particular, we may turn to stories that are ambiguous, and that ambiguity may lead us to tell more stories. When, then, did the sit-ins begin? Did they begin when the first students were arrested? Or did the impulse behind them go back further: to the Montgomery bus boycott in 1955 or the Brown v. Board decision in 1954? Did the sit-ins begin with the first slave rebellion? With the first song sung, or African tradition preserved, or Christian ritual reinterpreted in what James Scott calls an infrapolitics of dissent stretching back to Africans' enslavement in this country? The question of origins is historical but also personal. When does collective action begin? When does individual action become collective and resistance become opposition? When can I call myself an activist? The impossibility of answering these questions may call for more stories and more actions to recount.[25]

Let me expand on this possibility with an origin story from another movement. According to framing theorist Robert Benford, a story called "The Hundredth Monkey" proved to be an extraordinarily effective mobilizing tool for organizers in the American antinuclear movement. The story opens with a parable, which I quote at length:

The Japanese monkey, *Macaca fuscata,* has been observed in the wild for a period of over 30 years. In 1952, on the island of Koshima scientists were providing monkeys with sweet potatoes, but they found the dirt unpleasant. An 18-month-old female named Imo found she could solve the problem by washing the potatoes in a nearby stream. She taught this trick to her mother. Her playmates also learned this new way and they taught their mothers too. This cultural innovation was gradually picked up by various monkeys before the eyes of the scientists. Between 1952 and 1958, all the young monkeys learned to wash the sandy sweet potatoes to make them more palatable . . .

Then something startling took place. In the autumn of 1958, a certain number of Koshima monkeys were washing sweet potatoes—the exact number is not known. Let us suppose that when the sun rose one morning there were 99 monkeys on Koshima Island who had learned to wash their sweet potatoes. Let's further suppose that later that morning, the hundredth monkey learned to wash potatoes. THEN IT HAPPENED!

By that evening almost everyone in the tribe was washing sweet potatoes before eating them. The added energy of this hundredth monkey somehow created an ideological breakthrough!

But notice. The most surprising thing observed by the scientists was that the habit of washing sweet potatoes then spontaneously jumped over the sea—Colonies of monkeys on other islands and the mainland troop of monkeys at Takasakiyama began washing their sweet potatoes!

Thus, when a certain critical number achieves an awareness, this new awareness may be communicated from mind to mind. [. . .] You may furnish the added consciousness energy to create the shared awareness of the urgent necessity to rapidly achieve a nuclear free world.[26]

Benford argues that the story was so widely used by organizers because it conveyed a sense of efficacy, demonstrating to potential recruits "the power of the new awareness and your role in the unfolding drama." But does the story actually do that? Does it demonstrate the power of conscious individual action? "THEN IT HAPPENED," the story goes, but it is not clear just *what* happened, nor why all the Koshima monkeys and monkeys in distant tribes suddenly, "spontaneously," began washing potatoes. How did monkeys that were not in contact with the original tribe learn the practice? The story raises more questions than it answers. My own guess is that the story was successful precisely because it failed to supply a logical explanation for action. The story promises to explain the link between action and outcome but then simply places us, the reader/listener, at the victorious end. Penetrating the mystery of collective action requires more stories and more actions to recount. So framing theorists may be wrong to insist that people need a clear specification of agents, antagonists, and targets, and an easily interpretable rationale for participation. The stories protesters tell to make sense of what is happening may compel others to listen and to act not by providing a sense of the ease or efficacy of protest, but by reproducing its inexplicable character.[27]

Ambiguity operated similarly in the sit-in narratives. The word *spontaneous* means voluntary *and* instinctual (involuntary). Contradictory meanings are contained in the same word. In the sit-in narratives, in this reading, spontaneity functioned as a kind of narrative ellipsis in which the movement's beginning occurred. "BOOM—It Happened," as one account put it, and the non-narratable shift from observer to participant took place. This ellipsis strengthened the engagement of those hearing or reading the sit-in narratives in at least one of two ways. Either the story's underspecification of the mechanisms of participation forced readers to fill in the missing links, to become co-authors of the story, or the story could not fix the motivation for participation and so required its retelling. Either way, it was not the sit-in narratives' clarity about the antagonists, protagonists, and stakes of struggle that made them so compelling but their containment of mystery and risk within the familiarity of a ubiquitous discursive form.[28]

Institutionalizing Spontaneity

How compelling were the sit-in narratives? By September 1961, seventy thousand people had participated in the demonstrations. Of course, we do not know that the sit-in narratives were directly responsible for that. However, the challenges that were created for the sit-in movement's new organization by those narratives suggests their potency. Spontaneity, emblematic of students' independence and their unique contribution to the movement, became an organizational commitment that both animated and constrained strategic action. Students called for coordination but resisted direction, wanted the movement to speak to the nation but were wary of leaders, wanted to expand the scope of protest but distrusted adult advice. At a college workshop sponsored by the Highlander Center in April 1960, just before the formation of the Student Nonviolent Coordinating Committee, seventy-five students discussed "the spontaneous origin and spread of the sit-ins," and complained about adults' interference. They were determined that no organization should control the protests. Participants at SNCC's first and second conferences delineated only a modest role for their own organization in which it was "made quite clear that SNCC does not control local groups."[29]

SNCC's administrators found themselves repeatedly called upon to defend the organization's very existence to its members and supporters, and specifically to reassure them that organization would not stifle the spontaneity of the movement. SNCC's Jane Stembridge responded directly to a donor's concern: "We believe that the spontaneity will not die and the coordination will speed the coming of genuine equality." She and SNCC Chair Marion Barry reassured another supporter, "The purpose of the Coordinating Committee meetings is not to control the movement but to make an attempt at coordination of efforts." In funding appeals, newsletters, and speeches, SNCC leaders represented the group as an extension of the spontaneity of the sit-ins and of the values of moral imperative, local autonomy, and radicalism that spontaneity connoted.[30]

These statements never contrasted spontaneity to effectiveness. To the contrary, student activists believed that it was their capacity to move fast that was responsible for the remarkable scale of the demonstrations. At this point, the conventional oppositions between spontaneity and organization and between instrumental and expressive action simply did not hold. However, spontaneity's more capacious meanings would eventually yield to its conventional ones. In the next few years, a view of direct action as moral *rather than* political occasionally crept into SNCC workers' discussions. The conventional interpretation associated spontaneity not only with moral and immediate action but also with nonpolitical and nonstrategic action. The message of the sit-in story, in this interpretation, was that moral action demanded spontaneity and *not* planning. The minutes of a 1963 SNCC strategy session record that when participants had reached an impasse, older SNCC advisor Myles Horton observed, "It appeared that most of the participants wanted to deal with political questions, and wanted to deal exclusively with the political orientation. SNCC has continually had debates of whether the emphasize [*sic*] should be political or religious, spontaneous or rigidly political." By contrasting "spontaneous" to "*rigidly* political," Horton was leaving room for a view of direct action as political but not conventionally so. But he and others lacked the language for describing a politics that was not "rigidly political."[31]

That said, a tendency to view direct action as nonstrategic and nonpolitical by definition was much more pronounced among the white new leftists who were building their own movement—one that was profoundly influenced by the southern sit-ins. Students on northern campuses were impressed by the protesters' courage and by their unabashed sense of moral purpose. Their determination to act for their ideals now, without calculation or compromise, was a challenge to what historian Christopher Lasch called the "hard-boiled pragmatism" of the left. University of Michigan student Tom Hayden saw the sit-ins as "risky, shoot for the moon affairs," the beginnings of "a revolution that would reduce complexity to moral simplicity." He joined a new group named Students for a Democratic Society and described it as a northern counterpart to the southern student movement. But Hayden and his SDS colleagues were not shy about identifying what they saw as the limitations of that movement. Hayden criticized it in 1961 for lacking a "precise political vision"; even a "real political consciousness" to match its "moral clarity." His colleague, SDS founder Al Haber, criticized a focus on direct action as "non-political." Another SDS leader wrote, "The focus of action on Negro campuses in the non-violent protest movement has been largely 'non-political.'" The sit-ins were admirably moral, SDS leaders agreed, but not yet properly political.[32]

The sit-ins and, more broadly, direct action, were thus viewed as immediate, expressive, and powerfully moral—all meanings associated with "spontaneity"—but also as nonpolitical, and nonstrategic. This perception endured for the rest of the decade. Antiwar activist Staughton Lynd expressed a minority position in 1966 when he asked, "[W]hy should it be assumed that direct action is 'moral' rather than 'political'? If enough people act, or if the act is of a particularly strategic kind, there is a political impact." Lynd was a longtime pacifist and well-schooled in the Gandhian techniques of direct action that pacifists had developed before and after World War II. While often trained by those pacifists, black student protestors had transformed direct action. They put it on a mass scale, stripped it of its somber asceticism, and made it exuberant. But they never denied the discipline and training that preceded their actions. However, those features dropped out as the story of the sit-ins was retold. Historians have argued that direct action in the new left and antiwar movement tended to be poorly organized, with participants rarely trained in nonviolence or even clear on the principles guiding their actions. Partly responsible was the antinomy between spontaneity and strategy on which conceptions of direct action came to rest. The conventional story line, which has people acting out their moral commitments in emotional and impulsive protest, eclipsed one in which people acted emotionally, morally, *and* in politically instrumental ways.[33]

Destiny Stories

I have argued that when students called the sit-ins spontaneous, they were not saying that their actions were unplanned. Rather, they were conveying the sit-ins' urgent, moral, and local character. Calling the sit-ins spontaneous also captured the impossibility of fixing the point at which individual intention became collective will, the point at which resistance became opposition. Describing the sit-ins as spontaneous or using phrases like "BOOM—It Happened!" did the same thing that the ellipsis (. . .) did in the antinuclear movement's story of the hundredth monkey. It contained without explaining the unexplainable point at which protest began.

A similar ellipsis (often, literally three dots . . .) has figured in the mobilizing stories of other movements. For example, in his best-selling manifesto for community organizing, *Rules for Radicals*, published in 1971, Saul Alinsky imagined a conversation between an organizer and a resident. "Organizer: Do you live over in that slummy building? Answer: Yeah. What about it?" The organizer suggests that the residents should demand building repairs, and the resident counters that it will not do any good. "Organizer: Hmmm. What if nobody in that building paid their rent? Answer: Well, they'd start to throw . . . Hey, you know, they'd have trouble throwing everybody out, wouldn't they?" Again, the transformation takes place in the three-dot ellipsis, where the resident realizes the potential of collective action. His next line is "Hey, you know, maybe you got something—say, I'd like you to meet some of my friends. How about a drink?" He has become an activist.[34]

Another example comes from the first issue of the new magazine of the women's movement *Ms.* in 1972. In an article entitled "The Housewife's Moment of Truth," journalist Jane O'Reilly described a workshop she had attended where participants were asked to imagine themselves as animals. One woman told the group that she had been a snake:

As I was moving through the grass, enjoying my slithering, curving progress, I realized I had no fangs. No bite. I couldn't even hiss. My only protection was that I could change color in reaction to the people that passed by. I started to go through my garden and I saw that there were panthers draped over all the lawn furniture. I went into my house, and there were panthers everywhere, filling every chair, curled up in groups in all the rooms. They were eating, rather elegantly, and no one paid any attention to me, even when I asked if they wanted anything more to eat. I was interested but I was different, and finally I withdrew.[35]

There were both men and women in the workshop but O'Reilly and the other women had an immediate reaction. "The women in the group looked at her, looked at each other, and . . . click! A moment of truth. The shock of recognition. Instant sisterhood. 'You became a *housewife,*' we said, excited, together, turning to the men to see if they understood. 'She is describing a housewife. Do you know that?'" According to O'Reilly, the men did not get it, did not, as she put it, "recognize the click! of recognition, that parenthesis of truth around a little thing that completes the puzzle of reality in women's minds—the moment that brings a gleam to our eyes and means the revolution has begun." The article went on to recount story after story of men taking women's subservience for granted in mundane ways: men casually instructing their wives to pick up the toys, pooh-poohing the onerousness of housework, expecting a colleague to perform secretarial duties. Episodes like these were common, a dime a dozen, but for some reason, *this* time, they ended differently. The conclusion to each was "Click!" and then the woman's resistance, telling her husband to pick up the toys himself or sharply protesting her denigration. The dénouement of the panther story was actually not the confusing and unsatisfying ending that the woman herself gave it—"I was interested but I was different and finally I withdrew"—but the response of the other women: the three dots and then the new consciousness: ". . . click!" And that click, said O'Reilly, meant that "the revolution has begun."[36]

O'Reilly's article prompted thousands of letters to the editor, the vast majority of them telling personal stories of injustice and many of them beginning or ending with "Click!" The first letter, for example, began "Click!" then described a dinner party where the men professed their puzzlement at inner-city rioting: "Jesus, in their own neighborhoods, what's the matter with those people?" The letter-writer continued: "And one of the women said, very quietly, in a kind of wondering voice, 'Sometimes I think I know just how they feel . . .' The three of us women looked at each other: Click!" Again the banal comment, again *this* time, a profoundly different, rebellious response. What accounted for the change? In each case, only the three dots. According to *Ms.* magazine's historian, the O'Reilly article and the response to it had a profound impact on the magazine and the movement. So many readers wrote in with their stories that "click" became a "feminist term of art." And the magazine's editors realized that whatever format they chose for the magazine, they would have to plan for multiple columns of reader mail. But it was a certain kind of reader mail. From O'Reilly's story on, readers would recount episodes in their own lives as a way to make a point about an article they had read. Telling stories, personal stories, was political action. This would remain a hallmark of the women's liberation movement.[37]

In Alinsky's account of community organizing and in the feminist Click! accounts, narrative motivated action precisely by its capacity to represent without explaining the point at which resistance became opposition and/or individual action became collective. However, if this suggests that origin stories may operate similarly in all movements, there is another possibility. The critical discursive ellipsis, the point in the story where the non-narratable movement beginning takes place, may in fact be distinctively modern. In earlier eras and other places, understandings of the logic of individual action and of historical time may have made for narrativity of a different sort. The counterpart of modern narratives' suspenseful "Who or what is responsible for what is happening to me?" may have been "How does one come to know God's will?" or "Is our fate to be one of victory or defeat?" Viewed in a broad historical sweep, the sit-in stories' emphasis on spontaneity may have reflected an age in which the relations between agency and fate had become poignantly unclear.

In fact, we have evidence that people in other eras have acted collectively on the basis of quite different logics of agency. For example, in sixteenth-century France, people petitioning authorities for the remission of punishment for crimes they had committed often described their actions as the unfolding of a religious ritual. In her study of French pardon tales, historian Natalie Zemon Davis found that petitioners rarely invoked the historical circumstances of their actions, which included participation in tax riots and other forms of collective action. One petitioner, accounting for her involvement in a riot in Vermandois in 1539, described tax collectors breaking into peasants' homes and seizing the possessions of those who had refused to pay. Women took up pitchforks and pots and fought back. In her plea for pardon, the petitioner explained her action not by the excessiveness of new taxes or the overzealousness of those collecting them but by the fact that she mistook the tax collectors for soldiers. Perhaps the woman believed that the king would be more likely to grant pardon in a case of mistaken identity than one of incipient rebellion. But Davis argues that this unwillingness to invoke the historical contexts of action was characteristic of family histories and autobiographical writing of the time, which focused on moral and psychological circumstances rather than historical ones.[38]

If they were largely inattentive to their political historical setting, petitioners did invoke ritual and festive time to account for their actions. The compulsion to challenge or the obligation to retaliate made sense when put in their ritual context. For example, one account opened with the petitioner and his friends entombing themselves in imitation of the Lord on the day of the Holy Sacrament of the Altar. Later that evening, the narrative went on, the petitioner was insulted by a man he passed on the street with the words, "I see the god on earth. Did you keep your virile and shameful member stiff in playing God?" Passing by the man again, the petitioner was once more subjected to words that were "insulting to our Lord Jesus Christ and to the holiness of the day," and then assaulted by him. The petitioner responded "in hot anger" by fatally wounding his assailant. In this and other accounts, the acts of individuals became the unfolding of a narrative plot line, with insult become defilement and retort remade as retribution. Indeed, Davis observes, group fights between Catholics and Protestants often took place on religious occasions. The riots were experienced by participants either as an extension of the religious ritual or an exposition of its hypocrisy. Either way, action supplied the narrative reversal that drove the story.[39]

Sixteenth-century petitioners relied on narratives to make sense of their actions, just as participants in the 1960 sit-ins did. They too relied on a narrative trope of reversal, with a shift from peaceable gathering or harmonious relationship to confrontation. What differed were the relations between agency and structure embedded in their respective plot lines. This suggests that although people everywhere rely on stories to make sense of breaches with the conventional, the stories readily available to them reflect culturally distinctive understandings of the relations between individual and group and between agency and fate.

Strategic Storytelling

I have argued that narratives are a common form of discourse in fledgling movements, before formal organizations are established and while the idea of a collective actor is still tenuous. Narratives' endowment of events with coherence, directionality, and emotional resonance provides an explanation for confusing developments at the same time as it provides rationales for participation. In the stories students told, the 1960 sit-ins were a break with the incomplete engagement and gradualism of adult leaders (spontaneity denoted a moral imperative to act). They were a break with the action-impeding bureaucracy of mainstream civil rights organizations (spontaneity denoted local initiative). And they were a break with the sober asceticism of prior direct action (spontaneity denoted a joy and freedom in action). Narratives of the sit-ins helped make normative a physically dangerous form of activism. To be sure, representing the surge of student protest as spontaneous discredited charges of outside planning by left-wing groups. And tying SNCC to the sit-ins effectively legitimated the organization. However, my account suggests that such an instrumentalist view is limited. Rather than simply being persuasive devices used by strategic collective actors, narratives helped to constitute new collective actors and stakes in action. Multi-authored and told in formal and informal settings, stories made participation normative.

What role does storytelling play after formal movement organizations have been established, complete with strategic agendas and deliberate recruitment campaigns? Activists tell stories in courtrooms and in congressional hearings, in press briefings and on doorsteps. They craft their stories to make what they are up against seem intolerably unjust, their own actions seem worthy, and their opponents and competitors seem familiarly villainous or deluded. They use stories strategically. But stories also set the terms of strategic action, defining what is an opportunity or an obstacle, a success or a failure, and a cost or a benefit. I show how in the next chapter.

THREE

Strategy as Metonymy: Why Activists Choose the Strategies They Do

Picture a group of activists meeting to discuss strategy. Their demonstrations to protest the construction of a new nuclear power plant have produced little media coverage. Nor have they elicited any response from the government. The question now is whether to hold a protest *on* the site rather than outside it. This will involve cutting through wire fences, and it will constitute illegal trespass. What kinds of concerns shape the group's decision about what to do? In one view of strategic choice, activists seek to exploit whatever opportunities they can. If authorities have cracked down on protesters before, an illegal demonstration may lead to scores of arrests and the group's demobilization. On the other hand, if there is evidence of a split within the government over the merits of nuclear energy, a media-worthy demonstration may give the group's political allies just the kind of leverage they need to fight against new plant construction.

If this picture of how activists choose from among the strategies, tactics, and targets available to them is right, movement scholars should be able to account for activists' choices (and even predict them) by identifying the conditions in which some strategies are more likely to be effective than others. Scholars in this vein have argued, for example, that where political systems are relatively closed to citizen input, movement groups are likely to rely on disruptive

tactics rather than assimilative ones. Where state bureaucrats are ame-
nable to movement goals even if elected officials are not, movement
groups often target elected officials, either lobbying them not to stand in
the way of desired legislation or endorsing an alternate candidate in the
next election. Where movement groups on the same side face strong
competition for funding, they are likely to "product-differentiate" their
tactics in order to carve a niche for themselves.[1]

This all makes sense. But now imagine that someone in our imaginary
activist group speaks up: "If we are as committed to nonviolence as we
say we are, then we simply cannot cut through the fences. It doesn't
bother me that it's illegal but it is violent." The speaker's concern does
not have to do with the environmental opportunities and constraints
the group faces but with the need for the group to stay true to its ideological commitments. Activists are principled actors as well as practical
ones, in this picture. To account for movement groups' strategic decisions, scholars must pay attention to the cultural beliefs that make some
tactical options attractive or unattractive regardless of how effective
those options are likely to be. For example, groups committed to radical
equality are unlikely to adopt hierarchical organizational forms; those
committed to nonviolence are unlikely to accept support from funders
with ties to weapons manufacturers; those committed to feminism are
unlikely to elect a man as chair—even if there are strategic benefits to
doing all these things. Of course, few activist groups are altogether indifferent to the demands of instrumental effectiveness. They juggle instrumental concerns with ideological ones, and scholars should be able
to analyze the trade-offs they face in doing so.[2]

Neither of the pictures I just sketched is wrong. But both reproduce a
strategy/ideology divide whereby activists' strategic considerations are
by definition non-ideological. Activists are considered capable of identifying likely effective courses of action regardless of their consistency with
the group's political beliefs. In other words, activists self-consciously decide whether to privilege strategy or ideology. That formulation misses
the fact that what counts as effective action is likely be informed by ideological assumptions. As sociologist Charles Tilly points out, in any given
era, activists make only limited use of the range of claims and strategies
available. Their repertoires reflect prevalent understandings of what
forms of claims-making are "possible, desirable, risky, expensive, or prob-
able, as well as what consequences different possible forms of claim-
making are likely to produce." Such understandings constrain the kinds
of claims that political actors can make and the strategies and tactics that
they use to press those claims.[3]

While Tilly and other scholars have sought to explain broad transformations in repertoires over the course of whole centuries, they have not accounted for how particular strategies, tactics, or claims come to be part of an established repertoire. Nor have they examined the consequences for movements' trajectories of the constraints exercised by repertoires. Presumably, activists' notions of what is appropriate circumscribe their range of action. Presumably, too, we can look back with hindsight on activists' strategic choices and identify strategies that would have proven more effective had they been part of the established repertoire. But that tells us nothing about how repertoires actually operate to foreclose options. We need a better understanding of the processes by which options are ruled in and out of consideration in activists' strategic decision making. One need not assume an across-the-board mystification to hypothesize that cultural myths and chains of symbolic association operate to marginalize some options in ways that are subjected to little scrutiny or debate.[4]

Sometimes, of course, activists are explicit about the symbolic dimensions of their choices. For example, radical feminists in the 1970s were quite clear that they were repudiating bureaucratic organizational forms because they were symbolic of men's privilege. At other times, however, the symbolic connections that guide organizational choice operate less overtly. For example, in studying an alternative health clinic that was run along firmly collectivist lines, sociologist Sherryl Kleinman was surprised by members' insistence that each meeting be recorded in "minutes that had a bureaucratic look—lengthy, well-typed, with lots of headings, subheadings and underlinings." One staffer created an uproar when she submitted the minutes of a previous meeting in longhand and with illustrations. Staffers carefully rewrote the minutes line by line. Kleinman had never seen anyone actually refer to the minutes from earlier meetings and she found no evidence that staffers thought imitating mainstream organizational procedures would get them more clients or funding. Rather, Kleinman argues, they associated conventional minute-taking with "serious organizations." Had she asked members, they would likely have denied any desire to model themselves on mainstream health organizations. To the contrary, ideologically, they were vested in their status as an alternative organization. But the stability and standing of mainstream organizations—features that were symbolized by minute-taking—were nevertheless appealing.[5]

Just as the cultural assumptions that drive tactical choice may actually run counter to the group's ideological commitments, so they may also have instrumental costs. For example, sociologist Marshall Ganz argues that union officials who were involved in organizing California farm workers in the 1960s missed an important opportunity when they refused to participate in boycotts and marches aimed at building national support. "This is an honest to goodness trade union fight, not a civil rights demonstration," one union organizer insisted when the idea was proposed. Referring to the march organizers as ministers and as involved in a religious crusade, he vowed, "We will continue in our own union way." "Our own union way" stood for a variety of things: political secularism, an unwillingness to engage in moral and emotional appeals, and, most important, an approach that was *not* that of the civil rights movement or a religious campaign. The result, however, was that union representatives failed to consider tactics that might better have served their unions' cause.[6]

Minute-taking for the health workers and marching for the unionists were thus rated by their identification with a cluster of organizational virtues and liabilities. These identifications made sense to the people in the discussions I have just described but might not have made sense to different people or to the same people at a different time. To say that the union way was not to participate in marches would have sounded strange to unionists through much of the American labor movement's history. So would a refusal to join forces with other movements whose fortunes were in the ascendant. Similarly, one might imagine that to call an organization serious solely on account of its adherence to bureaucratic procedure would provoke some retort, especially in an organization that was wary of mainstream organizations. The symbolic associations of "union way" and "serious organization" were conventional but within a limited space and time.

"Union way" and "serious organization" were metonymies, things that stood for other things. What is interesting about metonymy, as a literary device, is that its meaning is at once figurative and conventional. Metonymies imply certain causal relations while granting them the status of the already known. As a kind of shorthand, metonymies both assume the existence of a group for whom the shorthand makes sense and signal membership in the group. That makes them difficult to question, since to do so can be interpreted as a sign of one's ignorance and, possibly, one's insecure place in the group. As I have argued before, it is always possible to think outside canonical story lines and the tropes on which they rest. But to articulate those alternatives is risky, whether in a public hearing or in a group of like-minded activists. By tracing how metonymic structures are established in group discourse, we can see how accounts become canonical, how they marginalize alternatives, and with what effects.

I explore these processes over a short period in the life of the organization that I described in the last chapter: the Student Nonviolent Coordinating Committee. The group was founded in 1960 as the national organization of the student sit-in movement. By 1961, it was coordinating direct action against segregated restaurants, movie theaters, and interstate bus lines. By 1962, it had switched course, trading desegregation efforts for voter registration campaigns in the most repressive areas of the deep South. Young, militant, smart, and fearless, SNCC workers inspired a generation of activists—not with their daring alone, but with something as prosaic as their organizational form. Rejecting hierarchies of all kinds, SNCC workers determined to enact in the here and now the radically egalitarian society they hoped to bring into being. They decentralized administration and strove for consensus in meetings that often went on all night. By mid-decade, SNCC's organizational form had a name—participatory democracy—and it was being adopted by northern white activist groups. By decade's end thousands of groups operated as participatory democracies: health clinics, newspapers, schools, bookstores, and law firms, as well as activist groups in the antiwar, new left, and feminist movements.[7]

By then, however, SNCC had imploded. Scholars have attributed its collapse in part to the participatory democratic ethos that for a time made its star shine so bright. Participatory democracy, they have argued, was worthy in principle but unworkable in practice. As long as SNCC was a small organization with little political influence, it could afford the inefficiencies of consensus-based decision making and decentralized administration. However, by the fall of 1964, the organization had become large and far-flung. Its political successes had opened up new avenues for political clout. In that context, the standard interpretation goes, SNCC could no longer afford inefficient administrative and deliberative procedures. The democratic purists who resisted the move to more centralized structure—"freedom high," their critics called them—were simply at odds with the new demands of political effectiveness. Some scholars have cited ideological pressures more than instrumental ones in accounting for SNCC's abandonment of participatory democracy. In their view, the group's new Black Power agenda emphasized gaining power rather than appealing to a liberal establishment now perceived as corrupt. Efforts to model an egalitarian society were therefore viewed as futile. At this point, however, the two explanations converge. Whether pressed by the demands of environmental adaptation or ideological consistency, freedom highs were forced to bow to the demand of the "hardliners" for more bureaucratic structure and clearer lines of administrative command.[8]

I argue that neither explanation can account for SNCC's abandonment of participatory democratic decision making in 1965. The first misses the fact that those who argued for retaining participatory democratic practices did so on instrumental grounds—grounds that for a time made sense to most SNCC workers. The notion that a Black Power agenda mandated a more centralized and hierarchical structure misses the fact that SNCC workers adopted such a structure *before* they embraced a Black Power agenda. I offer a different explanation. Participatory democracy was abandoned when it came to be metonymically associated with the organization's programmatic paralysis and with the dominance of whites in the organization. I say metonymically associated because no one could say just how decentralized and consensus-based decision making stymied program development nor how its abandonment would curb the role of whites. Rather, in SNCC workers' collective narrative of the problems they were facing in the fall and winter of 1964, participatory democracy stood in for organizational dilemmas that were difficult to confront, let alone solve.

The effects of the metonymic associations established during this period were lasting. For SNCC workers, participatory democracy came to be seen as principled rather than pragmatic, aimed at personal self-liberation rather than political change, and as white rather than black. Because SNCC was widely considered to be the cutting edge of militant black protest, moreover, its recasting of participatory democracy may have contributed to fixing that incarnation of the form as what participatory democracy *was*—for activists in the 1960s and after. Before I trace this history, I want to say a little more about adapting the literary concept of metonymy to the study of movement decision making.

Metonymy and Strategy

Metonymy is common figure of speech in which one word or image is invoked for another. So we might refer to a decision made by "the crown" rather than the king, or describe journalists as "the press," or refer to a child as "my pride and joy." Metonymy, like metaphor, involves the substitution of one thing for another. The difference, according to literary theorist Roman Jakobson, is that in metaphor, the relationship between the terms is one of similarity, and in metonymy the relationship is one of contiguity. When we use a metaphor, we substitute for something familiar another item that has similar properties but is from a different domain. So when I refer to a woman I know as a rose, I convey her delicate beauty and perhaps her combination of prickliness and fragility. In metonymy, the thing referred to explicitly and that which it denotes already have a relationship outside the text. We assume that relationship when we hear or see the word. The relationship may be one of cause and effect or one between a thing and a property of the thing. For example, when we say "the pen is mightier than the sword," we mean that writing, and more generally, persuasion, is more powerful than physical force. Synecdoche, in which a part of a thing substitutes for the whole, is one kind of metonymic relation. For example, we say, "all *hands* on deck" when we mean all the sailors to whom the hands belong. The object used in a metonymic relation often denotes a whole cluster of objects. So, when we say, "Washington is wary of recent Palestinian moves," we have in mind not a single person or organization but a cluster of organizations that together represent Washington: State Department and national security officials, congressional representatives, the president, perhaps the pundits who comment on national affairs.[9]

Metonymies may also condense chains of cause-and-effect relations. The important point is that the relation (or relations) between the thing referred to and the thing (or things) denoted is conventional. We talk about "the crown" to mean the king because the two are commonly associated. Kings often wear ceremonial robes but we don't talk about a decision handed down by "the robe." As literary theorist Hugh Bredin puts it, "A metonymy neither states nor implies the connection between the objects involved in it. For this reason it relies wholly upon those relations between objects that are habitually and conventionally known and accepted. We must *already know* that the objects are related, if the metonymy is to be devised or understood." Without disagreeing with that assessment, I want to suggest that the metonymic relation is creative as well as conventional in at least two ways. The power of metaphor, again, comes from the conjoining of objects from quite different domains. Calling a man a hammer, a teddy bear, or a creampuff is evocative because a word from the domain of tools, toys, or food, respectively, is being used to characterize a human being. The power of metonymy, for its part, comes from the particular object that is chosen to represent the relation. In this respect, although both metaphor and metonymy involve using one term for another, one can more usefully think of metaphor as involving substitution and metonymy (as well as synecdoche) involving deletion. When we say, "all hands on deck," we delete ". . . of the sailors." When I refer to my child as "my pride and joy," I delete "child who produces in me . . ." But the items that are deleted in a metonymy are not those that are logically dispensable, as literary critic David Lodge explains. The deletion makes a point. For example, when one waitress says to another that "the ham sandwich is waiting for his check," she is using a kind of shorthand (the man who ordered the ham sandwich is waiting for the check) that is not obvious to someone outside the food service industry. We see the man (eating a ham sandwich); the waitress sees a ham sandwich (being eaten by a man).[10]

In her use of metonymy, the waitress may be doing even more than highlighting what is most important about a customer in her line of work. She may also be forging a bond of solidarity with the other waitress by suggesting that the people they serve are no more than their lunch orders. This brings me to my second point. Bredin argues that the associations on which metonymies are based are long-standing, deeply rooted in a group's culture. But that may not always be true. The relationship between the word used and the thing denoted must be obvious to its audience, but the audience may have only recently become a community. Consider the readers of a novel or the viewers of a film. For them, metonymy is the telling detail that conveys the story's larger meaning and that moves the action forward. It is the handbag that Tolstoy focuses on in Anna Karenina's suicide. It is the close-up in the film that relates the character's emotions, evident on her face, to the situation that produces those emotions. However, the knowingness on the part of the audience that makes it possible for the author to delete the causal connections between the term used and what it denotes may be created through the repeated use of the term or image. For example, the handbag in Anna Karenina's death scene resonates because it has appeared before in the narrative. Each time it appears, our associations with it widen and deepen. By the end, the handbag *is* Anna Karenina, but it is the pathos that she has come to represent—all her belongings in that gaily-colored bag, her last bit of finery flung away as she goes to her death.[11]

In real life, metonymy may work similarly. In movement discourse, as in novels, metonymic relations can be created through repetition. Stories circulate in which a metonymy figures, and activists count themselves in the know because they recognize the cluster of meanings associated with the term used. Such meanings are unrecognizable to those outside the group. The more the metonymic relation is referred to, the more conventional it becomes. Note, again, that the metonymy signals a cluster of terms and also that the relations among the terms are never specified. The relations are assumed to be obvious but that assumption discourages activists from considering whether the implied relations are empirically accurate. For example, anti–corporate globalization activists today often refer to styles of participatory democratic decision making as being "Californian," especially those relying on hand signals and "vibes watchers" to monitor the emotional tone of the discussion. They mean not only that Californian activists use those techniques, but also that they are part of an ethos that is less than political, more concerned with personal liberation than political change, even self-indulgent. The metonymy represents as common sense something that only those in the group know. Retellings of the group's organizational choices may reaffirm the association of the term *Californian* with self-indulgent apoliticism. The clear message is that adopting hand signals or other process-oriented techniques would make the group vulnerable to the same critique. Whether or not such techniques would in fact make the group more effective is not broached. Similarly, the union representative who argued against conducting marches and boycotts in support of the farm workers because that was not "the union way" avoided counterarguments that unions had often participated in marches and that the adoption of tactics associated with the civil rights movement could energize the labor movement. The members of the alternative health organization who insisted that minute-taking was required of a serious organization avoided awkward questions about what value taking minutes actually had for the organization.[12]

This does not mean that activists use metonymies deliberately to avoid challenges to the causal relations they imply. The union organizer probably spoke from a deep sense that to launch marches and boycotts was wrong, was at odds with what the labor movement was most fundamentally about, in ways that he could not fully articulate. Still, to question those relations risks signaling that the questioner is unfamiliar with the basic idiom of the group. Since being in the know is a sign of belonging, questioning the meaning of a metonymic association may jeopardize one's place in the group. At times, of course, one can question the basis for metonymic associations with impunity. But especially when the group or one's membership in it is fragile, doing so is difficult. A waitress new on the job is unlikely to protest that diners are more than what they eat. A waitress a long time on the job is unlikely to notice the strangeness of the metonymic substitution at all.

Metonymies figure in discursive forms other than stories. And activists sometimes tell stories deliberately to press for particular tactical options. But stories also gain currency among group members that make some problems seem urgent and some conditions seem responsible; that make reform seem more or less necessary; and that make certain courses of action seem apt or out of bounds. Such stories are rarely told in full. Rather, metonymies function as a kind of causal thread in the stories that appear in fragmented form in activists' descriptions, claims, nonnarrative explanations, and references. In what follows, I concentrate on how metonymies figured in the accounts given by SNCC workers of what was wrong with the organization in a period of crisis.

Participatory Democracy's Early Story, 1960–1964

For the SNCC activists who worked to register voters and build black political organizations in Mississippi, Georgia, and Alabama in the early 1960s, participatory democracy was an effective organizing tool. Far from simply tolerating the impracticality of consensus-based and decentralized decision making, SNCC organizers saw such decision making as practical. To be sure, it was not only practical. Radical pacifists played key roles in SNCC's founding, and they gave the group's founders an appreciation for Quaker consensus. To operate in radically democratic fashion was to prefigure the radically democratic society SNCC wanted to build on a grand scale. Consensus-oriented decision making was also a way to keep sophisticated northern students from dominating discussion with their ready command of parliamentary maneuver. In that sense, a practical rationale for participatory democracy mingled with an ideological one from SNCC's beginning.[13]

As SNCC activists shifted from direct action aimed at desegregation to voter registration efforts, however, a different political tradition influenced their organizing style. SNCC mentors Ella Baker and Myles Horton had been trained in a form of radical labor education whose inspiration was Deweyan. They saw participatory decision making on local projects as a means to build leadership among people who had been denied opportunities for regular political participation. As SNCC evolved from a coalition of campus sit-in groups into a cadre of organizers in the Deep South, that rationale for radical democracy became more important. On local projects, SNCC workers sought to defer to local residents' agendas and aspirations. Bottom-up decision making helped people without political experience to assess the costs and benefits of alternative courses of action and to link tactical decisions to long-term visions. "We were trying to give the people we were living and working with ownership of the movement," Mississippi project head Bob Moses explained later. "The meeting—that's your tool for building. So how do people take ownership

of meetings? And there you get into what has come to be called participatory democracy . . . in which the people who are meeting really get
more and more of a feeling that this is [their] meeting."[14]

Discussions on local projects about what counted as leadership
chipped away at local residents' belief that only those with proper
credentials could lead. A decentralized organization, for its part, allowed
organizers to tailor movements to local conditions. Among SNCC staff,
many of whom were political novices themselves, participatory decision
making was a way to train a new generation of political activists. In
SNCC's early years, then, the tension between principle and pragmatism
that is supposedly at the heart of participatory democracy just was not
there. That would change, but not because of changes in either the
group's principles or its practical needs.

Letting the People Decide, 1964

SNCC's shift to political organizing did not bring immediate rewards.
To the contrary, voter registration programs in Mississippi met with
stepped-up intimidation, threats, and violence by whites against pro-
spective voters and organizers. The federal government, for its part, was
consistently unwilling to intervene to protect civil rights workers and local citizens exercising their constitutional rights. SNCC's organizing was
slow and dangerous. By the spring of 1964, SNCC workers reluctantly decided to invite hundreds of northern white volunteers to the state to
help with voter registration efforts. Although doing so ran counter to
their emphasis on empowering local black activists, it was their only
hope of securing the national attention that they believed would compel the government to intercede.

The Mississippi Summer Project, as it came to be called, thrust SNCC
into the national limelight. After three voter registration canvassers were
kidnapped and an FBI manhunt begun, the project was rarely out of the
news. In early August, the canvassers were found murdered. Shortly after, SNCC helped organize a challenge to the seating of the segregation-
ist Mississippi delegation at the Democratic National Convention. While
the challenge proved unsuccessful, with the Mississippi challengers rejecting the Party's compromise offer of two seats, both it and the summer project demonstrated SNCC's ability to mobilize national support.[15]

If SNCC had a new external profile, it was also a very different organization internally. A number of volunteers stayed on in the fall, doubling
SNCC's staff. SNCC now had projects across Mississippi as well as in

southwest Georgia and Alabama, a sophisticated fund-raising apparatus around the country, and a million-dollar budget. For the group's executive secretary, James Forman, these changes called for a new organizational structure. Forman was older than most SNCC staffers and had experience with the organizational competition that characterized the old left. He now saw opportunities for SNCC to capitalize on its recent success by restyling itself as a mass organization rather than a roving cadre of organizers. At a minimum, he believed it should implement the kind of centralized structure and clear lines of command that would allow it to compete with the other civil rights organizations for political influence. Forman was scathing in his criticism of those who resisted such a change. SNCC's anti-elitism had once been a source of political creativity, he wrote later, but the opposition to all authority that began to surface in the fall of 1964 was debilitating. "No one, including myself, foresaw the crippling effect of certain habits and values common among middle-class students: a fear of one's own power, egoistic individualism, lack of discipline, generalized rebellion against authority, and self-indulgence," he wrote later. "Freedom high," he and others began to call them.[16]

Forman's reading of the organizational battle that emerged in SNCC in late 1964 has been the basis for numerous scholarly accounts. Like Forman, chroniclers have characterized the battle as one pitting practical centralizers against utopian decentralists, pragmatists against ideologues. But records show that the objections to Forman's plan for restructuring were initially made on practical grounds. Organizers worried that centralizing authority in Atlanta would restrict their freedom of action in developing local organizations and movements. Some organizers also saw centralized, bureaucratic, and parliamentary structure as unappealingly associated with northern whites. One field-worker complained that "white college-educated Northerners have a tendency to take command of an assembly through rapid-fire parliamentary maneuvers which leave local people baffled and offended."[17]

Certainly, most staffers recognized that SNCC's formal structure, which still vested power in campus representatives, was obsolete. They complained bitterly about the administrative logjams that prevented resources from reaching local projects. But they were not convinced that a centralized bureaucracy was the answer. In response to Forman's proposal for a conventional structure with an executive secretary in charge of administrative staff, some SNCC organizers proposed what they called a loose structure, in which programmatic work groups would meet periodically to solve problems and coordinate common efforts. Loose-structure proponents cited not the requirements of ideological consistency, that is, of enacting a participatory democracy in the here and now, but the need of Mississippi field organizers for organizational flexibility.[18]

The two proposals were discussed at length at a staff retreat held in November, but the discussion failed to yield any consensus. Instead, SNCC workers simply reaffirmed their commitment to letting local people set the course of the struggle. Their recent experience with national Democratic party operatives and professed liberal allies in Atlantic City had been disillusioning. Even civil rights leaders had treated the farmers and domestic workers who made up the Mississippi Freedom Democratic Party (MFDP) dismissively, urging them to pack up and let political professionals take over the show. SNCC workers left Atlantic City more convinced than ever that their radicalism lay in their determination to let the people decide the course of the struggle. As MFDP leaders wrote in response to those who criticized them for not accepting the party's compromise offer, "This kind of dictation is what Negroes in Mississippi face and have always faced, and it is precisely this that they are learning to stand up against." The story of local black Mississippians standing up to the civil rights leaders who wanted to blunt their challenge, and of SNCC workers standing alongside them, was repeated in press releases, field reports, meeting minutes, and personal correspondence. As a volunteer in Shaw, Mississippi, wrote to a northern supporter about the project's decision to picket a local merchant, "That is, the people, residents of Shaw, decided. . . . This is where we differ from M. L. King and his officers. In their work the staff people make the decisions, rather than letting the people in the town where they're working decide what they want to do, when and how."[19]

Alongside this collective narrative, fragments of a more anxious one were surfacing in the fall of 1964. In field reports, organizers worried that letting the people decide was not yielding the radical programs it was supposed to. "So far I've been using the SNCC technique of prying and prodding with questions until the idea comes out—" wrote one organizer, "but it is slow . . . people really have no ideas for programs." The author of a field report from Monroe County, Mississippi, noted, "There has been a stopping of all projects, with an attempt to let the local people say what they want," but confessed, "the programs have been very slow. In fact I can't think of one program that is progressing." In Hattiesburg, "Apathy stems from problems of [developing a] program; . . . voter registration has worn off as a 'novelty.'" In Meridian, "What we've had so far is discussion and workshops, but no programs." In Holly Springs, "There is no plan."[20]

Why was it so difficult to develop new programs? There were several reasons. The failure of the challenge to the Democratic Party made many

SNCC activists question a strategy of appealing to national liberal groups. The federal government's unwillingness to protect voter registration workers threw into doubt the likely payoff of continued voter registration work. What they should do instead was unclear, however. The easy answer was that the people should decide. The local Mississippi activists with whom SNCC organizers worked should choose the programs they wanted to pursue. However, local Mississippians had no better information than SNCC staffers did on what initiatives would prove successful, and, like SNCC workers, they differed among themselves over the best course of action. There was another problem: What if the local programs together did not add up to a radical strategy? Especially at a time when other civil rights groups were launching their own projects in the state, SNCC workers were eager to come up with initiatives that were different from ones they saw as insufficiently radical. "Too damn many nursery schools, and milk programs," one organizer phrased a not infrequent complaint. "Many of us do not see the relationship between community centers, sewing classes and political and economic freedom," said another. And the notes from one meeting report, "Question of whether we are a social service agency or a band of revolutionaries. . . . It was decided we were the latter."[21]

Organizers were also hampered by the fiction that SNCC had not come up with programs on its own in the past. Voter education classes, the voter registration program, the Mississippi Challenge—all these had been devised by SNCC workers. The genius of such programs had been their combination of radical potential with fairly moderate aims. That combination had allowed student activists of varying political stripes to work with local black leaders and national civil rights organizations in a surprising coalition. Now, with no obvious program capable of connecting local claims with national ones and winnable issues with radical possibilities, SNCC workers became increasingly aggressive in their efforts to push local people to articulate their real interests and increasingly critical of each other for failing to draw out in black communities the radical interests they knew were there.

The endless injunctions to let the people decide were thus a reflection more than a cause of the group's programmatic uncertainty. Still, the pressure to avoid imposing an agenda created problems of its own. Project workers confessed that they vacillated between exercising leadership and renouncing it. And in their own staff meetings, they began to attack each other for their failure to let the people decide. Arguments for particular lines of action were castigated as manipulative, and proposals for new programs were denounced as power-mongering. In field reports, organizers complained about provisional decisions attacked for being imposed on staff and strategy sessions halted to discuss "why people don't speak." "Who decided that?" became a familiar rebuttal to any proposal or plan. A staffer described a Mississippi meeting as follows: "I asked someone to deal with the two personnel problems. . . . [W]e sat there and nobody talked, and Stokely said he was the only one there who was willing to make decisions. He said people were afraid someone would ask them who gave them the right to make a decision."[22]

When Forman introduced his proposal for centralization in the fall, he had found little support. However, by early winter, many organizers were beginning to rally around proposals for more centralized structure as a way to get past the group's programmatic paralysis. "Southern staff workers favor strong leadership and structure," a staffer reported in February. Yet no one made clear just how a centralized structure would generate the programs that were desperately needed. In fact, in the past, SNCC's most effective programs had been the products of the individual initiative and local experimentation that the organization's decentralized structure made possible. The enthusiasm for conventional organizational structure that was now surfacing, like the exaggerated concerns about organizers imposing their own agendas, was a response to the programmatic crisis. But it was a response in transmuted form. "Sometimes it's more comfortable to talk about structure, because it's so concrete," one staffer explains now. "And goals were so much more difficult to talk about." In other words, SNCC workers battled over how to make decisions and allocate resources because the real problem, namely, generating the sense of radical purpose that would reenergize organizers and appeal to residents, was difficult to get a handle on.[23]

Minutes of meetings during this period show that when issues of agenda were introduced, the discussion often shifted, sometimes abruptly, to organizational structure. Some staffers recognized that this was going on. "People here are incapable of dealing with the real problem, which is lack of programs," one complained. But drawing attention to the group's avoidance of the topic did not seem to remedy it. For all contenders, then, the preoccupation with structure, whether tight or loose, radically democratic or hierarchical, both substituted for and thwarted a discussion of goals. "If you're locked in this structural struggle," a staffer who was in the thick of the battle explains now, "then you're not thinking what are we going to do next."[24]

Why, then, the appeal of tight structure? In part, it was simply that it was an alternative to what SNCC had now. Tight structure came to stand for programmatic direction, as well for the vigor and larger sense of purpose that seemed now to be so palpably missing. The relationship between structure and programmatic direction was not specified. But as SNCC workers recounted to each other what was wrong with the organization, the need for tight structure increasingly became the endpoint of the story. Through repetition, the association between tight structure and programmatic coherence came to be a matter of common sense.

Another reason for the increasing appeal of centralized and hierarchical structure was that it was coming to be seen as a bulwark against the dominance of whites in the organization. That perception represented a real shift. As late as 1965, someone described southern black "old guerrillas" in SNCC who "distrusted any and all kinds of organization, which they associate with white, bourgeois Northern culture." Consensus decision making, for its part, was seen as a way to prevent northern whites' domination through their command of parliamentary maneuver. However, that view was losing currency.[25]

Freedom Highs and Hardliners, 1964–1965

In late 1964, a SNCC staffer circulated a sketch of people in the organization whom he referred to as the "New Mystics." "Politics is concerned with masses of people and practical considerations of law—power and economics," he wrote. "The new mystics are concerned with individual salvation, purity, self-expression, metaphor and symbolism." In spite of their proletarian pretensions and their determination to be of the people, they were "alienated middle-class college dropouts, the children of the middle class with the middle-class intellectual penchant for nuance, metaphor and symbol, impelled one suspects by middle-class neurosis and guilt." Finally, the author blamed SNCC's lack of direction on the New Mystics' self-indulgent hypersensitivity. "The tendency would be to think of the Black Belt as being populated by 1½ million individuals all unique and different and whose problems must be approached [in] 1½ million different ways. Consequently any attempt to formulate programs, no matter how general and vague, become[s] immoral because it fails to consider the precious uniqueness and individual problems of each person in the area."[26]

The piece was jocose, but its terms were echoed in field reports and meeting minutes during this period. Some people were "freedom high," staffers began to charge. The phrase "freedom high" referred to advocates of decentralized structure and consensus. But it also denoted a generalized animosity to organization and a passion for personal freedom over organizational responsibility. Freedom highs were "against all forms of organization and regimentation," staffer Cleve Sellers wrote later:

If a confrontation developed in Jackson, Mississippi, and a group of freedom high floaters was working in Southwest Georgia, they would pile into cars and head for Jackson. They might return to Georgia when the Jackson confrontation was over—and they might not. . . . They loved to bring meetings to a screeching halt with open-ended, theoretical questions. In the midst of a crucial strategy session on the problems of community leaders in rural areas, one of them might get the floor and begin to hold forth on the true meaning of the word "leader."

Sellers was not the only critic. Other staffers began to tell stories of freedom highs as more concerned with their own liberation than with political power for black Mississippians and as indulging their penchant for challenging all authority at the expense of any kind of concerted action. As their critics saw it, freedom highs' reverence for the untutored wisdom of the poor amounted to a kind of "local-people-itis." Their preoccupation with democratic decision making was compromising SNCC's ability to formulate new programs.[27]

Who were the freedom highs? They were seen generally as northern and white. "The 'freedom highs' are essentially white intellectuals, hung up in various ways," a staffer wrote in the spring of 1965. "Maybe these whites are trying to break free of the need to be like the strong people (which they can't ever be like 'cause they're not black) and their role as supplements to the work of the 'strong people.'" In metonymic fashion, the label "freedom high" implied connections between whiteness, a preference for decentralized and consensus-oriented decision making, a philosophical antipathy to organization and leadership, and a refusal to be bound by any organizational rules. But each one of these connections was questionable. Many of the proponents of decentralized structure were black, and some of the proponents of centralization were white. When SNCC's executive committee went through a personnel list to root out unproductive workers in April 1965, most of those identified as floaters, a term that was often paired with freedom high, were black. Indeed, earlier in the debate, "floater" referred to the mainly black project workers whose exhaustion after months of organizing in dangerous conditions had led them to abandon their assigned projects.[28]

To be sure, many of those now labeled freedom highs were more interested in the philosophical underpinnings of their work than were other SNCC workers, more willing to make bold statements in meetings about the virtues of a leaderless movement, and more sensitive to breaches of a radically democratic ethos. Some proponents of decentralized structure were in close contact with white new leftists who were finding in SNCC's collectivist decision making a wholesale challenge to conventional notions of politics and organization. But a liking for philosophical rumination was responsible neither for the disciplinary problems that SNCC was facing nor for the fact that no one knew what to do next. Today, black SNCC staffers see the freedom high/hardliner debate as having class and regional dimensions, pitting Atlanta staff against Mississippi field organizers, and northern student sophisticates (black and white) against less well-educated Mississippians. However, in the accounts that SNCC workers gave of their organizational travails at the time, those conflicts were gradually displaced by a black-white cleavage—fought out through positions on organizational structure.

There was good reason for the sharpening racial tensions. Black staffers who had been skeptical of the summer project to begin with had seen their fears materialize. White volunteers' ignorance of the intricacies of southern race relations created awkward and even dangerous situations. Whites sometimes offended black southerners by flouting southern norms of dress and demeanor and they intimidated with their command of formal political skills. Black workers had worried not only that whites would inadvertently reproduce patterns of racial deference but also that their own roles in the movement would be overshadowed. With a press corps focused almost exclusively on the white volunteers, this concern too seemed to materialize. After the summer, far more volunteers stayed on than expected, and eighty-five of them were added to the staff in a decision that many longtime staffers perceived as simply handed down by Atlanta headquarters. No matter the benefits of more manpower, staffers lamented the erosion of what had been a tight-knit group of friends. "They didn't know who the hell you were; you didn't know who they were," a black staffer later said of the newcomers. "It used to be a band of brothers, a circle of trust, but that's not true anymore," a staffer complained in a meeting at the time.[29]

White newcomers, for their part, came South awed by SNCC organizers and were taken aback by the barely concealed animosity they encountered. They were bombarded with rules about not leaving the project, not using cars for their personal needs, not socializing with local young people, and then exposed to SNCC workers ignoring the rules. They wanted guidance from project directors but found them taciturn. In response to the antagonism they were encountering, some white newcomers began to hector staffers to adhere to their democratic commitments. Records show that an enormous amount of time was spent in project meetings discussing the roles, responsibilities, and prerogatives of project directors. "Problem is that people can't trust [the] project director," a white volunteer complained on one project. "Who decides who goes where and what to do if people don't work out?" Another volunteer questioned the "whole concept of a project director as a feudal lord." And a third said plaintively, "There are people who are in positions of power and they are interested in retaining this power and then there are the have-nots." Comments like these were understandably annoying to black southerners who had long ago proved their commitment to the struggle. One project's long and contentious battle with its black project director prompted local black activist Annie Devine to intervene. "Unless you forget yourself and relate to the people, you'll go away without doing anything," she warned. A white project worker protested, "All here agree that our commitment is to the people . . . discussions of this sort are perfectly in order; they help us function better and work better for the people of Mississippi." Another put in: "How can I hope to get rid of authoritarianism in Miss. if I leave it in the Canton staff? . . . It's like the bossman telling his sharecropper to get off the land just because the sharecropper thinks differently from the owner." A northern white volunteer comparing her situation to that of a black sharecropper sounds downright embarrassing. On the other hand, these statements were made after the black project director had announced that whites would have to leave Mississippi permanently to go home and raise funds.[30]

"If a white man were project director, I wouldn't be in the movement," a black project worker declared in an interracial discussion in late 1964. "We have to organize something for ourselves." By late 1964, many black activists were interested in issues of racial identity and consciousness. Some wondered whether these issues could truly be addressed in integrated gatherings. "Although it had always been an issue in the organization," black staffer Cleve Sellers wrote later, "the role of whites had never really been openly discussed"—and was not, he says, until 1966. Other former staffers say that there was open discussion about the role of whites in the movement after the summer. But it tended to be about the liabilities of white organizers in black communities, not about staffers' ambivalence about an essentially black organization becoming interracial. Mississippi project director Bob Moses observes now, "There's a real need for black people to close the door and meet in their own group, and people were threatened by this. It was a need in the SNCC meetings. The SNCC meetings dragged on interminably partly because they could never do this. So people could never say what they felt." After the long debate in one project about the nature of legitimate authority that was prompted by the volunteer's complaint that "people can't trust [the] project director"—just the kind of discussion that hardliners criticized— an older minister who was participating remarked, "The thing that bothers me is that there really is a basic black-white problem here which you don't say but which is at the bottom of a lot of what you're saying. Why don't you deal with your black-white problem?"[31]

The "black-white problem" was tough to confront, let alone resolve. After all, SNCC had always been proudly interracial, and many of the whites on staff had long ago proved their commitment to the struggle. Unsurprisingly, field reports during this period made occasional but never more than passing reference to racial conflicts within the group. With decision making the central organizational concern and racial antagonisms difficult to talk about, debates over organizational structure and decision making both engaged and stood in for those thornier antagonisms. Earlier tensions between northerners and southerners, newcomers and veterans, and field staff and office staff had been supplanted by new ones between proponents of tight and loose structure and, less overtly, between blacks and whites. By the spring, a form of organization that black southerners had pioneered was becoming unappealing because of its association with whites. "Whites tended to be for loose structure and southern Negroes were the ones most resentful of whites," as staffer Julian Bond put it a few years later.[32]

The new account of the problem absorbed other organizational problems. Recall that a metonymic term refers to a cluster of things. As I noted, "floating" had initially referred to people abandoning their projects more because of exhaustion than because of any ideological opposition to rules. But floating, along with other disciplinary infractions such as people misusing cars, drinking, and flouting community mores were now characterized as "anarchist" and "obstructionist" and seen as reflecting an ideological opposition to authority. "Look at the people at Waveland who supported loose structure," one staffer paraphrased the story that had become standard (Waveland was the site of the retreat where proposals for tight and loose structure were debated in November 1964). "Look what they've been doing since Waveland; don't you think it's strange that the very people who don't want structure are off doing whatever they like without anyone in a position to ask them for an account of their actions?" Loose structure's proponents found themselves battling the perception that their preference for decentralized and egalitarian decision making reflected a politically careless anarchism. Thus a participant in a February meeting was thankful, she recorded, that "for the first time anyone spoke [about] loose structure as not being 'no structure' but different structure." But that distinction was rare. By February, whites had come to be seen as insisting on participatory democratic practices to retain control of the organization. A white staffer reported that the drive for looser structure was being described in terms of "conspiracy theories about white intellectuals."[33]

Those promoting centralized and more hierarchical structure were not an organizational faction bent on gaining acceptance for a particular agenda or ridding the organization of whites. The appeal of top-down structure lay rather in its relationship to inchoate preferences and problems. A preference for centralized authority stood in for programmatic certainty and an organization not dominated by whites. The relationship was metonymic. No one said just how a top-down structure would produce programmatic coherence or reduce whites' role. Indeed, a decentralized structure that vested personnel decisions in project directors would arguably have enabled them to curb the role of whites on their projects if they proved to be a block to effective organizing. As I noted earlier, SNCC's most successful projects in the past had been launched by individual organizers. Decentralized and informal structure here, as in other movements, had facilitated individual initiative and tactical innovation. The source of top-down structure's appeal was not its capacity to yield more efficient outcomes or its consistency with an existing ideology but its symbolic resonance.

Organizational Reform, Spring 1965

By SNCC's February 1965 staff meeting, the hardliners had organized to gain control. They were accused of intimidating local people and silencing opposition. But by the meeting's close, they had gained the upper hand, winning a reformed executive committee and plans for firmer administrative structure.[34]

Of the nineteen people on the new executive committee, eleven were Mississippi field-workers, most native Mississippians. Since proponents of decentralized organization had argued that such a structure would give field organizers more power, they might have considered this a victory. But by the February meeting, Mississippi organizers were firmly on the side of tight structure. Shortly after the staff meeting, a new personnel committee conducted a systematic review of every SNCC staffer in order to root out those who were insufficiently productive. Organizational hierarchy, not its absence, was now associated with political militancy. SNCC's efforts at "tightening up" were being guided by an image of "how a tough militant organization is supposed to work," rather than by what had proven effective, one staffer complained. But the tide had turned. "We're not individuals anymore—just 'screwed up' or 'freedom high,'" a white proponent of loose structure wrote.[35]

So far I have argued that decentralized and consensus-oriented decision making was rejected not because it had proven ineffective but because it had become symbolically associated with the group's programmatic paralysis and with whites' high profile in the organization. What, then, was the relationship between SNCC workers' bid for a more centralized structure and its new Black Power agenda? As I noted earlier, analysts have argued that when SNCC workers abandoned efforts at moral suasion in favor of gaining independent black political power, they also adopted the kind of top-down organization that could effectively mobilize people for power. I have argued, to the contrary, that SNCC's adoption of a more centralized and hierarchical organizational structure preceded rather than followed its espousal of Black Power. But the two developments were not unconnected. During the period of organizational reform that I described, components of what would come to be called Black Power surfaced in informal conversations: skepticism of liberal alliances, an attraction to political organizing outside the Democratic Party, frustration with nonviolence, and a growing belief that the movement should be all black. But these ideas were still tentative and difficult to voice in an interracial group, as well as one whose commitment to nonviolence was expressed in its very name. The progressive association of participatory democracy with whites may have made it easier for SNCC workers to begin talking about the virtues of an all-black organization.

Consider again a memo that circulated in the spring of 1965. "Who goes off to do work? Who goes off to do personal freedom? Who goes off to do irresponsibility?" the memo asked, answering,

The "strong people" who tend to fit the "rugged ragged" black SNICK worker image are the ones who go off to do work . . . the "freedom highs" are essentially white intellectuals, hung up in various ways. Maybe these whites are trying to break free of the need to be like the strong people (which they can't ever be like 'cause they're not black) and their role as supplements to the work of the "strong people." It sort of ties into the white-black question (which has simply taken another shape) and the need to have a black run and controlled organization.

The memo was written by a black staffer who himself had been associated earlier with the freedom highs. Now he not only connected the loose structure position with organizational problems and with the possibly inflated role of whites in the organization but cited those connections to ask explicitly whether whites should be excluded from SNCC. Stories about whites' antipathy to organizational structure thus helped to crystallize leanings toward racial separatism. This explains self-described hardliner Cleve Sellers's later observation that the hardliners "were primarily black" and that they "were moving in a Black Nationalist direction." Just as it was unclear how centralized structure would generate the programmatic initiatives that were needed, it was unclear why pursuing a nationalist agenda required a top-down organizational structure. Rather, ideological positions and racial allegiances had been mapped onto organizational preferences.[36]

Once established, however, those alignments proved influential. While a number of whites labeled freedom high drifted away from the group after the February 1965 meeting, most black staffers associated with that label remained. By November, SNCC's staff meeting included only one of the whites who had advocated loose structure. If the hardliners' victory began to solve the racial problem, however, it did not solve the programmatic questions the debate had also reflected. Clear lines of command could not by themselves supply the programmatic direction that was so desperately needed. Two organizers reported that "[p]eople really have no ideas for programs. . . . This is a reason that a lot of SNCC people have gone off to the frontiers of Alabama." SNCC's Alabama head reported in April that dozens of Mississippi staffers were leaving their projects to come to Alabama in spite of efforts to dissuade them. "People came because of frustration on their projects." By November, SNCC's Mississippi staff had dropped to one-third of what it had been the previous fall.[37]

Varieties of Leadership, 1966

The metonymic associations that were established during the debates over organizational structure also had more enduring effects. The recoding of participatory democracy as principled but impractical, oriented to transforming selves rather than gaining power, and implicitly as white rather than black went on to shape SNCC's tactical choices after the debates were over.

This was evident in SNCC's May 1966 conference. In the meeting, staffers openly discussed the role of whites in the organization. They also questioned the group's long-standing commitment to nonviolence and called for independent political organizing. In electing Stokely Carmichael chair, staffers signaled their desire to move in a new national-ist direction. In wide-ranging discussions during the meeting, SNCC workers recounted the history of the organization over the previous few years as a way to chart new directions. Speakers criticized what they saw as the organization's period of self-indulgent individualism. "[In] 1964–1965 people tried to be individuals. But they were begin-ning to realize there is no room for individual black people in the movement. The essential question is: How do we as technicians and organizers develop the black community?" Their mistake, they agreed, was that they had "assumed that when we went into a community, we did not assume leadership." They referred to this as their misguided "Camus period." They were determined not to make the same mistake again.[38]

The moral of the story that SNCC workers now told was that strong leadership was a good thing, distinguished from the "local-people-itis" that had prevented organizers from taking any action at all. However, that development ended up narrowing SNCC's range of tactical options and made it harder to organize. Granted, SNCC organizers faced many obstacles after 1966. In addition to continuing violence by local white Southerners, they now faced competition on the part of moderate groups and, in the North, militant ones, along with unremitting government surveillance and harassment. Add to that what seemed a single-minded media focus on the separatist implications of the Black Power slogan, which Stokely Carmichael had first used in June 1966. Confronted with a firestorm of publicity and attack, SNCC workers found themselves ab-sorbed in trying to interpret a phrase that, they say now, they had not fully defined. They ended up spending much more time giving speeches and press conferences than they had intended. As staffer Stanley Wise later put it, they were beginning to trade "leadership by sweat" for "lead-ership by rhetoric."[39]

This shift had little to do with SNCC workers' conceptions of indi-vidualism, participation, and democracy. But their repertoire of organiz-ing *had* changed. For one thing, a nondirective organizing style had become associated with white freedom highs' penchant for endless, unproductive talk. SNCC workers now were willing to abandon time-consuming discussions about the proper relationship between organizer and community. Stokely Carmichael, who had been clearly aligned with neither side in the structure debate, did reject what was seen now as a romantic refusal to exercise leadership. When he launched the organiz-ing project in Lowndes County, Alabama, that would be the incubus for Black Power, he "got out of that bag of manipulation," he said shortly after. "I went in there with certain ideas. One idea was to organize people to get power. And if that is manipulation, so be it."[40]

In fact, the drive to establish the Lowndes County Freedom Organization proved to be a remarkable exercise in community-wide organizing, and its local leaders were fully capable of running their own show. However, in SNCC workers' public statements about Black Power, giving voice to the voiceless sometimes shifted to speaking in the people's putative voice. "An organization which claims to speak for the needs of a community—as does the Student Nonviolent Coordinating Committee—must speak in the tone of that community," Carmichael said in a typical formulation. Speaking in the "tone" of the community became a way to radicalize it—as SNCC workers variously put it, to "break open the chains in the minds of people in black communities"; to "awaken . . . the black community"; to "educate the black people who have in the past been brainwashed." Of course, all organizations speak in the name of their constituencies. But internal SNCC discussions also suggest worries among some staffers that others were beginning to see themselves as an ideological vanguard. Executive secretary James Forman, who had been one of the fiercest critics of SNCC organizers' unwillingness to exercise leadership, nevertheless found this new approach discomfiting. "The whole generalizing about 'the black community feels this' and 'the black community feels that' has to stop," he insisted. "It is presumptuous of us to feel that we know what all the black community is saying and doing."[41]

The danger of claiming radical spokesmanship for the black community and abandoning efforts to wrestle with the relations between organizers, leaders, and residents was that it represented black people as a passive mass awaiting direction by leaders. Whether leaders were thought to lead on the basis of their mainstream political credentials or their racial authenticity, the model remained one in which leaders' accountability was an individual characteristic. The alternative was that institutionalized mechanisms for citizen input, scrutiny, and challenge would keep leaders accountable. SNCC workers had begun to envision and experiment with just such mechanisms in their Mississippi projects. Under the mantle of radicalism, they began to revert to a more traditional notion of leadership.[42]

For a number of reasons, this just one among them, SNCC never managed to revive its organizing efforts. By the time the organization collapsed in 1968, its activities consisted mainly of speechmaking and battles among pan-Africanists, Marxists, and cultural nationalists in the group. What of the participatory democratic organizational form that they had made famous? By the time of SNCC's demise, thousands of white activists in the peace, back to the land, feminist, and other movements had taken participatory democracy as their watchword. Decentralized and consensus-based organizations proliferated. However, for many activists, it was participatory democracy's antipathy to instrumental rationality that made it appealing. That was not the case early on, when Students for a Democratic Society coined the term *participatory democracy* in 1962 to describe a society in which institutions were controlled by their constituents. As I noted in the last chapter, the founders of SDS openly admired SNCC activists, and they described their own movement as a northern counterpart to the southern civil rights movement. They similarly credited SNCC in their conception of participatory democracy. But it was the macropolitical vision inspired by SNCC's work—of ordinary people making the decisions that affected their lives—rather than a mode of organizational decision making that SDS leaders had in mind. Indeed, at the time, and for several years after, SDS relied on a hierarchical structure, with formal offices of president, vice president, and national secretary; a paid full-time staff; and decisions between conventions made by a National Council.[43]

Over time, however, participatory democracy came to be embraced by many within SDS and then by the broader new left as an organizational form. This occurred in part through the stories that new leftists told about SNCC. One influential story appeared in *Studies on the Left* in 1965. Editor Norm Fruchter returned from a trip to Mississippi to herald profound changes in the civil rights movement. Black Mississippians and the SNCC activists they worked with had "abandoned the goal of eventual integration into existing Mississippi society as both unrealistic and undesirable," he wrote. Rejecting the "totemic demands" of the left—for federal housing and employment programs, national health insurance, and the like—they were rather working to create counter-institutions and relationships "based on assumptions about identity, personality, work, meaning, and aspirations not accepted in the majority society." And probably even more "disconcerting" to "orthodox left-wingers," Fruchter speculated, they were questioning what counted as radical organization. "Primarily a movement . . . only incidentally an organization," SNCC was seeking "to raise the question of just how well all the organizations operating on bureaucratic assumptions within the majority society have served human freedom."[44]

Fruchter's piece provoked an indignant response from Old Left stalwart Victor Rabinowitz. SNCC was more interested in getting black southerners' rights enforced than in questioning assumptions about identity and personality, Rabinowitz sniffed. To do that required a "disciplined, efficient organization," which SNCC strove to be by operating as a conventional bureaucracy. The piece also provoked a response from SNCC staffer Mike Miller, which was not published. Both Fruchter's and Rabinowitz's accounts bore "so little resemblance to the day to day realities" of SNCC "as to be almost frightening," Miller wrote. SNCC's goal was not to develop new assumptions about identity and personality, as Fruchter claimed, but to gain "power to break into the society and get a share of its resources." SNCC workers were indeed experimenting with decentralized forms of administration, and their commitment to local control and leadership from below did distinguish them from the Old Left, Miller observed. But their purpose was practical: they sought organization "designed to effectively service the staff and field without controlling all activity at the local level."[45]

No matter the inaccuracy of Fruchter's account, its depiction of black civil rights activists determined to transcend organizational hierarchy of all kinds struck a chord with northern white students who had come of age in 800-person college lecture halls and reading about grey-faced organization men. As white new leftists launched their own experiments in radical democracy, they were "heavily influenced by the SNCC legend," as one put it. Yet, as Miller's account suggests, the practical purposes of consensus-based and decentralized decision making that had been so important to SNCC dropped out as the legend grew.[46]

Ironies of Strategic Choice

I have argued that SNCC workers abandoned a fully participatory democratic form of organization when it came to stand in for the organization's lack of programmatic direction and the dominance of whites. The relations between loose structure, programmatic paralysis, and an overrepresentation of whites were never specified. Rather, those relations were metonymic: loose structure denoted a range of problems without ever showing how it was responsible for those problems. On one hand, the metonymy did allow SNCC workers to regain a sense of organizational purpose even in the absence of any clear program. And it did make it easier to talk openly about the virtues of an all-black organization. On the other hand, once the symbolic associations between participatory democracy, programmatic incoherence, a self-indulgent individualism, and the dominance of whites became conventional, those associations ruled out tactical choices even as they made others appealing. In particular, they discouraged an organizing style that focused on building local leaders in favor of a more conventional and directive leadership style.

Highlighting the metonymic relations that were established in SNCC workers' characterizations of their organization and movement during this period thus helps to explain key features of SNCC's shift in strategic commitment. It does so better than accounts that have focused on the group's growth in size and stature or on the ascendance of a Black Power ideology. More broadly, this case suggests that instrumental rationality and ideological consistency do not exhaust criteria for strategic choice in movements. I have argued that some strategies, tactics, organizational forms, and deliberative styles may be appealing mainly on account of the social groups or conditions with which they are symbolically associated. The emergence of metonymies in activists' discourse should alert us to the likelihood that such associations are becoming conventional. Again, metonymies figure in discursive forms other than stories. But in the accounts that activists give about what is happening to them as a group and movement, and why they need to change or stay on course—the kinds of stories that are prominent in tactical discussions—metonymies may supply a causal thread that links past events to desirable or undesirable futures. Metonymic associations can be negative or positive, and they can shift over time. But once established, they have staying power, since to question them is to question the basic idiom of the group.

I have not speculated about the kinds of groups that activists are likely to take as negative or positive models. Nor have I sought to identify the points at which metonymic associations between particular strategies and particular strengths or weaknesses are most vulnerable to challenge. Instead, I have highlighted a set of historical ironies. An organizational form whose cachet for white activists lay in its association with the cutting edge of the southern civil rights movement became unappealing to the cutting edge of that movement on account of its increasing identification with whites. Black activists rejected participatory democracy as good only for personal change rather than political reform. Then a generation of white activists celebrated it for that very reason.

The ironies continue. Today, even as consensus-based decision making has enjoyed renewed popularity, especially in the anti–corporate globalization and social justice movements, it has come under fire by some activists in those movements. To familiar complaints about the inefficiency of consensus decision making has been added the charge that the form alienates activists of color and working-class activists. As an organizer wrote in a movement periodical, "When labor people or African-American people have to organize within the consensus model they are

uncomfortable with it and the culture that comes with it." Another organizer observed that in black communities "the reality is that certain individuals play roles (whether by choice or not) that are similar to de facto
traditional leadership roles"—and that made black activists more comfortable with hierarchical organizations. After a national anti-sweatshop
organizing conference, a participant described consensus-based decision
making, along with veganism and "not raising your voice in meetings,"
as among the "white activist cultural norms" that alienated participants
of color. For these and other critics, consensus-based decision making is
one of the "cultural trappings" of middle-class, white, progressive activism. In a sense, it *is* white. Or, rather, I have argued, it has *become* white.[47]

FOUR

Stories and Reasons: Why Deliberation Is Only Sometimes Democratic

Stories are commonly viewed as persuading through their appeal to emotion rather than reason, through an affective identification that supersedes logic and evidence. If that is true, then does storytelling jeopardize fair and effective political decision making? In one view, it does. Storytelling produces mobilization rather than deliberation, galvanizes the mob rather than guiding the citizenry. Concerns like these have become especially significant in the context of political theorists' new enthusiasm for public deliberation. Champions of deliberative democracy argue that ordinary people are capable of recognizing the legitimacy of preferences that are different from their own and of modifying their own preferences when faced with compelling evidence. Discussion of even the most emotionally charged political issues can yield areas of consensus and compromise if participants are required to back up their claims by providing evidence and appealing to universal principles. One can see that stories—particular, subjective, ambiguous in their policy implications, and impossible to adjudicate by reference to evidence—could impede that kind of deliberation.[1]

There is another view, however. Storytelling can overcome precisely the limitations of deliberation as conventionally understood. What counts as rational discussion is deeply biased, say critics of the deliberative democratic vision I just sketched. The kind of discourse that is privileged is passionless, coolly logical, and abstract. That style is both more accessible to traditionally privileged groups and likely to be seen as characteristic of them, no matter how they actually speak. The widely shared values or universal principles that deliberators are supposed to appeal to, moreover, are far from universal. To the contrary, norms of fairness and equality incorporate the experiences of traditionally powerful groups. Opening deliberation up to storytelling can remedy both these flaws. When members of disadvantaged groups recount their experiences of particular policies, they expose the disparate impacts of supposedly neutral policies and invite in their fellow deliberators an empathetic understanding of their distinctive needs and priorities. Far from simply asserting personal experience as the basis for policy, such stories serve to reveal the false universality of existing standards—and that may open the way to construct more truly universal standards.[2]

Can storytelling in deliberation actually accomplish these things? Arguments on both sides of the debate have remained almost exclusively within the realm of theory. We know little about whether and how people tell stories in deliberative forums, who tells them, and what effects storytelling has on deliberation. This is surprising, since exercises in public deliberation have proliferated in recent years. Hundreds of thousands of Americans have participated in citizen juries, public issues forums, citizen assemblies, electronic town meetings, deliberative polls, online dialogues, and visioning workshops. Citizens in other countries have engaged in similar deliberative exercises, some even larger in scale. Although many of these forums are aimed at raising the level of civic discourse, without any direct connection to policymaking, some have been convened by local and national governments as part of the policymaking process. Whether or not personal storytelling can make for fairer deliberation thus has real political ramifications. Yet there has been no systematic analysis of narrative's role in deliberation.[3]

In this chapter, I respond to that gap by analyzing storytelling in twelve groups that were convened to deliberate about the future of the World Trade Center (WTC) site in the wake of the September 11, 2001, terrorist attack. The discussions took place online, involved about a dozen active participants each, and went on for two weeks. Participants were asked to discuss a variety of issues having to do with the rebuilding of the WTC site and the surrounding neighborhood, including transportation, housing, public space, and economic development issues; the design of buildings to replace the towers; and a memorial planned for the victims of the disaster. I combined a quantitative analysis of how storytelling and classical reason-giving were distributed across groups, topics, kinds of claims, and kinds of responses with a qualitative analysis of storytelling exchanges.[4]

What I found should give pause to those on both sides of the story-telling debate. Personal storytelling fosters deliberation, but not for the reasons given by its champions. And it impedes deliberation, but not for the reasons given by its detractors. I argue that neither side in the debate has fully grasped the *narrative* character of personal storytelling. Detractors have treated personal stories as unmediated representations of individual experiences, missing the fact that stories depend for their coherence on their capacity to link particular experience with more general normative principles. This opens up opportunities for jointly assessing preferences and principles that are unavailable to deliberators in the classical conception. Stories also may help to move deliberators from diverse and contradictory preferences to compromise positions, but less as a result of the clarity of stories' normative conclusions than of the ambiguity of those conclusions. As I argued in chapter 1, narrative's political effectiveness may have much to do with this distinctive feature of the form. Narrative's champions, for their part, have failed to account for how popular views of storytelling's credibility shape its rhetorical force in actual deliberations. In particular, I argue that a common view of personal storytelling as at once normatively compelling and politically unserious works against already disadvantaged groups in deliberation. In short, storytelling's liability in deliberation stems less from its rhetorical capacities than from its social status relative to other discursive forms.

Democracy and Storytelling

Arguments for the virtues of deliberation go back to Aristotle, but they have taken on special force in the context of widespread concern about the low levels of citizen engagement in contemporary democracies. If democracy requires the consent of the governed, the governed are doing very little active consenting. Voting rates in the United States and Western Europe are low. In 2000, only 28 percent of American first-year college students believed that "keeping up to date with political affairs" was "essential" or "very important"—the lowest percentage since the survey began. Nor can citizens' consent be assumed from their failure to participate: polls show that large and increasing numbers of citizens are dissatisfied with and distrustful of the political system. Even when people do participate, as they did in the 2004 American election, the polarized character of political discourse has contributed to a deeply divided electorate.[5]

As a growing number of democratic theorists see it, the solution to this state of affairs is to create opportunities for public deliberation. Proponents of deliberative democracy count among their ranks such thinkers as Jürgen Habermas, Benjamin Barber, Amy Guttman, Dennis Thompson, Joshua Cohen, James Bohman, and John Dryzek. Their arguments differ, but they share a common belief in the value of deliberation, as distinct from voting and bargaining, as a way to approach diverse preferences. For discussion to be deliberative, it must be open to all, and participants must be unconstrained in the arguments they make, save by the requirement of civility. In such a setting, deliberation takes the form of reason-giving. Participants seek to justify their preferences by making arguments that others can accept as persuasive. Deliberative democrats differ on whether the values and principles to which participants appeal should be shared by all participants already or whether it is the possibility of unity that motivates them. Most deliberative theorists, however, talk easily about the "universal standards," the "common good," or the "impartial values" to which deliberators should appeal.[6]

Even if participants do not change their minds as a result of their deliberations, they will likely come to recognize a greater range of preferences and preference orderings as legitimate. Once that recognition occurs, people are likely to accept a decision that does not match their preferences exactly. This means that public deliberation can be integrated with existing electoral, legislative, and administrative processes. It should lead to policy that is better because it is grounded in informed public opinion, as well as to greater citizen engagement and more legitimate political institutions.[7]

Arguments for deliberative democracy have been subjected to a variety of criticisms. In particular, political theorists Iris Marion Young, Lynn Sanders, and others question the assumption that rational deliberation as it is conventionally understood is equally available to all participants. To the contrary, they say, deliberation works better for those who are skilled in its discursive requirements: men, white people, native speakers of standard English, and those with cultural as well as economic capital. Moreover, rational discourse is usually taken to be passionless and neutral. Since women, in particular, are trained to respond compassionately, they are likely to be seen as less than rational, as are members of groups that use expressive discursive styles. No matter how they speak, groups that are commonly identified with passion over reason are less likely to be seen as rational deliberators.[8]

What passes as rational deliberation is biased in another way, say theorists in this vein. Deliberators are supposed to justify their claims in terms of widely shared values and universal principles. But those principles unfairly universalize the experience of particular, powerful groups. For example, as feminists have argued, supposedly universal standards of workplace equality have embedded the experiences of men in a way that has made it difficult for women to invoke those standards to gain the right to pregnancy leave, to be protected against sexual harassment, and to be hired for jobs traditionally defined as male. To claim that women have "special" needs has risked subjecting them to penalties. As legal scholar Martha Minow writes, when universal standards reflect particular experiences, difference becomes deviance.[9]

The solution to these problems, as some see it, is to legitimize diverse forms of discourse in deliberation. Among them, storytelling has special virtues. In a deliberative setting, storytelling is equalizing, since everyone has his or her own story. Encouraging disadvantaged groups to tell their own stories can counter the silencing that comes with privileging abstract, rationalist discourse. More than that, personal storytelling can gain an empathetic hearing for experiences and values that are different from those of the majority. Storytelling can also help to get new issues on the deliberative agenda. When people recount their experiences of daily injustice and exploitation, some among their audience may begin to recognize themselves in the stories. For an expanding circle, what seemed personal troubles become social problems in need of political remedy. For example, women's stories of fending off unwanted sexual overtures, told first in small circles of intimates, gradually forged the ground for what has come to be recognized as sexual harassment. In formal deliberative settings, too, personal storytelling may lead to the identification of new issues demanding discussion.[10]

Stories of personal struggles can make real the consequences of governmental actions that are too often conceived abstractly. They can also counter the stereotypes that underpin supposedly neutral policies. For example, when a woman on welfare recounts her struggles to find work and to care for her children, she may effectively debunk the stereotype of the welfare queen who is exploiting the system. Finally, personal storytelling by disadvantaged groups can help more advantaged groups to recognize the particularistic character of the ostensibly universal standards that deliberators are supposed to appeal to. This can lead the group to begin the work of crafting more inclusive standards.[11]

Deliberative democrats in the classical mold remain unconvinced by these arguments. John Dryzek argues that personal stories fail the minimum requirement of deliberative discourse: that it "connect the particular to the general." If a person's story is just her own, then there is no point in recounting it. If she tells her story to illuminate the experience of her group, her audience has no way of knowing how representative her story is. Should we take a quadriplegic's account as representative of the experiences of disabled people? More troubling still, if not formulated carefully, a group's story may widen perceptions of difference rather than narrowing them, making listeners even less responsive to the group's claims. Conversely, if listeners do identify emotionally with the victimization described in a story, they may be prone to unreasoned action, to vengeance rather than reasoned remedy. In sum, unless storytellers make a special effort to "appeal to universal standards," in Dryzek's words, or, as David Miller puts it, to "invoke reasons and principles that are widely shared," along with their stories, then storytelling is likely to inhibit deliberation rather than advance it.[12]

Deliberative democrats are clear that telling stories and appealing to shared values are separate discursive acts. Personal storytelling can usefully *precede* an appeal to shared values, and good storytellers can even integrate shared values into the story itself. But without special effort, personal storytelling is unlikely to make for fairer deliberation. Disadvantaged groups may have the satisfaction of expressing their particular needs and values in their own distinctive voices, but they thereby engage in a "politics of futile gesture" that leaves the status quo intact.[13]

The problem with these criticisms is that they ignore precisely the narrative character of personal stories. Deliberative democrats tend to treat personal stories as a raw account of personal experience rather than as personal *stories*. In fact, champions of personal storytelling do the same thing, arguing that storytelling should be combined with appeals to "general normative arguments," as Iris Marion Young puts it. Again, the two are seen as separate kinds of discourse. But stories, more than other discursive forms, depend for their very coherence on the connections they forge between storyteller and audience and between particular experiences and more general normative standards. Stories "reach out" to their audiences in precisely the way that deliberative democrats urge deliberators to do.[14]

This is true in several respects. As I noted in chapter 1, stories require that listeners or readers enter a reality that is separate from the present one. Narrators rely on a variety of devices to effect that transition, including indicators in the conversation that a story is about to be told; an orientation to the time and place of the story ("Once upon a time . . ." or "When I first came to Manhattan . . ."); and a shift in verb tense. These devices help the reader or listener to suspend initial skepticism about the credibility or salience of events recounted in the story and instead to strive to grasp the motivations of characters and the logic of unfolding events.[15]

Stories also reach out to their audiences in the sense that they depend for their very understanding on plot lines that are familiar to the audience. An account of a personal experience makes sense against the backdrop of similar stories. The story is recognizable as a "David and Goliath story" about the little guy triumphing over the big guy, or a "pride before a fall" story about the guy biting off more than he can chew. Such plots are normative as well as explanatory. That is, they organize events so as to yield meaning that reaches beyond the events. To grasp the story is to grasp its moral implications. This is different from saying that people can combine their stories with an appeal to shared values. Rather, the values are built into the story itself. They seem to be given by the events rather than asserted by the narrator. Indeed, it is difficult to tell an intelligible story *without* communicating the normative values associated with a particular plot line.

All stories have a moral, but a narrator rarely announces the moral explicitly. Rather, readers or listeners know that they must interpret the story to extract its meaning. They also know that their initial interpretation may be wrong; that the same events can be recounted in different ways to reveal different meanings; and that the same events recounted from the point of view of another character may yield a different normative point. A story's meaning is allusive. Of course, all discursive forms are, at some level, allusive. But audiences *expect* good stories to be interpretable more than they do good arguments or good reports. I have talked about narrative's openness to interpretation before. Here, I emphasize what may be a corollary: the frequently collaborative character of storytelling. Scholars of ordinary conversation have found that when people tell their stories, listeners often participate in interpreting and even telling the story. The narrator may offer the point of the story, which may then be modified or amplified by her interlocutors, who may then tell other stories that take up the point but reformulate it. Or the narrator's interlocutors may supply the point of an account that the storyteller presented as ambiguous. In these respects, far from being oriented merely to self-expression, stories are a way for their narrators to involve others in making sense of experiences and options.[16]

In sum, stories draw their audiences into the world they create; integrate novelty into familiar frameworks; and involve audiences in defining their moral meaning. These features provide important deliberative resources. Indeed, telling personal stories may help deliberators not only to register their differences (which deliberative democrats see it as well-equipped to do) but also to discover areas of unanticipated agreement (which deliberative democrats see it as spectacularly unequipped to do). By deliberative democrats' own account, if deliberators are to move toward agreement, they must be able to hear different opinions and experiences as different but not incomprehensible or threatening. Deliberators must also be willing to scrutinize their own experiences, the opinions to which their experiences have given rise, and the principles that they have usually called on to justify those opinions. Deliberators must be able to think themselves into other people's opinions, into other ways of interpreting their own experience, into new definitions of problems and solutions. Much more than is suggested by images of argumentative joust and parry or the legalistic application of principles to cases, deliberation requires an effort of imagination. Finally, even if they hold fast to their opinions in the end, deliberators must be able to recognize the legitimacy of opinions that differ from their own. Simply saying that they do is probably insufficient. Rather, they must find ways to demonstrate to a skeptical audience their understanding of and respect for competing opinions.[17]

Telling personal stories can help with each of these tasks. When audiences enter the storyworld created by the narrator, they know that they are making a projective leap. This allows them to understand and empathize with the narrator without assimilating his experience to their own. The fact that stories integrate novelty into the familiar form of canonical plot lines should also make it possible for audiences to comprehend people's experiences both as unique and as similar to more familiar experiences. When people tell stories, they make their experiences available to be interpreted by their audience, sometimes in ways that had not occurred to them previously. Their stories may lead others to tell their own stories, with the normative conclusion crafted jointly through an exchange of stories. Personal storytelling thus encourages deliberators to collaborate in scrutinizing their opinions, experiences, and principles. Finally, by retelling other people's stories or imagining the experiences associated with a particular position, deliberators can demonstrate their empathetic understanding of an opinion with which they do not agree, or at least their appreciation of the experiences that gave rise to it. In at least these ways, then, personal storytelling may foster good deliberation.

But there may be a downside. Even if the opposition between storytelling and reason-giving is conventional rather than inherent, it may still have powerful effects. If certain groups are seen as prone to storytelling rather than reason-giving, their stories may be devalued, or they may be valued for their authenticity rather than for their persuasive power. If stories are commonly seen as appropriate during discussions that are personal, social, and conversational, they may be seen as inappropriate during discussions that are public, political, or technical. Storytelling may be discouraged in precisely the kinds of discussions where it could be most useful.

These possibilities point to a set of empirical questions that I address in the context of an episode of online deliberation. How do people in real life use stories in deliberation? Do stories counter the narrowness of existing deliberative agendas and standards by inviting identification with the needs of disadvantaged groups and a glimpse of more truly universal standards? Or do stories simply assert idiosyncratic demands without offering any means of adjudicating among them? Finally, do the social conventions around storytelling make it a more or less powerful tool in forging understanding across difference?

Listening to the City

Between July 31 and August 12, 2002, more than eight hundred people deliberated online about the future of Lower Manhattan. The online dialogue was convened in conjunction with a 4,300 person face-to-face forum called Listening to the City. The online component began immediately after the face-to-face forum and followed roughly the same agenda. Participants were assigned to twenty-six closed dialogue groups and asked to discuss preliminary plans for the WTC site, as well as housing, transportation, economic development issues, and the memorial planned for the site. The results of their discussions were registered in individual polls and group summaries, synthesized by forum organizers, and forwarded to rebuilding authorities. Some of the issues in the discussions were prickly: for example, whether to build on the original footprints of the towers and whether to build low-income housing on the site. And many participants—562 were active discussants—had a real stake in these issues. Some had lost friends and family in the disaster, and others lived or worked near ground zero. Still others had no direct connection to the site at all, and some lived outside the city and even outside the state. Groups would thus deliberate across significantly different experiences. The recommendations agreed to in group discussions were not binding on officials or participants. However, this is by no means atypical of public deliberative forums. Most of them operate on a model of civic education that is aimed more at better informing and engaging participants than at reforming particular policies, and even those that are aimed at policy reform rarely secure more than officials' agreement to consider their recommendations.[18]

Two other features of this particular forum bear note. Convened in the wake of a national tragedy, Listening to the City attracted many people with a high emotional investment in the discussion but little direct material stake in it. Yet, this could be said about other issues that have been the subject of deliberative forums, such as abortion and welfare reform. Although people did tell stories about their experience of 9/11 and its aftermath, they told many more stories about matters that were more prosaic, and they told stories far more often to express their opinions about redevelopment than to express their feelings about the 9/11 attack. The online nature of the forum, which lacked the verbal and visual behavioral cues that characterize face-to-face interaction, undoubtedly affected the character of discussion (and I speculate at several points about how storytelling might have been different had deliberation been face-to-face). However, the anonymity that is frequently cited as a key difference between the two modes of interaction was not a factor here. Group members were asked to introduce themselves both in an autobiographical blurb that was easily accessible to others throughout the discussion and in an "introductions" thread that led off most groups' discussions. That meant that participants generally knew fellow deliberators' gender, as well as, in many cases, their level of educational attainment, race/ethnicity, and income level. In addition, previous research on the two modes of communication has not noted the kinds of differences that would likely be reflected in patterns of storytelling and reason-giving. Perhaps more important, the lower cost and greater accessibility of online forums has convinced many observers that they, and not face-to-face forums, will be the public commons of the future.[19]

To study how storytelling figured in the Listening to the City online dialogues, I worked with John Lee and several other graduate students to identify every story told, 197 altogether, in twelve groups or 5,345 messages. Following Labov and Waletsky, we defined a story as an account of a sequence of events in the order in which they occurred so as to make a normative point. Stories typically were composed of (a) an orientation, which set the scene; (b) a series of complicating actions ending with one that served as dénouement; and (c) an evaluation, establishing the importance of the events related (the evaluation could come at any point in the story).[20]

The vast majority of the stories that appeared in the dialogues—more than 76 percent—were first-person stories. Although some were about the narrator's experience of 9/11 or about its impacts on his or her daily life, many others related more to redevelopment options; for example, stories about changes in the narrator's neighborhood over the years, visits to other memorials, the narrator's use of amenities in Lower Manhattan before the disaster, good and bad commuting experiences, the narrator's experience of local politics, and so on. Altogether, 23 percent of the stories were about the narrator's experience of 9/11 or the impacts of 9/11 on his or her life; the rest were about other issues. In some cases, people told stories to give group members a sense of themselves or to express their feelings about an issue without voicing an opinion or preference. However, 92 percent of the stories in the sample (182 of 197 stories) introduced or followed opinions or preferences. I call these *narrative claims*. Here are two examples of such claims:

As I stated in my bio, my youngest child, Paul, was murdered on Sept. 11. He was attending [a] conference at Windows on the World. He did not even work at the WTC. He was only 25 years old, standing on the brink of a wonderful future. Though Paul is dead, as a parent, my need to care for him has not gone away. To that end, I became the co-chairperson of the Memorial Committee [. . .]

All this started by my wanting to see Paul's name etched in stone. Many people resent calling Ground Zero a cemetery, but in fact, many people's remains have not been found, including Paul, and this site will be their last resting place. I want to see a respectful and dignified memorial. I want to see a museum that will tell future generations what happened in NY on Sept. 11. I don't want this event remembered as a mass murder, but the loss of many individual human souls. A museum will give a human face to this tragedy. I want Ground Zero to become a meaningful place that will honor those murdered as well as create a vital neighborhood in the city Paul truly loved. My immediate reaction cannot be described. I am no longer the person I once was and I will never ever recover from the fact that Paul will not be able to live out his life . . . and he truly loved life.[21]

Hmmmmmm. At first I was very gun-ho about rebuilding the towers. I, like many, thought that to not rebuild the towers was to "let the terrorists win" and I also feared that what was lost could only be replaced by rebuilding them exactly as they were.

But as time passed and information surfaced about the possibilities I began to change my mind. Now I am 100% for rebuilding but I do not think we should rebuild the towers.

The story of the first writer's son backed up her preferences for the memorial and a museum, but it did so by recounting how she came to hold those preferences, an account that took the form of a tragic but literarily familiar story of a parent's loss of a child. The second writer described coming to believe just as strongly that the new buildings should not be replicas of the originals as he had at first believed the opposite, the symmetry of his conviction providing the narrative reversal.

Both writers could have justified their preferences without telling a story. The first writer could have argued that honoring those who had died required a museum that recognized their individuality. The second writer could have argued that replicating the towers would forgo an opportunity to design something truly original. Justifications that appeal to shared values—here, respect for the dead and aesthetic originality—are consistent with deliberation in the classical mold. To capture this way of backing up claims, we coded every *non-narrative claim,* where those posting messages introduced or followed a preference or opinion with a reason rather than a story. We defined such claims broadly, as any statement that could be interpreted as reading, "I want or believe X because Y." Reasons could be practical ("that option has worked elsewhere"), normative ("that is the fair, or democratic, or honorable thing to do"), or symbolic ("that option signals our commitment to freedom, or strength, or environmental sustainability"). There were 1,484 non-narrative claims in the twelve groups that we coded.

People were thus much more likely to advance their opinions by way of reasons than stories. Conversational analysts argue that because telling a story takes longer than other kinds of utterances, people tend not to launch into stories uninvited. Instead, a person will preface a story with remarks like "Did I tell you . . ." or "Incidentally, . . ." and wait for some indication that the audience is willing to grant them the floor. Alternatively, a person will offer what I referred to in chapter 1 as a kernel story, in which an event is referred to rather than recounted, with the expectation that she will be asked to expand in a subsequent conversational turn. Neither expectation was realistic in the online dialogues, however, since exchanges were asynchronous. In other words, one would be unlikely to post something like, "that reminds me of something that happened to me . . ." with nothing further, and were one to offer a kernel story, it might be hours before anyone responded with an invitation to tell the whole story, if anyone responded at all. This may be one instance, then, of a difference between asynchronous online deliberation and in-person deliberation: the faster back and forth in in-person deliberation may encourage more storytelling.[22]

We compared narrative and non-narrative claims along a variety of dimensions, including the demographic characteristics of claimsmakers, the content of the claims, the discursive contexts in which the claims were made, and the ways in which other group members responded to them. In the following, I focus on the most striking findings from the point of view of storytelling's virtues and weaknesses for good deliberation. Of course, defining what counts as good deliberation is not easy. Evidence that group members were converging on a shared position might indicate that they were collectively reasoning their way to a consensus, but it might also indicate that some were coercing others or that the issue was not interesting. Since people are notoriously reluctant to acknowledge changes of opinion, relying on members' statements to that effect is also likely to be unreliable. Instead, I begin with a minimal requirement of good deliberation: that participants engage each other's claims. By that I mean that participants respond to claims made by others: that they agree or disagree, ask for clarification or elaboration, raise questions about the claims' relevance or general application, corroborate, or counter them.

Who Told Stories and Why?

Are people from classically disadvantaged groups likely to tell stories? And do people use stories to seek recognition for unrecognized needs and understanding for unfamiliar opinions? Online dialogue participants who had incomes below $50,000, those with less than a college education, and those who were not white were no more likely to make narrative claims than were people with incomes above $50,000, those with a college education, and those who were white. However, women were more likely to turn to stories than men. Women made up approximately 45 percent of the dialogue participants. But they made 52 percent of the narrative claims and only 40 percent of the non-narrative ones. Indeed, controlling for other variables, a woman was 1.75 times more likely than a man to make a narrative claim.[23]

An even more striking pattern had to do not with the kinds of *people* who advanced opinions by way of stories but the *kinds of opinions* advanced in that way. Members of all demographic groups who saw themselves as having opinions or experiences that were not shared often told stories to make their points. For example, the dialogue participant I quoted earlier noted, "Many people resent calling Ground Zero a cemetery, but in fact, many people's remains have not been found, including Paul, and this site will be their last resting place. . . ." In telling Paul's story, this writer sought to communicate a point of view she saw as unlike that of a particular group, namely people who resented calling ground zero a cemetery. Other writers combined their stories with statements like, "I guess I'm in the minority for thinking . . ."; "Reading through the group discussion, I know that I am in the minority . . ."; "I am also opposed to some people . . ."; "The difference I have . . ."; "I actually have a different reaction . . ."; "I know it will sound strange, but I think . . ."; and so on.

All told, where 29 percent of the narrative claims represented the writer's experience or opinion as unlike that of others, only 6 percent of the non-narrative claims did. People who mentioned their experiences or opinions as atypical were more than five times as likely to make a narrative claim as those who did not. For disadvantaged groups, then, there seems to be good precedent for using personal stories to convey marginalized needs and priorities—since personal stories are already being used by all groups for just that purpose.

This does not tell us *how* people used personal stories, however. Did they recount their experiences simply to register their different needs and priorities, as deliberative democrats worry? Or did their stories open possibilities for forging agreement across differences? Deliberators often told personal stories to establish their stake in an issue, for example, to explain why preserving the footprints of the original towers was so important to them, or to establish the credibility of their opinion. They also told stories to illustrate a point or a practical idea or to flesh out imaginatively the implications of a position. Narrative's champions, recall, point to stories' capacity to reveal the narrow or biased character of ostensibly shared values and neutral principles. Something like that may have been operating when participants told their own stories of loss to explain why it was so inappropriate to call rebuilding the site a "design opportunity," or an "economic development opportunity," as public officials and pundits were doing at the time. To talk about capitalizing on opportunities was to deny the paralyzing loss that many had experienced. Storytellers thus revealed the underside of opportunity, something that, under other circumstances, would likely be seen as a universal good.

Participants' stories also helped to define a new set of issues as worthy of discussion. As participants told stories of what the towers had meant to them personally, many expressed surprise and pleasure to find that there were others in their own group, as well as in other groups, who also wanted the towers rebuilt exactly as they had been. Before the dialogues began, several small groups had been advocating publicly for rebuilding the towers, and some of their members participated in the dialogues. However, their influence paled beside the groundswell of sentiment expressed by dialogue participants who were new to the rebuilding process and who found in fellows' personal stories similar desires and, increasingly, commitment. Complaining that their views were being ignored in the public debate, they began to strategize about how to press their case for rebuilding the towers outside the dialogues. They would eventually circulate a petition and organize a letter-writing campaign.

Dialogue participants used stories to introduce opinions that they characterized as possibly unpopular, to puncture reigning verities and values, and to call for the inclusion of new issues on the deliberative agenda. But people also told personal stories in ways that seemed aimed at advancing the give-and-take that deliberative democrats urge. Narrative claims were much more likely to be *occasioned* than were non-narrative ones; that is, they were explicitly connected to the previous discussion. Where 58 percent of the narrative claims were made either in direct response to another member of the group or in explicit response to a theme or argument that had surfaced in the discussion, only 34 percent of the non-narrative claims were. This suggests that people told stories as part of a dialogue. Again, this may have had something to do with people's inability to secure the invitation to tell a story that they commonly do in everyday conversation. In the absence of such invitations, people may have been more careful to link their stories explicitly to comments made by writers who had posted earlier, as a way to justify telling a story.[24]

Whatever the reason, the effect was to frame narrative claims as part of an ongoing dialogue. It worked on the other side too: in telling stories, participants invited commentary on, and, indeed, collaboration in drawing lessons from their experiences. In some cases, narrators recounted their experiences to convey their strong feelings about what should be built at the site. These were feelings that they had not yet connected to a principled opinion. For example, one participant wrote, "My friend in Tower One had asked me to apply at his company and I refused based on security concerns, especially after the first bombing. I can't really explain it, but NOW I would work in the new building, on the top floors." In other cases, participants suggested that their experience pointed to a different way to think about the principles at stake. So one writer objected to framing the choices as either rebuilding the towers for symbolic reasons or not rebuilding them in the interests of good design. He recounted his own experiences of visiting the towers to argue that they had been well designed, concluding, "I'm not advocating re-building a replica, and I believe that the footprints of the towers should be respected, but why not let what was there be a starting point for designing what is to be?" In stories like these, deliberators offered up their thinking to the group in a way that invited fellow group members to think along with them.

This was especially evident in the many stories, like the example I quoted earlier, that rehearsed the narrator's change of opinion. Such stories invited readers to identify with the narrator's own metamorphosis. They communicated, "I understand your position because I held it myself. What changed my mind was . . ." Their tentative, open-ended quality encouraged readers to see possibilities that were only dimly recognized by the narrator. Even where the writer sought to persuade others of the position she had arrived at, recounting the evolution of her views encouraged respondents both to imagine the shift she described and to volunteer their own views.

Some participants asked people with other points of view to tell their stories, like the writer who asked a proponent of rebuilding the towers to do so, explaining, "I just think it would help the group, as the issue of whether to build high or higher is so contentious." Or they told stories from vantage points they could only imagine. "When I think about the footprints, I place myself in the shoes of a person who lost a loved one and has no remains at all, not even ashes in an urn, to visit," one participant wrote, going on to imagine a family member's experience of the site. Another writer described the powerful emotional impact that the Vietnam war memorial had had on him despite the fact that he had no personal connection to the war. He concluded, "How is someone who was just a baby on 9/11/01 going to feel when going to this memorial and what will they leave with."

Surprisingly, online deliberators also told personal stories not to back up their own opinions but, seemingly, to back up a competing one. For example, one woman argued that honoring too many people as victims would render meaningless the concept of victimhood. But she then told a poignant story of a friend who had lost his job as a result of the attack, was now driving a cab, and, near penniless, was about to lose his apartment. "Isn't he a victim of 9/11?" she wrote. The story suggested that he *was* a victim of 9/11, even though the writer presumably believed that people like her friend were not true victims. The writer was not a bad storyteller. Rather, she made clear that she understood the pain and suffering of those whose loss was primarily economic. Another writer argued firmly for resisting victims' families' demands for a large memorial but then recounted how the attack had affected her, writing, "While I did not know any of the victims, I cried for them for days on end." And a third argued against improvements to a commuter railroad, writing in part, "My office moved to Jersey City 15 months ago. Since I live in Manhattan, I have a reverse commute that sucks[. . . .] So, I'm not being unsympathetic." The last writer explicitly recognized the complexity of the issues at stake, but other writers were just as clear in signaling their empathy with an opposing view. Their own opinion, they seemed to be suggesting, was hard won.

In sum, far from being aimed at personal self-expression rather than mutual understanding, personal storytelling in the online dialogues was both occasioned by other people's remarks and invited commentary, interpretation, and more storytelling. The narrative character of people's accounts—an orientation that drew readers in and a series of complicating actions with a reversal that made sense in terms of familiar stories of loss and enlightenment—engaged people imaginatively in experiences quite different from their own. The interpretatively open character of stories demonstrated participants' willingness to scrutinize their own assumptions. And in asking for and telling the stories of people with views different from their own, storytellers communicated their respect for those views.

How Did People Respond to Stories?

Did telling personal stories work? Did personal stories secure their narrators a respectful hearing and even support for unfamiliar or unpopular opinions? Did they gain a recognition of additional issues as legitimate and relevant? Did they foster a collaborative scrutiny of preferences and principles with the aim of carving out areas of agreement? To some extent, yes (see table 1).

To assess the deliberation-enhancing capability of personal storytelling versus reason-giving, we identified every response to a particular claim in a thread. Perhaps the most sobering finding was that, more often than not, people did not respond to their fellow participants' claims at all. Less than half of the claims people made, whether by way of stories or reasons, elicited at least one response. This suggests an image of a group of monologists more than dialogists. Again, the asynchronous character of the dialogue may be partly responsible for that image. One can imagine that a dialogue participant, logging on and reading several messages, might respond directly only to one of those messages while taking into account points made by the others. Still, this finding does nothing to assuage critics' worry that what passes as deliberation generally, and online in particular, may not be especially deliberative.

Table 1   Responses to narrative and non-narrative claims by response type

	Percentage of narrative claims (and count)	Percentage of non-narrative claims (and count)	z
Express appreciation	26.37 (48)	16.91 (251)	−2.78**
Agree	20.32 (37)	14.55 (216)	−1.85*
Acknowledge the claim's emotional impact	6.04 (11)	0.47 (7)	−3.14**
Acknowledge the claim's impact on opinions	1.65 (3)	0.67 (10)	−1.01
Make a corroborating claim	18.13 (33)	1.35 (20)	−5.84**
Disagree	14.29 (26)	5.12 (76)	−3.45**
Express doubts about the claim's generalizability or relevance	4.40 (8)	0.67 (10)	−2.43**
Request clarification or elaboration	1.10 (2)	2.35 (35)	1.45
Challenge interpretation of claim	2.20 (4)	1.21 (18)	−0.88
Other	1.10 (2)	1.28 (19)	0.22

Note: Percentages for each response type were calculated by dividing the number of each response by the total number of claims in each claim category (182 narrative claims and 1,484 non-narrative claims); the percentages therefore do not add up to 100.
*significant at .05; **significant at .01.

However, participants were more likely to respond when they heard stories than when they heard reasons. Almost half of the narrative claims were responded to in at least one subsequent message, whereas just over one-third of the non-narrative claims were. Controlling for other variables, narrative claims were still 1.5 times more likely than non-narrative claims to elicit a response. The kinds of responses elicited by narrative and non-narrative claims also differed. People were much more likely to express appreciation for narrative claims than they were for non-narrative claims. More than 26 percent of the narrative claims elicited at least one appreciative response, whereas less than 17 percent of the non-narrative claims did. People were also more likely to acknowledge the emotional impact of narrative claims than they were of non-narrative claims (approximately 6 percent of the responses to narrative claims acknowledged that kind of impact compared to less than .05 percent of the responses to non-narrative claims). Often, participants combined expressions of appreciation and emotional impact, as did the

99

one who wrote, "I meant to respond to Greg's story a few days ago—about flying your plane. It really touched me and I had a good cry over it. It's still in my mind. Thanks for sharing it."

Critics of storytelling might not be surprised by these findings. They might point out that expressing appreciation for a story, even describing its emotional resonance, is not the same as engaging the point that a deliberator makes by way of a story. To say that deliberative give and take is occurring, we would want to see people requesting clarification or further elaboration of a point, expanding on it, questioning its generalizability or relevance, agreeing or disagreeing with it, or acknowledging its impact on their opinions. Accordingly, we defined all such responses as *engaging* a claim. On that definition, a narrative claim was more than three times as likely as a non-narrative claim to be engaged.

I want to focus on one kind of response. A greater proportion of narrative claims elicited similar or corroborating claims (over 18 percent) than did non-narrative claims (1 percent). This was the largest difference in responses. More than simply agreeing with a claim, making a corroborating one indicates an effort to build on the prior claim in a way that makes it more nuanced, more broadly applicable, or more persuasive. People often corroborated narrative claims by telling stories of their own. But on closer examination, I found that a story told to corroborate another story often seemed to make a somewhat different point than the original one. For example, in one discussion where participants were highly critical of the tourists descending on ground zero, a former Manhattanite described returning with her husband and children to visit the site. She recounted her fury at the tourists and her shame in realizing she was now one herself. Another participant responded, "My thoughts exactly Moon10!" and then described a friend coming to visit who wanted to see ground zero. But, far from critical of her friend, the writer empathized with her: "She needed to comprehend it all. Its one thing to see it on TV or in the paper, but to be there . . . and to see St. Paul's [the chapel adjacent to the site] . . . its different."

This writer said explicitly that the story she was about to tell confirmed the one that the previous writer had told ("My thoughts exactly Moon10!"), even though it did not obviously do so. Narrative's openness to interpretation may have been important in allowing deliberators to reformulate each other's points in a way that advanced a different position without seeming to disagree. To clarify, let me continue with this particular exchange. After the second writer responded to the first writer's passionate criticism of World Trade Center "tourists" by describing sympathetically her friend's perspective, a third participant wrote, "I too want to respond to the issue of 'tourists,'" and then described volunteering at St. Paul's: "We at the gate made a point of speaking to the passersby, and what became clear to me early on was that that was an important element of our ministry. Another volunteer described these 'tourists' as pilgrims, and that is how I see them too." This author seems to have reconciled the first two points of view by recounting her own conversion on the issue. She modestly credited a co-worker with her new view of visitors as "pilgrims." Two more participants weighed in, both thanking the previous writers. The first one took issue with those who were critical of visitors to the site: "How ungenerous and needlessly judgmental. All I saw were witnesses and pilgrims." The other writer picked up on the earlier writer's mention of volunteers, describing people cheering volunteer aid workers on their way to the site. He went on, "For me, the nightmare of the buildings coming down has evolved into a strange dream that they were ever there in the first place. Folks aren't going to get that from a big hole in the ground or a T-shirt, but people should want to come and understand it in the ways that they can." Without drawing attention to the contrasting views of tourists thus far expressed, this writer too sought to reconcile them: Visitors wouldn't understand as the people who lived in Lower Manhattan did, he suggested, but they should try to understand as best they could.

In the course of this series of stories, then, visiting the site was remade from a reprehensible tourist activity to an understandable and, indeed, laudable, effort to make sense of the disaster. "Tourism" had become a normative obligation. Those who criticized visitors, by contrast, were recast as "needlessly judgmental." These shifts occurred without anyone acknowledging a difference of opinion. To the contrary, each writer represented her or his view as like that of the others. Telling personal stories may have made it possible to do that without seeming inconsistent. There was enough that was similar to make each story seem to follow on from the previous story, even though the moral in each case was quite different. It was in exchanges like this one that the deliberation-enhancing collaborative potential of personal storytelling was most fully realized.

Narrative's champions may be right, therefore, about narrative's capacity to foster deliberation, but they may miss some of the reasons for it. Because stories call for more stories, each one connected to and different from the previous one, and because the moral of a story is always more implied than stated explicitly, storytellers can advance different points, as well as compromise and third positions, all in the guise of telling a similar story. In other words, as I have suggested before, interpretive ambiguity may be a surprising resource in deliberation. Now, this may not always be the case. Where positions on an issue were well-known and conflicting, people probably would not let pass so easily a fellow deliberator's claim that a story corroborated their own opinion when it did not. Deliberators likely would be more resistant to rhetorical moves that glossed over differences. On the other hand, in such a situation deliberators would probably be suspicious of the authenticity of personal stories altogether. This only suggests that discursive styles should probably be different where parties are deeply mistrustful of each other.[25]

When Did People Tell Stories?

The problem with stories was not people's reluctance to engage them, but their reluctance to tell them in certain contexts. I noted that the dialogue groups followed the same basic agenda. Over the course of two weeks, organizers introduced a series of discussion threads with titles like "Hopes and Concerns," "Memorial: Values," "Economic Development and Employment," "Transportation." In many groups, participants also created their own threads. Table 2 depicts a typical group's set of discussion threads.

To determine the discursive contexts in which people were likely to tell stories rather than cite reasons to advance claims, we identified the discussion thread in which each narrative or non-narrative claim appeared.[26] Dialogue participants tended to make narrative claims in discussions of the memorial and discussions of broad themes in rebuilding. They tended not to do so in the discussions of housing, economic development, and transportation. The latter are established policy arenas, with long-standing agendas, institutionalized procedures, and credentialed experts. Discussions of the memorial and the rebuilding process would have implications for practical planning but they were less clearly within the domain of existing policy. Only 3 percent of the narrative claims appeared in the policy-oriented threads, but almost 12 percent of the non-narrative claims appeared there. Participants were only about one-third as likely to make a narrative claim as a non-narrative one in a policy-focused discussion. In other words, when people expressed opinions and preferences in areas of established policy, they tended to do so in more classically deliberative fashion rather than by telling stories.

Now, one could explain this disparity by arguing that the discussions of the memorial and rebuilding generally were more about normative values than about technical challenges and that stories are an especially

Table 2 Dialogue group discussion topics

Topic	No. of messages
1. LTC Core Discussion: Welcome	53
2. General Questions	89
3. LTC Core Discussion: Your Hopes and Concerns	36
4. Links to Related Stories and Articles	25
5. What Would We Do with Another Site Downtown?	24
6. LTC topic: Wrap-Up of Hopes and Concerns	8
7. LTC Topic: Elements of Rebuilding	33
8. LTC Topic: Revitalization Issues— Economic Development and Employment	9
9. LTC Topic: Revitalization Issues—Transportation	25
10. LTC Topic: Revitalization Issues—Housing	33
11. LTC Topic: Revitalization Issues—Parks & Culture	17
12. Memorial w/ Music???	8
13. How Is It Going?	26
14. Interesting Facts about Skyscrapers	9
15. The Swap: WTC Site for New York City's Airports	10
16. LTC Topic: Memorial—Values	19
17. LTC Topic: Memorial—Relationship to the Site	17
18. LTC Topic: Memorial—Process	26
19. Wrapping Up	10
20. Good-byes	15
21. Not Necessarily Really Tall Bldgs	2
22. LTC: What's Next	1

Note: LTC = Listening to the City.

good way to make values understandable and persuasive. That explanation suggests that decisions about housing, transportation, and economic development were *not* about values—but that was not true. Many participants in the dialogues had a real stake in decisions about where to locate new transportation facilities, whether to build low-income housing on the site, and what kinds of support to make available for those affected financially by the disaster. Some residents of Battery Park City, a neighborhood adjacent to the site, had signed up for the dialogues precisely because they were so concerned about a proposal to move a street in their neighborhood below ground. Small-business owners might have described their struggles to survive financially before and after 9/11 as a way to talk about the inequities in grants being given by the city to retain large businesses. Had low-income residents told their stories, they might have convinced their fellow deliberators of the importance of low and mid-income housing in Lower Manhattan.

If, as I suggested above, corroborating stories did indeed foster good deliberation, then it seems that the only thing that stopped people from telling such stories in the discussions of policy was the convention against it. And if stories allowed participants to clarify their own preferences as much as to gain support for them, then the fact that discussions of housing, economic development, and transportation discouraged them may have made it more difficult for people to work out their preferences on those issues. Either way, the norm against storytelling may have reproduced a view of policymaking as expert problem solving and as properly insulated from public input—even, paradoxically, as it was opened to public input.

What Did People Think of Storytelling?

Some clues to why personal storytelling was seen as inappropriate in discussions of transportation, housing, and economic development emerge from the passing comments that participants made about narrative in the course of the dialogues. I studied every reference to "story" or "storytelling" in the twenty-six dialogue groups, a total of 180 messages. I found that people talked about storytelling's purposes, virtues, and risks in contradictory ways. They described stories as at once moral and manipulable, authentic and artificial, powerful and powerless. For example, people often talked about victims' and survivors' stories as fostering a deeper understanding of 9/11 than a mere chronology of the events alone could do. One participant criticized a tendency to refer to "the events of 9/11" in a way that denuded them of their horror. "It is precisely this tendency in our society to euthanize memory, to paper over truth, that makes our work so important." He went on to say of survivors and victims of 9/11 who had been mentioned in the group that "the stories of Neighborhood Mother and Abby (and of Edwin, heaven rest him) must be remembered forever." Stories gave their audiences access to the unvarnished truth, in this formulation, and to the human dimension of history, in other formulations. But deliberators also worried that stories were vulnerable to manipulation. In that vein, one writer complained that forum organizers' promise to sum up the dialogues for rebuilding authorities was like "an advertising gimmick, a blip to show the world your own patched together story in the guise of ours."

Another tension was evident in participants' assessment of the normative power of storytelling. Telling and retelling the story of 9/11 was what stood between memory and forgetting, they said. It would ensure that future generations would remember the meaning of the tragedy, that the victims would not have died in vain. It would even help to ensure that a similar tragedy would never happen again. One participant wrote, "I don't care how many times people have seen the footage, the story needs to be preserved and retold for future generations." Another wrote, "As a country, we are the storytellers. It's our responsibility to redesign the WTC in a new chapter and verse. To reflect the lives lost . . . to encourage the living . . . and to bring hope to the new generation." Stories, in this view, had powerful normative force. At the same time, people often worried that stories lacked such force: they were, after all, just stories. Future generations would "only have a story in a history book," one participant complained. Another worried about how much money rebuilding the towers would cost, "Yes, we could float bonds, but is the legacy we want to leave to our children an inspiring story, a fine view and a pile of debt?" "Inspiring stories," in other words, were no match for financial imperatives in compelling action.

Even when dialogue participants did tell stories to argue for particular positions, they drew attention to their subjective and potentially confusing character. For example, one participant wrenchingly described replaying over and over in her mind the televised images of the towers' destruction, then wrote, "A purely personal reason that The Skyline must be restored??? So, I and the many others with similar feelings, can again look at pictures of the Twin Towers without that scenario, because they are now replaced by something Fantastic, Bold, and incomparable." Her powerful story introduced a "purely personal reason." I referred earlier to the participant who described being deeply touched by the Vietnam War Memorial despite his having no connection to the war. But he preceded this evocative story about the power of design to transcend subjectivity by cautioning that since everyone's opinion was "subjective, . . . we need to be careful." Not only were personal stories represented as personal but also as misleading. One woman described her brother going back into the towers to rescue people. People like him should be honored, along with the firemen and policemen who lost their lives, she declared, and suggested, interestingly, that the memorial could take multiple forms. But she introduced her story by saying, "I know I might be biased." Thus, ironically, even as deliberators' stories invited engagement, their comments about them discouraged that engagement.

One last clue to personal stories' status for dialogue participants comes from the organization of the dialogues. A number of groups on their own established a topic thread where members could talk about issues unrelated to ground zero. They called the threads variously "Bar and Grill," "Corner Lounge," "Coffee Shop" or other names for a café or bar. In introducing the new thread to the rest of the group, those who launched it often described it as a forum for storytelling. It was a place where people "could place . . . stories and/or tidbits of personal information"; ". . . share typical New York stories"; "Just kick back, hoist a glass, relax and trade personal stories, ideas, reminiscences, etc." Storytelling was associated with "kicking back," relaxing, and going off topic. Storytelling was a way to get to know people, but it was also a break from the serious business of deliberation.

Of what consequence are these tensions between storytelling as serious and unserious, powerful and powerless, authentic and artful? Certainly, as I noted in chapter 1, we have inconsistent views of many cultural forms: we see art as a universal language and as elitist; bureaucracy as efficient and as the height of inefficiency. At some times, we emphasize narrative's authenticity, and at others, its artifice; at times its morally prescriptive character, at others, its entertainment value. The question is whether these inconsistent views redound to the benefit of some groups more than others. Perhaps our negative views of storytelling are more likely to be triggered by some storytellers than by others. If so, then the capacity to tell authoritative stories may be unevenly distributed, not because of people's unequal facility in telling stories but because of the different ways in which their stories are heard. In the online dialogues, however, I found that such capacities were restricted less to certain groups than to certain topics. Storytelling was seen as powerful when it came to issues of culture and memory; powerless when it came to issues of policy and finance. That had indirect effects for disadvantaged groups, however. The rules around storytelling reproduced a view of policy as problem solving rather than politics. That, in turn, may have made it more difficult for groups who were traditionally excluded from policy elites' considerations to register their preferences, even as they were invited to do just that.

The Literary and the Deliberative

Is storytelling in deliberation good or bad for disadvantaged groups? Both. But neither narrative's benefits nor its liabilities have been fully captured in theoretical discussions of the topic. As narrative's champions promise, storytelling does seem able to secure a sympathetic hearing for people and positions unlikely to gain such a hearing otherwise. It is also well-equipped to convey the bias in ostensibly universal principles and to represent new interests and identities. Narrative's prowess in these respects stems from features that distinguish it from other discursive forms. The creation of an alternate reality allows audiences to identify with experiences quite different from their own while remaining aware of that difference. Stories' dependence on a cultural stock of plots enables storytellers to advance novel points of view within the familiar form of canonical story lines. And stories' openness to interpretation encourages tellers and listeners to collaborate in drawing lessons from personal experiences. While it might seem obvious that stories with a clear normative conclusion would better foster deliberation, I have argued rather that stories may be effective insofar as their normative conclusions are ambiguous or, better, open to alternative interpretations. That openness may make it possible for deliberators to suggest compromise or third positions without seeming to disagree with their fellow deliberators. It may allow them to advance and grasp practical possibilities that lie outside a familiar political idiom.

However, if personal stories further the give-and-take that characterizes good deliberation, they only do so in certain circumstances. People are less likely to tell stories in areas of formal policymaking than they are in more value-oriented discussions. Although storytelling is capable of communicating minority points of view, naming new issues, puncturing false universals, and opening established positions to reconsideration, the fact that it is discouraged in discussions of policy diminishes its capacity to do those things. In the end, narrative's utility in deliberation may be limited less by its intrinsic rhetorical capacities than by popular views of storytelling as normatively powerful and politically unserious.

Does this case yield lessons for how to do deliberation better? Encouraging participants to tell personal stories at the beginning of a deliberative forum, as the organizers of such forums often do now, may be effective in building solidarity and trust. But to capitalize on stories' capacity to foster unforced agreement, personal stories should be encouraged throughout the course of a deliberative forum. This includes discussions that are often labeled technical or policy-oriented. Personal stories can do more than make concrete the consequences of different policies. They can also serve as a kind of check on values that are assumed to be universal and standards that are assumed to be neutral. When a decision is cast as one between competing principles—between fairness and efficiency, for example, or diversity and expertise—a story can expose the falseness of those oppositions. Storytelling can be used, then, to expose gaps in the kind of classical reasoning that deliberative democrats favor.[27]

But stories can do more than that. In the Lower Manhattan dialogues, people often told stories because they were not certain as to what principle best applied to their preference or because they were not certain how to articulate their feeling as a preference. Their stories invited other deliberators to collaborate with them in making sense of their own experience: to figure out what preference emerged from a recounted experience or what principle it best supported. The organizers of deliberative forums might do well to exploit even further narrative's openness to interpretation. In a deliberative forum, participants could be encouraged to think through alternative normative punch lines to a story. They might imagine together what would happen if events in the story had unfolded slightly differently, if the same events were told by someone else, if the story was their own rather than someone else's. Recounting the evolution of their views over time might help others to imagine modifying their opinions. These possibilities remain speculative. They simply reflect the belief that tools for deliberation may come from literature as much as logic.

FIVE

Ways of Knowing and Stories Worth Telling: Why Casting Oneself as a Victim Sometimes Hurts the Cause

In a book that made headlines in the mid-1990s, Princeton graduate student Katie Roiphe leveled an angry broadside at contemporary feminists. The movement's success in winning protections against date rape and sexual harassment had turned college campuses into dystopias of sexual Puritanism, she complained. Gone was the unapologetic experimentation of yesteryear as every harmless joke and awkward grope was scrutinized for sexually coercive intent. And gone were the women who could turn away unwelcome advances on their own. Now "hothouse flowers," they relied on legalistic codes of sexual conduct and talked longingly about the *in loco parentis* rules of the 1950s. Where men had never done so, women had succeeded in turning themselves into helpless victims.[1]

Roiphe's attack on contemporary campus feminism was advanced through a pastiche of personal anecdotes and broad generalizations, some based on factual inaccuracies. Still, her critique resonated with attacks on a contemporary "culture of complaint" that were circulating in the media at the time. It also resonated with feminists' concerns, voiced in more nuanced ways, about the dangers of portraying women as victims. Naomi Wolf, another young feminist with a wide audience, faulted Roiphe for naïveté born of privilege. Easy for Roiphe's Princeton pal to repel an unwanted suitor by dumping a glass of milk on his head, Wolf wrote: "[I]n real life, where the provosts might not be drinking sherry nearby, the spunky lass might find herself dragged into an alley and peremptorily sodomized." But, like Roiphe, Wolf worried that feminists were "identify[ing] with powerlessness even at the expense of taking responsibility for the power they do possess." The victimization of women was real, but feminists had made it into a moral virtue. As a result, they refused strategies that had the unappealing stink of autonomy, seeking instead the kind of special protections that had oppressed women a century ago. They made sex and power and success into male-identified epithets; they relied on persuasive appeal rather than seeking clout in a straightforward way; and they privileged intuition and "women's ways of knowing," over logic, reason, and the public voice. Women might be recruited to the movement by learning about what Wolf called "power feminism"; they were being alienated by victim feminism.[2]

In another line of critique, legal scholar Martha Minow argued that victimization's all or nothing character—one is either a victim or an oppressor—simply invited counterclaims of the "You're not the victim, *I'm* the real victim" variety. In separate books, Wendy Kaminer and Elayne Rapping saw a rhetoric of victimhood too easily co-opted by the personal recovery movement, in which the answer to one's victimization was not collective action but purely therapeutic efforts at "empowerment." And second-wave feminist stalwart Betty Friedan pulled no punches in arguing that women's victim mentality distracted from more important issues. "I'm sick of women wallowing in the victim state," Friedan was quoted in *Newsweek*. "We have empowered ourselves."[3]

Kaminer and Rapping put the blame for a victim mentality partly on the recovery movement and Wolf blamed a conservative political backlash that led to defensive claims of victimhood. But none of them spared the movement's own missteps. The "difference feminism" of the 1970s had defined the realms of politics and power as masculine and had renounced them, Wolf argued. Feminists took solace and even a kind of pleasure in their victimization. Rapping faulted feminists for acquiescing to, even embracing, the recovery movement's belief that the only solutions to women's problems were personal ones.[4]

Concerns like these were not new. A decade earlier feminists had battled over whether calls to regulate pornography reproduced a view of sex as aggressive and unladylike. (A decade later, they debated whether Naomi Wolf herself was guilty of the victim feminism she had once bemoaned when she recounted for the readers of *New York Magazine* the traumatizing effects of her college professor's sexual bullying twenty years before.) Nor were such concerns limited to feminists. Gays and lesbians have similarly wrestled with the question of whether styling themselves victims has proven tactically counterproductive. They *are* victims: of prejudice, violence, and inequality. But to trumpet that fact, some say, smacks of self-hate and forgoes the tactical benefits of representing themselves as aggressive challengers.[5]

The criticisms of victim stories are plausible. Surely, representing oneself as a victim, and as passive, pitiable, and generic, cannot but diminish one's sense of agency. Surely casting women or gays or lesbians as victims rather than as proud challengers worthy of respect and power will repel rather than attract potential recruits. And surely a role of supplicant, even if successful in gaining the sympathy of the powerful, will translate into protection at the expense of power, paternalism at the expense of equality. In this chapter, I argue that these assumptions are wrong. Familiar criticisms underestimate both the advantages and the dangers of telling stories of victimization. To claim oneself a victim is not necessarily to trade agency for passivity. The victims of social injustice have sometimes cast themselves as political irritants rather than supplicants and as tutors of moral uplift rather than objects of pity. Victims have been seen, and not only by activists, as capable of reforming audiences' rational faculties rather than only their emotional sensibilities.

This does not mean, however, that disadvantaged groups have been able to pick and choose how they style themselves as victims. To the contrary, I find that institutional and historically specific conventions have shaped the stories groups can tell. Such conventions take the form of canonical story lines, for example, about how proper victims respond to their treatment and when victims are justified in striking back against those who harm them. They also reflect prevailing beliefs about how audiences are expected to respond emotionally to stories, how credible narrative is thought to be relative to other forms of discourse, and what relation narrative is thought to bear to rational thought and right action. Together, these beliefs make up a popular theory of narrative and knowing, a narrative epistemology.

Canonical story lines are distinctive to institutional realms—for example, law, medicine, and the media—and they also reflect wider cultural narratives. The same is true of narrative epistemologies, which are institutionally specific and transcend institutional boundaries. Dominant story lines and epistemologies are historical and subject to revision. For example, as I explain below, an understanding of the victim as moral tutor that was familiar to nineteenth-century American audiences is no longer available to us. In an example of change over a shorter period, sometime between the late 1960s and 1972, American courts trying cases of discrimination in employment redefined what was necessary to tell a convincing story of victimization.

It only makes sense that activists have sought to conform to institutionalized conventions of storytelling. But doing so has created problems. In chapter 4, I showed how popular views of storytelling as morally compelling but politically unserious limited narrative's equalizing force in a public deliberative forum. Here I examine narrative's liabilities in the context of feminists' efforts to secure gender equality in court. Their main problem has not been that they have been forced to deny aspects of their experience in order to fit into a narrow mold of the victim, but that they have been penalized even when they have sought to fit into that mold. To make a plausible case for discrimination, harassment, or abuse, women have had to claim both poles of familiar cultural dichotomies. They are like men and unlike them; they are victims and agents; they are autonomous and dependent on others. But to make those claims in court, they have been equipped only with abstract legal categories and thin causal accounts that are no match for the richly developed and oft-repeated stories that define a cultural common sense about gender, work, agency, and responsibility.

Part of the answer to the problem is to tell women's stories better. Some feminist legal theorists have made a similar argument. Where I differ from them is on how to do that; specifically, how to account for motives that depart from those in familiar story lines and how to represent protagonists whose lives are quite unlike those of decision makers. Where legal theorists have argued that effective narratives invite audiences' empathy through the vivid immediacy of the events they recount, I argue that stories combining immediacy and distance, with events mediated by an obvious narrator, are better able to convey an understanding of women as both victims and agents. Where legal theorists have emphasized stories' capacity to elicit an easy identification with the story's narrator/protagonist, I argue that effective narratives may juxtapose discordant ideas and emotions in a way that initially prevents an easy identification, forcing the reader instead to discover the sense of an unfamiliar connection. In its incarnation as irony, the discord between the conventional meaning of things and their meaning in the story may work to illuminate the social forces shaping abusive or discriminatory relationships.

I make these arguments in part through a literary critical analysis of first-person stories that were used in a campaign for legal reform in the treatment of battered women. Then, turning briefly to a different institutional setting—the media—I show again how institutionalized epistemologies of narrative shape what activists can gain from telling victim stories. Here, though, I focus on how such epistemologies have opened up strategic possibilities more than shut them down. Throughout the chapter, I argue that if canonical story lines make it difficult to gain a hearing for previously suppressed experiences, activists can expand the canon by using familiar tropes to tell new stories. And if prevailing epistemological assumptions about how storytelling works make it difficult for members of a disadvantaged group to gain credibility, activists can set their sights on transforming those epistemologies.

Stories of Victims, Sinners, Tutors, and Experts

In her interviews with women who had experienced job discrimination, Kristin Bumiller found that the women often took pride, not in their willingness to bring to legal account those who harmed them, but in their determination not to do so. They were well aware that they had been paid less than men for the same work or passed over for a promotion, and they were usually unafraid to name their experience as injustice. However, they balked at lodging a formal complaint. To do so was to assume the identity of a victim. It was a totalizing identity: it was to become *only* a victim, to erase those parts of oneself that were self-sufficient, strong, and successful.[6]

Is there any way to assert one's victimization without becoming a victim? Bumiller contrasts our modern legal notion of the victim with a classical one. When Jesus and Socrates were tried, they were victims in a classical sense: forced to choose between good and evil, they sacrificed their own lives for the cause of good. Their trials were an opportunity to affirm their principles and proclaim for history the rightness of their cause. They died, but as historical personas, they lived on. By contrast, in modern trials, the victim is represented by the state. She has no historical status of her own. The legacy of the trial exists in the strategies of the prosecution and defense and the ruling of the judge, not in the words of the hero/victim. She is merely an instantiation of a larger oppression, a passive member of a legal class. The result, Bumiller argues, is that there is little incentive today to take on voluntarily the legal role of the victim.

Bumiller's discussion points to the historicity of our conceptions of victimhood. Hard as it is for us to imagine a victim who is not powerless, acted upon rather than acting, indistinguishable from other members of an unfairly treated group (indeed, indistinguishable from all victims), other historical imaginations have produced other kinds of victims. It has been possible to tell different stories of personal suffering. We need not turn to antiquity for examples. What sociologist Michael Young calls a *confessional* mode of political discourse gained currency in the 1830s in what were arguably the first national movements in this country—those for abolition and temperance, and against sexual licentiousness. In church meetings and private homes, outside saloons and in newspaper tracts, reformers confessed their sins as a way to mobilize sentiment for political reform. The effect was often powerful. An observer at a temperance meeting in New York described the response to the self-proclaimed reformed drunkards who told their stories: "During the first speech, a young man arose in the gallery, and though intoxicated, begged to know whether there was hope for him, declaring his readiness to bind himself from that hour to drink no more. He was invited to come down and sign the pledge, which he did forthwith in the presence of the audience, under deep emotion, which seemed to be contagious, for others followed, and during each of the speeches they continued to come forward and sign, until more than a hundred pledges were obtained."[7]

Storytellers sought to aid in the redemption of their audiences but also to sign people up for the cause. When abolitionist William Lloyd Garrison confessed in a speech to having long advocated gradualism in the dismantling of slavery, a minister described his own reaction, "Never before was I so affected by the speech of a man. When he had ceased speaking I said to those around me: 'That is a providential man; he is a prophet; he will shake our nation to its center, but he will shake slavery out of it. We ought to know him, we ought to help him. Come, let us go and give him our hands.'"[8]

Reformers like Garrison described themselves as victims of their own stupidity and weakness in acquiescing to palpable wrongs. However, their rhetoric was more one of moral responsibility for failing to act against those wrongs. Consider, by contrast, the stories told by abolitionists who were former slaves themselves. In these stories we might well expect to see victims as we commonly think of them: passive rather than active, to be helped rather than emulated. However, that was not the case. Abolitionists' use of slave narratives reveals a set of assumptions quite different from those we make today about how storytelling worked on listeners' reason, emotions, and moral capacities.

As political historian Kimberly Smith shows, abolitionists were convinced that appealing to slavery supporters' reason or sympathy would have little effect on their views. Pro-slavers seemed immune to reasoned arguments about the moral repugnance of slavery. And, like antebellum Americans generally, they were suspicious of sympathy, which, they believed, could be manipulated to produce an incorrect moral judgment. As abolitionists saw it, the problem was that slavery supporters lacked a moral sense. That lack made it impossible for them to recognize the merits of moral arguments or to be moved to moral action. Slave narratives would develop a moral sense in their slavery-supporting audiences, abolitionists believed. Such narratives were modeled on Christian conversion narratives, but with the slave's passage to freedom substituting for the sinner's passage to grace. As a discursive form, conversion narratives had emerged as a solution to the problem of knowing whether a petitioner to a congregation had genuinely experienced the conversion he claimed. In eliciting sympathy on the part of congregation members, the petitioner successfully demonstrated his understanding of God's glory and his suitability for membership in the church. But such sympathy was thought to lead to enlightenment also for members of the congregation. It enabled their access to God's truth and moral action. The relationship between narrator and audience was hermeneutical: at the same time as audiences ratified the conversion of the sinner, they themselves were transformed.[9]

The slave narrative reproduced that hermeneutical relationship, but in a political sphere rather than a religious one, and with the goal of liberty rather than salvation. Slave narratives were not sob stories, Smith emphasizes. Eliciting the audience's pity was not their aim. Narrators sought to produce a sympathetic identification, to make the audience feel about slavery as the slave did. This helps to explain a peculiar feature of the slave narratives: they did not spend much time making a case against the institution of slavery. For example, after describing her separation from her brother and sister, Sojourner Truth wrote, "I make no comment on facts like these. . . . [Readers] will draw their conclusions from the promptings of humanity and philanthropy." The assumption was that the story itself would educate the moral intuitions of readers in a way that would compel right action. On the template of the Christian conversion narrative, then, slave narrators were moral guides. They were victims, but also heroes.[10]

Movement storytellers as sinners and moral tutors seem very far from our idea of storytellers as passive, pitiable, and generic victims. Yet, alternative conceptions of the victim continue to exist. Victims of social injustice have styled themselves as political irritants, aiming to expose injustices that have been kept invisible; and as experts, aiming to transform what counts as expert knowledge. When women told their stories of rape, abortion, and domestic abuse in the public speak-outs of the women's liberation movement in the late 1960s and early 1970s, they shattered the silence that surrounded such acts. They refused the social contract that made them conspirators in their silencing. Women's liberationists believed that the more women spoke, the more other women would recognize their own experiences, too, as abuse, and the more they would join the rising chorus. The threat posed by this public storytelling was that all women would speak out. They would make the problem too big and loud and insistent to go away. Like the stories told by the reformed drunkards of the temperance movement, this was political discourse in a confessional mode. But these confessors talked about the most private area of social life—sex. And they made clear that, if there was shame in these stories, it was properly born by male abusers and misogynistic institutions such as the hospital review boards who denied them abortions and the police who refused to intervene in abuse that they called private. Telling their stories of victimization was self-transformative, but it was also the first step in transforming institutional practices.[11]

Women's speak-outs set the template for gay coming-out stories. Again, such stories were aimed not just at encouraging other gays and lesbians to acknowledge their homosexuality. They were also intended to force straight people to come to terms with the fact that some of their co-workers, co-congregants, friends, and relatives were homosexual. To tell a story of one's victimization, and, in particular, of being forced to live a secret life, was to make it impossible for people to require that secrecy of others. Storytellers in these movements described themselves as victims but also as people who transcended their victimhood through the stories they told. The stories often traced a narrative arc, from powerlessness and passivity to insight, enlightenment, and self-liberation. In movements against child sexual abuse and domestic battering, the notion of the "survivor" put the emphasis on the person's agency. She or he was not merely the object of abuse but had survived it. Where the term *victim* also suggested an immutability (one was and would always be a victim), the term *survivor* pointed to the possibility of change. The message was that survivors had been grievously hurt and traumatized in lasting ways but that they had not been destroyed.[12]

Yet another role claimed by movement storytellers in the last few decades has been that of expert. Victimhood, in this view, grants the narrator knowledge that is superior to that of established authorities. The women's liberationists who formed consciousness-raising groups believed that recounting their experiences as women would help to generate the political analysis of their oppression that was the first step to collective action. But it would also validate women's personal insights as political knowledge. A number of the women who pioneered consciousness-raising had come of political age in the southern civil rights movement, and the discussions that civil rights organizers had held with local black Mississippians were a model. Encouraging residents to share personal stories of their experiences and aspirations was a way to craft a common agenda, to build people's leadership capacities, and, not least, to challenge the idea that only credentialed leaders were capable of leadership. Similarly, for women's liberationists, women knew better than experts the sources of and solutions to their problems.[13]

In activism around AIDS, storytelling has been a challenge to standards of scientific expertise. In demanding a place for AIDS sufferers on the federal panels that reviewed proposals for drug research, activists argued not only that the stories of HIV/AIDS victims would make the effects of the disease more real to experts but also that AIDS storytellers *were* experts. Refusing the conventional antinomies of subjective and objective knowledge and of reason and emotion, they sought and won legitimacy for storytelling as a form of authoritative knowledge.[14]

Thus, conceptions of the victim as moral guide, expert, survivor, and truthteller have existed alongside that of the victim as a passive object of pity. That said, activists *have* often found it difficult to gain acceptance for these conceptions outside their movements. They have battled unsuccessfully against views of victims as passive, not active, as powerless, not struggling against constraints, and as identical, not as united only by their common experience of oppression. The fault lies less with the movements' strategy than with the institutional settings in which they operate. For example, in her study of activism by adult survivors of child abuse, sociologist Nancy Whittier found that when survivors gathered in movement conferences and at marches, they told stories of personal fortitude. They described fear and self-loathing yielding to grief, anger, and finally, to the strength that came from casting off shame. With titles like "Sing Loud, Sing Proud," and "Courageous—Always Courageous," movement magazine articles and workshops encouraged participants to emphasize their recovery rather than the details of their abuse. When survivors appeared in court, however, the stories they told were different. Legislation passed in the 1980s entitled the victims of child abuse to seek compensation as crime victims. In their court appearances, survivors described only the fear, grief, shame, and hurt produced by their abuse. These kinds of emotional performances were required, Whittier writes, in order to prove that the survivor was a victim deserving of compensation. Indeed, survivors were cautioned by movement leaders that betraying their anger or pride in court would hurt their cases. On television talk shows, another place in which child abuse activists appeared frequently in the 1980s, survivors' stories were different still. They concentrated more on the abuse and its traumatizing effects than on the survivor's eventual recovery. Guests often cried while clutching stuffed animals or speaking in childlike voices. They were usually joined by therapists who interpreted their stories to the audience, further reinforcing an image of victims as childlike.[15]

Activists worried about the effects of these storytelling norms. Advice articles in movement magazines warned those going to court that the experience would be demeaning. They were counseled to tell their stories in the ways expected of them but to find outlets outside court in which to tell other parts of their stories. Whittier argues that by representing child sexual abuse as deeply and permanently traumatic, storytelling on talk shows may have made it easier to see such abuse as aberrant rather than widespread. By eliciting pity and horror in audiences, talk-show storytelling may have made it more difficult for audiences to identify with survivors. And by representing themselves as passive and powerless, survivors may have repelled others suffering from abuse, who might have been mobilized by stories of focused anger and personal overcoming.[16]

We are back to Bumiller's concern about the liabilities of our current conception of victimhood. But Whittier's account points to the fact that activists face real constraints in how they portray themselves. The formal and informal rules of the institutional settings in which they operate shape the kinds of stories they can tell. Critics of victim storytelling have tended to underestimate those institutional pressures and may also have underestimated their consequences. As I show in the next section, conforming to stock images of the victim may not only cost movements recruits but may impede their efforts to secure legal equality. I focus on storytelling in court, first in cases of sex discrimination and then in cases of domestic abuse. In each case, I show that courts have encouraged women to present themselves as victims in a narrow mold. The irony is that doing so has made the goal of equal treatment even more elusive.

Liberal Stories and Good Victims

To give an account of one's victimization is not the only way to support a claim of injustice. When women made claims of sex discrimination in hiring and promotion under Title VII of the 1964 Civil Rights Act, they presented statistical evidence of women's underrepresentation in higher-paying jobs. Beginning in the early 1970s, however, they were encouraged also to present anecdotal evidence of victims experiencing discrimination. This would counter employers' arguments that the statistical disparities were meaningless because they reflected women's own choices. Women were generally uninterested in jobs that traditionally had been held by men, employers argued, even when the job paid better.[17]

Logically, however, the anecdotal evidence that courts called for was meaningless. Just as employers could not prove their argument by the testimony of a few women that they had *not* been interested in the higher-paying jobs, so the testimony of a few women that they *had* been interested in such jobs could not disprove it. Presumably, some women were interested in the higher-paying jobs and some were not, just as some men were and some were not. What such witnesses could not do was prove that they were representative of the larger pool of eligible workers. But plaintiffs who did present witnesses testifying to their stymied aspirations were more likely to win their cases. In a study of fifty-four sex discrimination cases brought under Title VII between 1972 and 1989, Vicki Schultz found that courts were three times as likely to reject employers' claims when the plaintiffs presented anecdotal evidence than when they did not. When judges accepted employers' arguments about women's lack of interest in higher-paying jobs, they often pointed explicitly to the fact that plaintiffs had failed to produce any individual victims.[18]

So what was the harm in plaintiffs' producing those victims, even in spite of the flawed logic behind it? By conforming to the story line expected of them by liberal judges, Schultz shows, plaintiffs ended up challenging only *some* of employers' discriminatory practices, leaving others intact. Actually, the problem was less a liberal story line than the lack of one. The conservative story told by employers and accepted by some courts was that certain kinds of work were inherently masculine: they were "heavy" and "dirty." They had these features apart from anything that employers did. It was hardly surprising, therefore, that women preferred not to do masculine jobs. It was a matter of common sense, as conservative judges often put it. The liberal story did not take issue with the idea that women's work preferences were set long before they entered the workplace. But it did reject the notion that such preferences were fundamentally different from men's. To think otherwise was to engage in stereotyping, which was prohibited by Title VII. If women's basic values and experiences were not appreciably different from men's, then, most likely, neither were their work preferences. Women's underrepresentation in nontraditional work could only reflect employers' discriminatory stereotyping.[19]

The liberal story suppressed gender differences rather than accounted for them. This explains why it was so important for plaintiffs to produce witnesses who could testify that they had wanted nontraditional jobs. Again, such witnesses could not prove that their experiences were representative of the larger pool of workers. But they were symbolic. They suggested that women were no different from men in their capacities and aspirations. The good victim, for the court, was one who was genderless, in the sense that she had always seen herself as capable of, entitled to, and likely to secure traditionally masculine work. As a judge in the famous Sears case commented, the Equal Employment Opportunity Commission's case would have been much stronger it if had produced "even a handful of witnesses to testify that Sears had frustrated their childhood dreams of becoming commission sellers."[20]

But this was not the only way to conceive of the victim. The courts had conceived of victims differently in the first Title VII cases, which were brought in the late 1960s and early 1970s. These cases centered on race discrimination. But employers made a similar argument: the underrepresentation of racial minorities in higher-paying jobs reflected minorities' own job preferences. The courts rejected the argument. In one early case, black physicians had declined to seek staff privileges in an all-white hospital. The court ruled that they had done so not because of preferences that were independently arrived at but because of their realistic assessment, given a history of discriminatory job treatment, that they would be unlikely to get such jobs. Employers' reputations for discrimination preceded them. In a context of long-standing racial inequality, statistical evidence of a segregated job market was enough to prove discrimination.

By the early 1970s, as the courts shifted to sex discrimination cases, they had adopted a very different framework. Now plaintiffs had to prove that their aspirations were long-standing and were unaffected by what they knew about the job market. But when they strove to do so, they found that their claims flew in the face of popular wisdom. Like most people, judges found unpersuasive the suggestion that women had the same skills and values as men. Employers, for their part, cited feminists' own argument that girls were socialized into feminine roles to support their contention that as adults, women aspired to feminine work. In some cases, then, plaintiffs probably lost because the conservative argument seemed more credible, if only in its acknowledgment that people's decisions about work are gendered.[21]

Even where plaintiffs were successful, it was a limited success. By hewing to the liberal story line, in which work preferences were formed through socialization processes outside the labor market, plaintiffs were ill-positioned to show that workers' preferences themselves were influenced by employers' practices. In their recruiting strategies, employers did more than simply publicize vacancies. They also tried to stimulate interest in those whom they hoped to attract, in part by describing the position and its ideal occupant. Doing so in masculinized ways discouraged women from even thinking about the job as one they should apply for. Yet few courts focused on these effects of sex-segregated advertising. Word of mouth recruiting had a similar effect, but it too remained largely unchallenged.

The problem for women charging sex discrimination was not only that they were forced to style themselves as victims who were, in everything but their sex, like men. The deeper problem was that in the absence of a convincing account of how women came to forge their job preferences, women effectively ceded terrain to conservatives, who did have such an account. The conservative account was detailed, variegated, and meshed with countless stories told in other settings about gender differences and socialization processes. The liberal account, which was made up of dry abstractions and denials of a causal chain rather than the assertion of one, was no match for that story.

What is the solution? Schulz argues that women need to tell a new story about women and work. That story, drawing on a now-extensive body of sociological research, should acknowledge the socialization processes that give girls different preferences and values than boys. But it should also make clear that early childhood socialization is only one among the influences on later choices. Grown women's work preferences are shaped much more powerfully by the kinds of jobs that they perceive as available to them. Confronting a labor market in which employer practices clearly signal women's unfitness for certain jobs, many women will give up on those jobs. The moral of the story then centers on the power of law to hold employers responsible for the practices that create a sex-segregated workplace.

Good Victims and Mad Women

Is a better story answer enough? Consider storytelling about a very different kind of inequality. When battered women are charged with having killed or assaulted their abusers, they have the right to tell the story of their abuse to defend themselves, often supported by expert testimony about the effects of domestic abuse on its victims. Winning that right capped years of struggle by feminist activists to gain battered women the same legal options that were available to men. As activists saw it, describing the context of abuse in which women acted would make clear that, in some cases, women had struck back at their abusers to save their lives. Expert testimony, for its part, would answer the all-too-familiar question, "Why didn't she just leave?" by describing the material, cultural, and psychological barriers to battered women's leaving.[22]

Yet, the difficulties that battered women faced even after winning these legal reforms point to the inadequacy of storytelling when ranged against the power of canonical story lines and institutionalized epistemologies of narrative. In the early 1990s only a quarter of the battered women who pleaded self-defense in homicide cases were acquitted. More significant, convictions of battered women who pled self-defense were overturned on appeal at a substantially higher rate than were convictions in other homicide cases (40 percent compared to 8.5 percent). Clearly, there were problems in how such cases were being tried. In some cases, judges did not instruct juries to consider the possibility of self-defense for fear that it would seem to condone vigilantism. In other cases, defense attorneys did not see defendants as capable of meeting the standards of reasonableness necessary for a self-defense claim.[23]

The problem was not, as some scholars maintained, that the legal standards for pleading self-defense—imminent danger, proportionality, and the duty to retreat—were inherently biased against battered women. Most jurisdictions did not impose a duty to retreat before using force, and those that did usually exempted a person attacked in her home. No jurisdiction prohibited the use of a weapon against an unarmed attacker. Standards for self-defense were just as capable of handling violence in which parties were intimates and where the imminence of danger extended over a substantial period. The problem was not the legal standards but the fact that judges, juries, and lawyers were unwilling to see battered women's use of deadly force as reasonable under those standards. Familiar stories of the soldier on the battlefield, the man defending his home against an unknown intruder, and the barroom brawler continued to shape the thinking of legal decision makers about what constituted legitimate self-defense. Against the backdrop of those stories, it was difficult for legal professionals to imagine that women were acting reasonably when they assaulted their partners.[24]

The challenge has been to see women as victims *and* as rational agents. As legal scholar Martha Mahoney writes, in our society the two are seen as unalterably opposed: "[A]gency does not mean acting for one-self under conditions of oppression; it means *being without oppression,* either having ended oppression or never having experienced it at all." That view has discouraged battered women from describing their efforts to end or change abusive relationships. It has discouraged them from talking about their efforts to protect themselves and their children, to seek help, to marshal the resources that would enable them eventually to leave their abusers, maintain some semblance of family in the midst of chaotic circumstances, and so on. When the battered woman has killed her abuser, emphasizing her victimization has undermined her claim of rational agency. That, in turn, has made it tougher to meet the standard of reasonableness necessary to claim self-defense.[25]

Here, advocates' victory in gaining the admissibility of expert testi-mony has had mixed effects. Legal expert Elizabeth Schneider, a key figure in winning that victory, explains that the point was not to make a special case for battered women, that is, to assert a "battered woman's defense." Nor was it to claim that at the moment battered women used lethal force, they were irrational. The latter would have justified pleas of insanity or manslaughter but not self-defense. The point was rather to demonstrate that in some cases, women had killed their abusers to save their own lives. "The notion of expert testimony was predicated on an assumption that battered women's voices either would not be under-stood or were not strong enough to be heard alone in the courtroom," Schneider explains. There were good reasons that women were not heard. As sociologist Kim Scheppele observes, women who have been the victims of domestic abuse, as well as those who have been the victims of rape, incest, and other forms of sexualized violence, often hesitate to tell their stories. When they do tell them, their narratives often have a frag-mented character. Scheppele writes, "Survivors of extraordinary brutal-ity often literally cannot say what they have seen or put into words the terror that they have felt. Picking through the shards of a former life, sur-vivors can no longer put the pieces into relation with each other to tell a coherent and compelling narrative about how things disintegrated." Their accounts also change over time as they piece together what hap-pened and begin to retreat from their initial impulse to normalize their experience. But judges and juries tend to assume that true stories are told immediately and stay the same over time. The stories that women tell later are often heard suspiciously. A prevailing narrative epistemology has thus operated to discredit women's accounts of their abuse.[26]

Scheppele argues that victims have some recourse in expert testimony, which can account for the discrepancy between a victim's earlier and later stories by citing the effects of post-traumatic stress disorder. In addition to strengthening the battered woman's credibility, activists believed, experts would describe not only the psychological mechanisms that prevented women from leaving abusive relationships but also the economic and cultural ones such as the lack of support services and the norms that encouraged women to keep families together at all costs. Experts would also help to expose the real possibility faced by the abused woman that she would be hunted down and attacked by her abuser if she left. Experts would show that the defendant's apprehension of imminent danger and great bodily harm was reasonable.

Yet lawyers representing battered women have tended to use expert witnesses to emphasize a woman's victimization, not her reasonableness. They have encouraged experts to testify to the defendant's so-called learned helplessness rather than the fact that she acted to save her own life. "Battered women's syndrome" has become a popular phrase and is often used simply to indicate the existence of a battering relationship. But its connotation of an impaired mental state has made it difficult for lawyers, judges, and juries to comprehend the reasonableness of the woman's act, and, therefore, to recognize her act as legitimate self-defense. So the woman who has killed her abuser faces two equally unacceptable options. She can assert her agency, telling a story of her actions in which she appears composed and in control of herself. But then she may not be seen as victimized at all. Or, she can emphasize her victimization. But then her actions may be seen as unreasonable. They are to be excused through an act of judicial solicitude rather than justified by her experience of abuse. Moreover, if she departs from the stock image of the victim—if she is too angry, aggressive, or insufficiently remorseful—she may not be seen as a victim, no matter what she says. If she is black, she is especially vulnerable to being seen as an agent rather than a victim, given popular images of African American women as strong and powerful.

So, does telling stories work for battered women? Lawyers, judges, and scholars hear the stories that battered women tell. But they hear them through familiar plot lines with stock characters. A battered woman tells her story of abuse and is heard as a passive, powerless, incapacitated victim, incapable of reasoned action. Or she is heard as unapologetic and provocative, hardly a victim. The problem is not limited to battered women who have assaulted their attackers. Battered women seeking custody of their children may describe their learned helplessness to explain why they stayed with their abusers for so long, but in doing so they risk being seen as insufficiently competent to care for their children. If they appear competent and responsible, that may cast doubt on their credibility. Again, victims are not really rational; rational women are not really victims. Stock stories operate to reproduce inequalities in other areas of the law. Think of the countless stories that circulate in popular culture extolling the virtues of self-sufficiency and autonomy. Such stories minimize the extent to which people in real life are both dependent and depended on. But by combining description and normative prescription, they seem to suggest that autonomy is both desirable and the common state of things. The effects of such stories on legal reform are profound. The reforms that created no-fault divorce equalized the relations between men and women by treating women, like men, as autonomous, unencumbered individuals. They thereby discounted women's caregiving role and penalized them for that role. Or consider another example: with the family seen as properly independent of the state and market, the notion of state assistance for single women who are poor has been widely condemned. So welfare and divorce reforms in recent years have aimed instead at reconstituting the "natural" family, which includes two parents and is male-headed, through paternity proceedings and child support proceedings against "deadbeat dads." Such reforms effectively reproduce a patriarchal structure even as they are intended to make women more autonomous.[27]

Real equality would require rejecting both poles of the dichotomies I have described. Women are like men in some respects and unlike them in others. Women in some situations are both victims and agents. Women, like men, are autonomous and dependent. What makes it so hard to combat these dichotomies is that they are reproduced in countless popular narratives, appearing in movies and magazine articles, political speeches and news stories, in self-help books and television commercials. The narratives are credible because they are both ubiquitous and diverse: appearing in many versions, they seem to capture a reality that is complex.

Telling Non-canonical Stories

What is the solution? I want to suggest two. Those with the power to represent disadvantaged groups or decide their fates must be instructed on how to hear new stories. In this regard, consider a 1998 opinion on the status of expert testimony in abuse cases by the Canadian Supreme Court. In the opinion, Judge Claire L'Heureux Dubé recognized the questionable value of substituting reliance on experts for an ostensibly objective "reasonable man" standard to authenticate battered woman syndrome. Then she wrote,

A judge and jury should be told that a battered woman's experiences are generally outside the common understanding of the average judge and juror, and that they should seek to understand the evidence being presented to them in order to overcome the myths and stereotypes which we all share. Finally, all of this should be presented in such a way as to focus on the reasonableness of the woman's actions, without relying on old or new stereotypes about battered women.

Judges, juries, and defense lawyers can be asked to suspend their narrative expectations and to truly listen to stories that depart from the standard plot lines.[28]

The best fictional narratives do just this. They recall familiar plot lines but depart from them. Their characters defy expectations but do so in ways that point to generalizable normative conclusions. The second answer to the problem of how to gain a hearing for experiences that defy the standard categories, then, is to figure out how to tell these kinds of stories. I mentioned Vicki Schultz's argument that women claiming sex discrimination should tell the story of how women's job preferences are formed. The story she described was long on information and research findings. It would persuade through the sophisticated logic of its argument. But some legal theorists have suggested that politically effective narratives work differently. Lynne Henderson argues that effective narratives produce an empathetic understanding in their audiences. They make it possible for audiences to put themselves in the narrator's shoes and to understand her experience "phenomenologically," and in all its particularity. When that happens, Henderson goes on, it becomes impossible to stereotype the narrator or her experience. Instead, audiences find themselves obliged to think about the law not abstractly but in terms of its effects on real people. Empathetic narratives have the same effect on legal decision makers, Henderson argues, pushing them to jettison the stereotypes that inhibit just decisions.[29]

Two cases illustrate the power of storytelling. In the 1969 Supreme Court case, *Shapiro v. Thompson,* lawyers challenged state residency requirements for welfare recipients. They did so by telling poignant stories of people who became destitute when they were forced to move to another state on account of family obligations or ill health. The Court responded favorably to plaintiffs' storytelling, Henderson reports, and indeed retold those stories in its majority opinion. By contrast, attorneys in *Bowers v. Hardwick* failed to tell an empathetic narrative, with disastrous results. The notorious case involved a man who was arrested under Georgia's antisodomy statute for having consensual sex in his home with another man. While attorneys for the state suggested that homosexual sex would lead to adultery, AIDS, and violent criminality, respondents took issue only with the infringement of privacy rights. The argument they made was one of "legality, not empathy," Henderson writes. They did not tell Michael Hardwick's story. The result was that, for the court, Hardwick "became another disembodied person onto whom fears, prejudices, and false beliefs could be projected." The statute was upheld.[30]

Henderson's argument that empathy-inducing narratives can counter the stereotypes that inhibit fair decisions makes sense. But it restates the problem more than it solves it. What kind of narrative is likely to produce empathetic understanding? One can imagine that stories told badly would confirm stereotypes rather than debunk them. For example, at the time of his arrest, Michael Hardwick was a former drug user and, according to neighbors, the host of often raucous parties. Had attorneys told his story ineffectively, they might well have fueled popular stereotypes of gay men as drug using, exhibitionistic, and sexually promiscuous. Beyond describing narratives that are long on description and emotion and that present plaintiffs as "human beings," Henderson does not say what kinds of stories are likely to invite empathy rather than indifference or a hardening of stereotypes. Indeed, the stories that the court told in *Shapiro v. Thompson,* which Henderson quotes approvingly as "crying with human need," make their protagonists into victims with very little agency: "[A]ppellee Vivian Marie Thompson . . . was a 19-year-old unwed mother . . . [who had moved to Connecticut] to live with her mother. . . . Because of her pregnancy, she was unable to work or enter a work training program . . ." "Appellee Minnie Harrel, now deceased, had moved with her three children from New York to Washington. . . . She suffered from cancer and moved to be near members of her family who lived in Washington." These stories give us no clue as to how to tell a story that departs from canonical story lines of bad women (who aren't victims) and mad women (who aren't reasonable).[31]

Rather than telling stories that are simply "human," perhaps the key to empathy is that we recognize ourselves in the stories we hear. For example, legal scholar Jane Murphy writes as follows about a collection of stories by victims of wife battering: "Even if we have not been victims of physical abuse at the hands of our intimate partners, we recognize ourselves in the stories of these women. These are women with varied backgrounds, women whose experiences defy the stereotype of the passive, grotesquely beaten victim." But do we need to recognize ourselves easily in other people's experiences in order to empathize with them? Later in the same article, Murphy reprints portions of personal stories that were told by battered women who were serving sentences for having killed their abusers. These were women who *were* "grotesquely beaten." These were women who killed another human being. I found it difficult to see myself in relationships in which extreme possessiveness was initially seen as an attraction and early acts of violence were tolerated. In fact, I did come to empathize with the women, but not because I saw myself immediately in their stories.[32]

Perhaps, then, effective stories are more complicated than that. Legal scholar Kathryn Abrams argues that feminists have mistakenly assumed that simple, linear narratives, in which the moral is unequivocal and the experiences depicted are easily generalizable, are the most effective in gaining recognition for needs that are currently ignored. To the contrary, she asserts that ambiguous narratives that recount experiences in all their particularity may better capture women's experiences. By *ambiguous,* she seems to mean stories in which women's responses to their experiences are ambivalent and self-consciously particular. But left at that, ambiguity seems a fairly vague goal to aim for in feminist storytelling. Instead, we should be able to identify the narrative strategies that enable groups to do certain things. In this case, how can storytellers get past the tendency of legal decision makers to hear new stories in terms of familiar ones that cast groups in stereotyped roles? How can accounts of people's personal experiences be made to illuminate the broader social forces shaping those experiences? And how can legal decision makers be made to empathize with the experiences of people who are quite different from them?[33]

Irony and Discord

In her book on the struggle to gain legal justice for battered women, Elizabeth Schneider argues that progress will only come when judges, lawyers, politicians, and the public listen to battered women's stories. She reprints one such story. It begins as follows: "Here goes. Broken nose. Loose teeth. Cracked ribs. Broken finger. Black eyes. I don't know how many; I once had two at the same time, one fading, the other new. Shoulders, elbows, knees, wrists. Stitches in my mouth. Stitches in my chin.

A ruptured eardrum. Burns. Cigarettes on my arms and legs . . ." The account continues with a list of graphic abuses:

Seventeen years of it. He never gave up. Months went by and nothing happened, but it was always there—the promise of it. . . . For seventeen years. There wasn't one minute when I wasn't afraid, when I wasn't waiting. Waiting for him to go, waiting for him to come. Waiting for the fist, waiting for the smile. I was brainwashed and brain-dead, a zombie for hours, afraid to think, afraid to stop, completely alone. I sat at home and waited. I mopped up my own blood. I lost all my friends, and most of my teeth. He gave me a choice, left or right; I chose left because he broke the little finger on my left hand. Because I scorched one of his shirts. Because his egg was too hard. Because the toilet seat was wet. Because because because. He demolished me. He destroyed me. And I never stopped loving him. I adored him when he stopped. I was grateful, so grateful, I'd have done anything for him. I loved him. And he loved me.[34]

The story is powerful because in its dull litany of abuses it captures both the horror and the mundanity of domestic abuse. It is powerful in conveying the combination of fear, resignation, hope, and love that make the abusive relationship. Finally, it is powerful because it is animated both by the abject victimization of the narrator and by her strong narrative voice, her refusal to whitewash either the cruelty of her abuse or her love for her abuser. This was a relationship, she makes clear. The clarity of that acknowledgment attests to her agency. Yet it does not make her any less a victim, does not justify her abuse in any way.

It is hard to imagine that an account such as this could not impress upon its audience the insufficiency of thinking about battered women as either passive victims or not victims at all. And yet the story is fictional. It was written not by a woman who had been battered but by an Irish novelist, a man, Roddy Doyle. That a man could convey so well the experience of battering shows the power of the literary imagination to capture experiences quite different from the writer's own. But it also suggests that telling the kinds of stories that can represent protagonists as victims and as agents, without one contradicting the other, requires literary sophistication.[35]

Consider several narrative strategies in the Doyle account. The narrator lists some of the reasons for which she was beaten, then stops and says, "Because, because, because." She seems to be reminding herself that there was always a reason for her abuse, that there was never not a reason, that, finally, the reasons were unimportant. The reader is both brought into her world, in which there were so many triggers to violence, and taken outside of it in the narrator's insight that the triggers were excuses, not explanations. The story's point of view is evident rather than obscured. We never lose the sense that these events are being related to us. Far from diminishing the emotional force of the events, the narrator's presence conveys a better understanding of her situation as both victim and agent. The story is told in the first person and crafted as a coherent and evocative account. It provides a phenomenology of abuse, to use Henderson's term. But it is not the statement of someone so incapacitated as to be limited to a fragmented stream of consciousness. Rather, the narrator conveys simultaneously her entrapment in the events she describes and the psychological remove that allows her, in retrospect, to appraise her situation. She alternates between describing external events and describing her own internal response to them in a way that demonstrates her grip on both. Far from unreasoned, she is sharply insightful.[36]

A second narrative strategy in the Doyle account involves the juxtaposition of discordant ideas. The abused woman says, "He demolished me. He destroyed me. And I never stopped loving him." The "and" connects two things that we do not ordinarily think of as connected: he destroyed her and she never stopped loving him. The narrator does not say, "and *yet* I never stopped loving him," which we might expect to precede an explanation for that fact. Instead she says, "and I never stopped loving him." For her, at the time, there was no "yet." The connection defied explanation. The juxtaposition is jarring, and it engages us as readers. It forces us to think about a situation that is not familiar, to try to figure out how such a connection could have seemed self-evident to the narrator. And we may well do so. We may begin to understand how a woman could have been so abused and so love her abuser. We may begin to empathize with someone who is very different from us. In another discordant statement, Doyle's narrator says of the violence that "it was always there—the promise of it." By "promise" she means "threat." But the confusion is understandable in a relationship in which tenderness followed cruelty and love and fear were so commingled. A statement that is at first disturbing helps us to understand why, against all evidence, a woman could believe that this time the violence would stop.

Of course, Roddy Doyle's narrator is an invention. So we cannot know the effect these narrative strategies might have had on real legal decision makers. But we can see similar narrative figures operating in a set of first-person narratives that *were* heard by decision makers. Battered women's advocates in Maryland launched a campaign in 1989 to gain admission for expert testimony in cases where women had killed or assaulted their abusers. To press their case, advocates sought out women who were serving prison sentences for those offenses and videotaped them as they told their stories. The resulting film, which focused on four women, was shown to legislators, the governor, parole commission officers, activists, and the public. These are the stories that legal scholar Jane Murphy cited as evidence of narrative's power to elicit empathy.[37]

The women's stories do seem capable of eliciting empathy in their audience but not in the ways predicted by legal theorists. All four stories portray women abused for long periods and fearful of the retaliation to which they would be subjected if they left. Three of the four narrators say that they do not remember taking the action that killed their partner. "I didn't feel my hand pull the trigger. I don't remember shooting him. All I remember was handing him the weapon and him grabbing it and I remember it going off . . ." said one. Another said, "I don't recall stabbing him no twenty-two times with no scissors . . ." And a third said, "[M]y daughter said that I loaded the gun, and it will be five years this September, and I still don't remember loading that gun." These narrators seem to be the quintessential helpless victims, so incapacitated that they were unconscious of their actions. Such actions seem the opposite of reasoned, and the women responsible for them the opposite of rational agents.[38]

Yet, in each story, the juxtaposition of discordant ideas, the use of irony, and the narrator's strong point of view combine to convey the narrator's reasonableness and her agency. The first narrator, a former policewoman, describes her fear and despair after years of escalating abuse:

Many times I thought I would die. Many times I didn't want to live anymore because of what was going on. I said, God, this will never end. I thought it wouldn't. Many times I said, if he don't kill me, I'm sure I'll kill myself, cause it was that painful. I know I want to live. No, I don't want to die. I don't want to have anybody beat on me or threaten my life.[39]

Halfway through this passage, the narrator changes perspective. From wanting to kill herself, she says, "I know I want to live." She does not introduce or explain the transition but her stark statement—"I know I want to live"—reads as a powerful act of will. Note the change in verb tense. After a series of feelings told in the past tense, she shifts to the present: "I know I want to live." Sociolinguists have argued that shifts from the past tense to the conversational historical present are generally used to introduce a new and critical segment of the story. Here, "I want to live" marks the key shift, the point at which the narrator refuses to acquiesce to her abuse. By rendering that decision in the present tense, the narrator effectively makes it the central transition in the story. That event, her decision to live, is the climax of the story—not her decision to strike back at her abuser.[40]

The same is true of another woman's story. She too believed her partner would eventually kill her and, like the other women, had stopped caring. The shift for her came when her boyfriend was beating her in the kitchen as his friend looked on. "But right in mid-stream, as he was beating me and as I was sliding down my refrigerator, something inside me was like I wanna live. You know, I have something to live for. Something is out there for me and I'm going to get it. And I'm not gonna die, and I'm not gonna let him kill me in here with his friend watching. I meant that." She decides she wants to live when she is "sliding down [her] refrigerator"—an odd combination of images. And she vows to herself that she will not die with her boyfriend's friend watching. It is the idea of someone watching her own murder that is repugnant to her.[41]

In their oddness, the juxtapositions involve the reader in trying to make sense of them. More than that, they also suggest that the narrator is well aware of the absurdity of her situation. Her tone is ironic. This is true in the other stories as well. The first narrator says, "He would hit me with anything. He would bite me all over. Pick up things and throw them at me and hit me with them. But I never went to the hospital for anything. It was too embarrassing. I was so determined that this was going to work if I would just stop and just make him happier." She sounds bemused by her certainty that she could make the relationship work, even as she was abjectly victimized. The strangeness is the idea that a relationship in which violence is kept at bay by the wife's unrelenting effort can be said to be working. The second narrator says,

Soon after we started dating I had noticed that he was kind of possessive and he was very jealous. But I didn't really count it as out of the ordinary; it kind of flattered me to be honest. I kind of thought, well, he loves me this much that he cares, he don't want me speaking to this one or he don't want me going there without him. And I kind of thought that was really kind of nice, so I must have been something really special.

The narrator comments ruefully on her own confusion of possessiveness and caring. The irony is that her dehumanizing abuse began, in her mind, as the recognition that she was special.[42]

An ironic stance is even clearer in the third story, where, long before the scene in the kitchen, the narrator's boyfriend had proposed that she quit her job: "I was like, girl, my boyfriend told me I don't have to work, he's going to take care of me so I don't have to go to work nowhere." She goes on, "I didn't know he was in the process of putting me in his own little prison . . ." Here, as in the previous account, the narrator mocks her misinterpretation of her partner's blandishments. But in doing so, she exposes the societal norms that make such misinterpretation easy. The real ironies, in other words, are that pathological possessiveness in our society is taken as a sign of romantic passion; that the line between violent relationships and ones that are thought to be "working" is so thin; and that women fantasize about rescue from the world of work. We, the audience, may begin to recognize that the narrators were trapped by social norms and popular fantasies as much as by violent men.[43]

Even where she is not ironic, the narrator is undeniably *present* in all four accounts, reflecting with hindsight on her beliefs and emotional states ("I know this sounds nuts . . ."; "I was hysterical . . ."; "And that day I promised to myself . . ."); and raising and answering questions that an outsider might have ("Sure, many people say why don't you just leave. But they don't understand . . ."). The narrator's presence diminishes the immediacy of the events she recounts. But it also casts her as in full command of her faculties at the time she killed her partner since she is so clearly in command of them now. She seems to have been driven to desperate behavior in desperate circumstances.[44]

The protagonists in these stories did not make it easy to identify with them. They were pathologically dependent on abusive men, they lacked supportive friends and family, and they killed another human being. The ironies and paradoxes, often noted with cool detachment by the narrators, and the sudden, subtle, and profound realizations were what drew me, as a reader, into the women's worlds. The disjunctures and juxtapositions—at first, strange, and then understandable—were what led me to understand, feel for, and finally admire these women.

My reaction seems to have been typical. Maryland's governor had never supported legislation or policy to help battered women. But, after viewing the film in which these women appeared, he asked to meet with them. The meeting converted him to the cause. He eventually commuted the sentences of eight women convicted of killing or attempting to kill their abusers and pressed successfully for legislation allowing the introduction of testimony about a history of abuse and about the phenomenon of battered women syndrome. In commuting the women's sentences, he said, "It's a startling experience for a governor to come in and sit across from women who committed murder." He went on, "This isn't something they made up. A long history of abuse, terrible abuse. . . . So I felt that some of them, there was not any question in my mind, that they were in danger for their own life" (ellipsis in original). The governor referred to the women's victimization but then made clear that these women were acting in self-defense. In the story form that I described in the last chapter as being especially persuasive, the governor recounted his own change of opinion, from "First of all you think: They committed murder . . ." to his not having any "question in my mind" that the women acted in self-defense, with the shift occurring at the ellipsis points between "a long history of terrible abuse" and "So I felt that some of them, there was not any question in my mind, that they were in danger for their own life." As it did in the sit-in narratives that I described in chapter 2, the ellipsis captures both the leap and the connection: that the long history of abuse made the women's actions reasonable.[45]

A *New York Times* story on the clemency decision quoted additional portions of the governor's comments: "'Some of these stories are hard to believe—difficult, horrible stories,' said Mr. Schaefer, adding that some of the women would probably have been killed themselves if they had not struck back." Again, the governor referred to the combination of horrible abuse and reasonable self-defense, and the rest of the story reported sympathetically on efforts by advocates to get testimony of abuse and battered women's syndrome admitted into court. In subsequent news stories, the governor's criticism of a justice system that made it difficult for abused women to plead self-defense was as prominent as his description of their horrific abuse.[46]

Success in this case may thus have been due in part to the narrative strategies of point of view, irony, and antithesis by which battered women conveyed their experiences both of victimization and agency. Of course, neither the abused women nor the activists who put their stories on film need to have been especially conscious of these literary tropes. Rather, some women knew how to tell evocative stories and the film's director knew how to choose evocative stories.

Early in this chapter, I rehearsed Kristin Bumiller's worry that victims had come to be associated with pathos rather than tragedy. When viewed as tragic, victims elicit admiration. When viewed as pathetic, they elicit only pity. Stories of tragic victims encourage learning; stories of pathetic ones, catharsis. Yet the battered women's stories that I described suggest a literary genre that, according to literary critic Northrop Frye, has become increasingly popular in the last hundred years. The hero in stories of what Frye calls *tragic irony* is victimized through no fault of his own. Rather, his lot is arbitrary. He is a scapegoat. If he is innocent in a legal sense, Frye goes on, he is guilty "in the sense that he is a member of a guilty society, or living in a world where such injustices are an inescapable part of existence." I noted earlier that nineteenth-century abolitionists capitalized on readers' expectation that narrators would help them to achieve moral uplift. Battered women's advocates may have been able to rely on a different expectation among their contemporary audiences: an expectation that stories illuminate broader social forces. This is critical because illuminating broader social forces is essential if battered women are to secure justice. The question "Why didn't she just leave?" can only be answered by reference to battered women's financial dependence on their abusers, the lack of support services and protection for women who have left, and the cultural norms that, variously, expect women to keep families together, treat pathological possessiveness as romantic, and regard the relations within families as properly private. Tragic irony's political virtue is that it directs our attention to the social determinants of the hero's fate. The victim is more than a victim; she is also a guide. The proper response to such a story is not just the cathartic experience of sympathy but empathy in which the emphasis is on understanding as much as identification. With or without knowing it, battered women's advocates may have been able to capitalize on a distinctly modern genre of storytelling.[47]

Victims' Stories in Other Institutional Contexts

In describing how canonical story lines and narrative epistemologies have operated to shape the strategic options available to activists, I have focused on the legal arena. But similar processes operate in other spheres, determining, for example, how well activists can get their message out through the media and how effective they are in winning legislative reforms.

Prevailing assumptions about personal storytelling's truth value determine what activists can gain from telling personal stories to the press. Indeed, paying attention to how consumers assess the information that is presented to them in different forms in news reports should revise our ideas about how well the media serves those trying to effect social change. The standard view among scholars is that the media's tendency to focus on individuals is unequivocally bad. Political scientist Lance Bennett comments in this vein that "if there is a single most important flaw in the American news style, it is the overwhelming tendency to downplay the big social, economic, or political picture in favor the human trials and triumphs that sit at the surface of events. In place of power and process, the media concentrate on the people engaged in political combat over the issues." Audiences can relate to these "personalized human interest stories," Bennett writes. But that does not necessarily lead them to a deeper engagement or even interest in politics: "[T]he meanings inspired by personalized news are not the shared critical and analytical meanings on which a healthy democracy thrives. Personalized news encourages people to take an egocentric rather than a socially concerned view of political problems."[48]

However, recent social psychological research has pointed to another possibility. When people hear or read stories in which someone affected by an issue is profiled, they are likely to see that person's views both as widespread and as persuasive. Researchers have studied audiences' response to what they call "exemplars": stories, examples, and firsthand accounts that describe an issue from the perspective of an individual. When audiences are presented with exemplars and with information that casts doubt on the representativeness of the exemplars, they tend to see the exemplars as reflecting majority opinion. In one study, subjects heard a simulated radio news broadcast in which an ordinary citizen expressed his disapproval of military intervention in a regional conflict, followed by a reporter who said that "two-thirds of Americans support military intervention." Despite the polling evidence to the contrary, subjects believed after the broadcast that more Americans opposed intervention than supported it. Audiences are also likely to modify their own opinions in line with those of exemplars. This is true even when the issues are controversial. Researchers' best explanation is that because processing information is time-consuming, audiences tend to take cues from the reactions of other people, even when those people are not experts and even when they present a distorted picture of the issue in question. What this means for activists is that the well-placed man on the street may serve to popularize the movement's views.[49]

Jason Salzman, a media consultant to activist groups, makes a similar argument. Reporters want to hear from the people who are affected by the issue: the person living next door to the toxic waste dump or the worker denied health coverage. Salzman calls such stories entertainment, but he is not dismissive of them. To the contrary, such stories are engaging. They are the hook that brings the audience to the larger issue. And journalists do want to engage the larger issue, Salzman maintains. Activists can provide both the storyteller and the information on the trend illuminated by the story. *Boston Globe* reporter Kimberly Blanton agrees. Certainly, when an advocacy organization gives her the names of people to contact, she is prepared for the possibility that her interviewees may toe the party line. But she trusts her own ability to recognize the genuine experiences people describe and to communicate those experiences to her readers. In fact, she goes on, sometimes she has had to pester advocacy organizations to provide her with people to interview, a strategic misstep on their part that may cost them valuable coverage. But, as Salzman points out, activists too often move in different circles than the people directly affected by their issues.[50]

Personalizing the movement's cause may not undermine it. At least, this is the case in the United States. In a study of media coverage of the abortion debate in the United States and West Germany, sociologists Myra Marx Ferree, William Gamson, Jürgen Gerhards, and Dieter Rucht found that the American media were much more likely to include personal stories in their coverage. Of the forty-six articles that the authors sampled from the *New York Times* and the *Los Angeles Times* in 1994, 13 percent of them profiled activists on both sides of the issue. Few personal stories appeared in the German press. This was not surprising, say Ferree and her colleagues, given the preference of the German press for detached rational argumentation over what journalists saw as the emotionalism of storytelling. The researchers also found that, in the absence of strong political parties and party spokespeople, American reporters were much more likely to turn to movement groups and their members as sources for their stories. German reporters relied overwhelmingly on state and party representatives. The prominence of grassroots actors and a narrative style in American news stories may also reflect a populist wariness of experts that extends to news reporting. As media scholar Herbert Gans puts it, "'[G]rassroots activity' is one of the most complimentary terms in the vocabulary of the news, particularly when it takes place to foil politicians or bureaucrats."[51]

Popular respect for the kind of experiential knowledge that personal narrative conveys may open up strategic possibilities in still another context. As I noted earlier, some feminists have argued that in a popular culture dominated by the therapeutic language of recovery, talk about victimization has been stripped of its political dimensions. The television talk shows that dominated in the 1980s, programs such as *Donahue, Sally Jesse Raphael, Ricki Lake, The Oprah Winfrey Show,* and *The Montel Williams Show* are often exhibit A in that critique. Elayne Rapping writes that the women who appeared on these programs described problems in ways that sounded feminist: they talked about unsatisfying relationships with men and other women, and about their frustration with their jobs and self-perceptions. But they accounted for those problems in terms that were individual and therapeutic. Women were victims not of political powerlessness and institutional inequalities but of their own addictions. The solution, then, was to embrace a twelve-step recovery program.[52]

However, other studies of daytime talk shows suggest that they may have conceived of victimization in more complex ways. When talk shows in the 1980s tackled issues such as rape, domestic abuse, addiction, and crime, guests usually included activists along with professional experts such as academics and psychologists as well as the ordinary people who had suffered from the issue in question. Activists were staffers of rape-crisis centers and battered women's shelters; they had founded gang-prevention programs or legal aid centers; or they were leading HIV/AIDS support groups and advocacy efforts. Sociologist Laura Grindstaff found that activists on daytime talk shows often had a more prominent place in the guest line-up and were given more airtime than professional experts. Experts, especially academics, complained about being relegated to the end of the segment (colloquially referred to by producers as Siberia). Academics' more complex analyses of an issue were edited out, they said, and they were often attacked by guests and audience members when their comments departed from the frame that had been established before the program even began. They were also challenged for their distance from the issue in question. Audience members and guests often asked them outright whether they had experienced teenage pregnancy, drug addiction, or sexual abuse themselves. Activists, by contrast, often *had* experienced the issues about which they spoke. Indeed, some of them had appeared previously on the program as guests and were brought back as experts. Activists' firsthand experience gave them a more trusted kind of expertise. For example, when a representative from the Prisoners' Rights Union appeared on a show about sexual predators to make the unpopular case that ex-offenders were entitled to full civil rights, he "came on like gangbusters," he said, and was eventually able to persuade a hostile audience to consider the "side of the prisoner and the ex-con." His status as an ex-con himself, Grindstaff observed, gave him an edge that the academic expert lacked. Talk shows' privileging of personal experience over expertise thus gave victim-activists credibility. And activists used that to call for mobilization, support, and political reform, not therapy.[53]

Certainly, talk shows have never been just a mouthpiece for movement messages. Sociologist Joshua Gamson found that such programs moved the conventional line on sexual deviance slightly and then redrew it even more firmly: homosexuality was acceptable but bisexuality and transvestism were not. I noted earlier the charge that talk shows' sensationalistic treatment of child abuse made the behavior seem more aberrant than it actually was. The value of the venue therefore remains mixed for activists. My point, though, is that activists can exploit the conventions of storytelling and, especially, the presumed relations between personal storytelling and authoritative knowledge. Like canonical story lines, they both offer strategic opportunities and impose strategic constraints.[54]

Conclusion

Is playing the victim good or bad for those who want to change laws, policies, and social practices? The standard critique is that telling stories of victimization trades autonomy for passivity. It invites pity and protection rather than respect and power. I have argued that, depending on prevailing views of victims and of stories, telling stories of victimization may not have those effects. And I have argued that those effects may not be the worst of it.

Victims have styled themselves moral tutors, policy experts, abuse survivors, and political provocateurs. None of those roles deny the victim's suffering and none of them emphasizes his or her helplessness. Instead, each one foregrounds the political insight or moral responsibility that comes from suffering. In news stories, audiences are likely to see victims' opinions as widely representative and as persuasive. On television talk shows, audiences commonly see victims who have become activists as appealingly down-to-earth. Their storytelling is granted an authority that is not given to professional experts. These views of victims and their stories are historical, reflecting both familiar genres of victim narratives and prevailing assumptions about what kinds of discourses and what kinds of stories are likely to be true.

In courts, too, disadvantaged groups have told stories of victimization and agency, suffering and insight. When women in low-paying jobs testified that they really did want the more competitive jobs that had been denied them, they were more likely to win their claims of sex discrimination than when attorneys presented only statistical evidence of women's underrepresentation in such jobs. When battered women who were on trial for homicide told of the cruel and unrelenting violence they endured without seeing any means of escape, they became for lawyers, judges, and juries something other than cold-blooded killers.

But telling their stories has not won women equality. Their accounts of sex discrimination and self-defense have been heard by legal decision makers against the backdrop of more familiar stories, ones that are richly developed, that come in enough different versions to seem to encompass a broader range of experiences, and that have the status of common sense. A battered woman tells a story of killing her abuser to save her life, and she is heard as a brutalized woman who finally snapped, killing in a fit of irrational rage. Or she is heard as strong-willed and unapologetic; not a proper victim but someone using her abuse to get herself off the hook. A woman tells a story of aspiring to the same jobs that men have aspired to and she is heard as claiming that there are no differences between men and women. Or she is successful in proving that an employer's use of male-biased job tests was discriminatory but not in proving that the employer's use of word-of-mouth advertising also was. In these cases and others, stories that are familiar to legal decision makers have variously trumped, discredited, and limited the impact of challengers' stories.

Does this mean that storytelling inevitably reproduces the status quo? No. Canonical story lines and institutionalized ways of knowing may limit storytelling's influence, but activists have sometimes succeeded in extending those limits. AIDS activists effectively redefined the protocols of biomedical research to award a greater role to those suffering from the disease being researched. Activists chipped away at the long-standing opposition between storytelling and science to show that science was improved by incorporating the accounts of disease sufferers. Battered women and their advocates have also been able to chip away at familiar oppositions. They have sometimes gained a hearing for stories in which battered women are both victims and rational agents, and in which the obstacles they face are social and financial as much as psychological. They have done so, I have suggested, by using narrative strategies that are familiar to literary critics. By combining discordant ideas or feelings, their stories have forced the reader or listener to struggle to make sense of an unfamiliar experience. The author's strong narrative voice has conveyed an impression of agency and reasonableness, even as she has described experiences of dependence and dehumanization.

Critics worry that to claim one's victimization is to make oneself into a pathetic figure. And indeed, unlike the tragic figures of old, victims today tend to inspire pity, not admiration, and they invite catharsis, not learning. But the situation is not entirely bleak. Insofar as victim stories follow a popular genre of tragic irony, they may effectively illuminate the cultural norms operating even in violence between intimates. Abolitionists almost two hundred years ago were able to draw on the template of Christian conversion narratives to style victims as tutors in moral uplift. So, with the right narrative tools, disadvantaged groups today may be able to style victims as guides to the social bases of inequality.

SIX

Remembering Dr. King on the House and Senate Floor: Why Movements Have the Impacts They Do

In previous chapters, I have talked about the virtues and liabilities of storytelling for ordinary citizens and for organized groups. People with unpopular views, whether participants in a forum about what to build on the site of the former World Trade Center, abolitionists in the antebellum South, or advocates for women who have killed their abusive husbands, have been well served by telling stories. Narrative's reliance on familiar plot lines has made it possible for people to gain an empathetic hearing for needs that have been ignored by policymakers. Narrative's openness to interpretation has helped groups to reach agreement across differences of opinion and alliances across differences of agenda. The distancing effect of shifting among points of view in a story has created authority for groups that have normally lacked it.

But telling stories also carries risks. People with unfamiliar experiences have found those experiences assimilated to canonical plot lines and misheard as a result. Conventional expectations about how stories work, when they are true, and when they are appropriate have also operated to diminish the impact of otherwise potent political stories. For the abused women whom juries disbelieved because their stories had changed in small details since their first traumatized call to police, storytelling has not been especially effective. Nor was it effective for the citizen forum participants who did not say what it was like to search fruitlessly for affordable housing because discussions of housing were seen as the wrong place in which to tell stories.

Of course, it is not only the powerless who tell political stories. There is a voluminous literature on how governments have used accounts of the past to legitimate themselves. States ritually recount myths of their origins to revitalize the bonds of citizenship. They tell stories of past insurgency to mobilize national action and stories of stoic suffering to discourage further insurgency. Such stories appear in diverse versions and forms: in school textbooks and officials' speeches, in the commentary that accompanies national holidays and the dramas that appear on state-sponsored television networks, just to name a few. The stories states tell invariably involve inventing as much as reporting and forgetting as much as remembering.[1]

This does not mean that it is always easy for states to produce useful pasts. To the contrary, governments have been confronted with suppressed episodes in the triumphalist stories they have told. Occasionally, they have been called on to tell the stories they had long denied, as with South Africa's Truth and Reconciliation Commission. Governments' efforts to control access to historical archives have sometimes failed. Political careers have been destroyed by an otherwise innocuous story told at the wrong time. There have been spectacular battles over government agencies' efforts to authorize a particular version of history, whether in museum exhibits or holiday commemorations. Even without open conflict over which version of the past is accurate, alternative versions have always circulated quietly in opposition to the official ones.[2]

Scholars of collective memory have referred accordingly to the conflicting interests in the past of "political structures and ordinary people"; "dominants and subordinates"; and the creators of "official" and "popular memory." But we should be wary of implying that the state has a single interest in how the past is represented. Competing accounts of the nation's history jockey for prominence in routine political processes as much as in the public controversies that punctuate those processes. Democrats hold to a different American history than Republicans do; hawkish Democrats tell different stories than dovish Democrats do. Certainly, elected officials seek to appeal to their constituents in the stories that they tell. But their constituents are diverse; the stories that will appeal to them are often not obvious; and, in any case, officials seek as much to shape constituents' preferences as to accommodate them. All this makes for complex and sometimes conflicting tasks of narration.[3]

Consider, in this respect, the awkward storytelling position of officials whose election or appointment is the result of long mobilization efforts. Women elected after feminist mobilization, environmentalists elected as the result of the environmental movement, African Americans elected in the wake of the civil rights movement—each of these can be counted as evidence of the movement's success. Yet, new officials may find themselves struggling to prove to their constituents that their proximity to those in power has not tempered their desire to effect real change. They can easily be charged by critics with co-optation. At the same time that they make the case to their constituents for pursuing institutional routes to collective power, they must persuade their colleagues within the institution to implement policies that benefit a constituency that still has relatively little clout. If their status as outsider-insiders demands that they present themselves as the embodiment of progress toward the movement's aims, their status as insider-outsiders demands that they represent those aims as unfulfilled. Their stories of the movement and its lessons should reflect those competing demands.

Yet their efforts may also be constrained not by what really happened in some pristine sense but by powerful institutional conventions of storytelling. This is what I found in an analysis of how African American legislators told the story of the civil rights movement and its most famous leader, Martin Luther King, Jr. Through a content analysis of the *Congressional Record,* which is the official transcript of House and Senate floor activity, I studied who invoked King, in relation to what topics, and how they represented his struggle and his legacy. Note that my interest in this chapter is less in how congressional speakers used storytelling as a discursive form than in how they used different versions of a well-known past for different political projects. I try to piece together the story of the civil rights movement evident in their statements: the movement's protagonists and antagonists, its major events, its dénouement, and its moral. Although I draw comparisons between Democrats and Republicans and between white and black members of Congress, my main interest is in how African American legislators referred to King and the movement. How did they narrate the past to overcome difficulties posed by their position in Congress as at once insiders and outsiders? I argue that they assimilated King into a pluralist framework by representing community service and institutional politics as the proper legacy of his activism. In the story they told, elected officials, not extra-institutional activists, were the bearers of King's dream.

So far, my argument is an instrumentalist one. African American officials referred to King in a way that legitimated their own role as advocates for black interests. This is supported by a second content analysis that I present in the chapter of the stories told about King by black protest leaders. Unsurprisingly, these storytellers emphasized King's protest as disruptive and unfinished, and represented themselves as the standard-bearers for the next phase of the movement. Yet the limitations of an instrumentalist approach to political storytelling are revealed by a second feature of African American legislators' stories of King. Black legislators struggled rhetorically to represent the purpose of telling the story of King and the movement, to retell the past in a way that neither deprecated the movement's accomplishments nor claimed that its aims were fulfilled. The awkwardness of legislators' attempts to do this, in contrast to their customary eloquence, suggests the power of the narratives of progress and unity that are built into an American discourse of remembering. But it also points, once again, to specifically institutional conventions of narration. Such conventions shape not only what one can do with the past, that is, what stories one can tell, but also when one can do it, that is, the occasions on which stories are acceptable.

In chapter 4 I showed that citizens deliberating in a public forum were much less likely to tell stories in discussions that were explicitly policy-oriented. In this chapter I find once again that the line distinguishing appropriate and inappropriate occasions for storytelling is politically significant. Black legislators intended their stories of King to criticize and challenge the present state of things, but they told them mainly on occasions that were removed from the legislative process. This has implications for how we understand the effects of movements more generally. For groups wanting to effect political change, the fact that a movement's leader is quoted approvingly by legislators should be sign of institutional success. But if those references are confined to commemorative occasions, then the success may be illusory. Stories about protest may reinforce institutional politics—both by legitimating institutional political actors as protest's proper heirs, and by strengthening the symbolic boundary between decision making and commemoration.

Dr. King on the House and Senate Floor

The *Congressional Record* is the official record of floor activity in the House and Senate, and it is published daily. It includes proposals for new legislation and legislative debate. It also includes *one-minute speeches* on topics of national or district concern delivered by House members at the start of the day's business, and *special orders:* five-minute speeches in the

Senate and prearranged, sixty-minute sessions in the House, usually at the end of the day's business. My analysis of African American legislators' storytelling about Dr. King is based on an examination of all speeches between January 1, 1993, and May 31, 1997, in which Dr. King was explicitly mentioned. The *Record* is not a verbatim record of legislators' speech. Speakers may edit their remarks, insert longer statements from which they draw only selectively in their floor speeches, and, with permission, insert previously published reports, articles, and op-ed pieces. For my purposes, this means that speakers have had an opportunity to cast their remarks in what they see as coherent form. When I refer to "awkward formulations," therefore, these are less likely a function simply of the messiness of spoken speech than of the problems generated by the content and context of the utterance.[4]

For each congressional session, I read all the documents that referred at least once to "Martin Luther King" or "Dr. King"—in total, 843. I discarded references that were to an institution, place, or event named after King as well as those that appeared in the text of a proposed bill or resolution, a list of sponsors, or other procedural matter, or that were not made by the legislators themselves (for example, newspaper editorials inserted in the *Record*). That left a total of 305 *Record* entries over the four-and-a-half-year period that referred to King at least once, and a total of 420 speeches. Are 420 speeches mentioning King over four and a half years a lot? There were a total of 612 entries during the same period in which "Abraham Lincoln" or "President Lincoln" was invoked at least once, less than the 843 for King. The comparison with King's civil rights contemporaries is more striking. Roy Wilkins, head of the NAACP, Whitney Young, head of the National Urban League, and James Farmer, head of CORE, who were, together with King and John Lewis of SNCC (now Congressman John Lewis), the leaders of the major civil rights movement organizations, were barely mentioned. Wilkins appeared nine times in four and a half years, Young four times, and Farmer five times. A. Philip Randolph, who was the head of the Brotherhood of Sleeping Car Porters and organized the 1963 March on Washington, was mentioned twelve times.[5]

Who invoked King? Overwhelmingly, Democrats. One hundred and twenty-two Democrats, that is, 33 percent of the 370 Democrats who served in both chambers between 1993 and 1997, made speeches referring to King. Democrats accounted for 344, or 84 percent, of the 420 King speeches. By contrast, only 34 Republicans, or 10 percent of the 333 Republican legislators, made speeches referring to King (as did both Independents). People of color were more likely than whites to refer to

Dr. King. Thirty-five of the 49 African American representatives (71 percent) made speeches that referred to King, as did 8 of the 18 Hispanic representatives (42 percent), and 3 of the 7 Asian Americans and Pacific Islanders. By contrast, only 17 percent of the 641 white representatives referred to King in their speeches. Of the 420 King speeches, 182, or 43 percent, were made by African American legislators. Former civil rights activist and current Georgia congressman John Lewis invoked King most frequently: he did so in 24 speeches over the four-and-a-half-year period. Nine other House and Senate members, all but one of whom were African American, made 7 or more references to King.[6]

In what discursive contexts did speakers talk about King and the movement? Five kinds of speeches predominated. The largest group were *tributes* to other people, 151 in total, 112 of which noted the individual's relationship to King (other tributes simply quoted or paraphrased him). Recipients of such tributes were often former civil rights movement activists from the legislator's district (for example, a lawyer who represented activists or a local minister who marched with King) or nationally known former activists (for example, Rosa Parks, James Farmer, Thurgood Marshall, and César Chávez). They were also often people little known outside the legislator's district who were "inspired by Dr. King," "shared Dr. King's goals," or worked "in the spirit of Martin Luther King, Jr." Another large group of references—there were 93—came in *speeches honoring historical events:* Freedom Summer, the Selma to Montgomery March, King's birthday and assassination, and Black History Month. Fifty-one speeches citing King were *commentaries* delivered by a representative on a topic of interest but not pending legislation. Thirty-one speeches were about legislation proposed to extend the federal King Holiday Commission or to *commemorate King* or the civil rights movement in other ways, for example, with memorials, commemorative coins, or congressional resolutions. The remaining references came in 94 speeches that were part of *legislative debates.* Since members of Congress speak to issues of policy concern in extensions of remarks, one-minute speeches, special orders, and resolutions that are not part of debate over specific legislation, I combined commentary speeches with legislative ones when the commentary spoke to a politically salient issue. Multiple references to King were made in calls for federal legislation to assist in prosecution of church arsonists in the South (17 King speeches), in debates over legislation to toughen penalties against pro-life protests at abortion clinics (11 King speeches, both pro and con), in support for affirmative action policies (11 King speeches), and in opposition to the withdrawal of U.S. troops from Haiti (6 King speeches).

What was the substance of the references to King? How was King represented in these speeches? Congressional speakers styled him as an orator and moral leader, not as a shrewd political strategist. He was remembered for his rhetorical eloquence, for his "dream" of racial harmony, and for his "message," "lesson," "principle," and "spirit" of nonviolence. The dream reference was from King's famous "I have a dream" speech delivered at the 1963 March on Washington. Congresspeople referred to the speech forty-eight times and to some portion of its most famous line thirty times: "I have a dream that my four children will one day live in a nation where they will not be judged by the color of their skin but by the content of their character." When congresspeople referred to King's "dream," however, they rarely described it and sometimes conflated it with an American dream of individual success ("One of Dr. King's philosophies revolves around the promise that every individual can achieve his or her dream in America"). Interestingly, Democrats and Republicans interpreted King's dream in different ways. Democrats interpreted it as a vision of a future society in which people would be judged by the content of their character. Republicans interpreted it as injunction to treat people in the here and now on the basis of the content of their character. For example, one speaker declared, "If we are to move forward as the world's most diverse and successful multicultural nation, we must stop defining each other by the color of our skin, and strive to judge one another by the content of our character."[7]

The targets and antagonists of the civil rights movement did not appear in either Democratic or Republican legislators' speeches. Instead, King was represented as bringing about change by "inspiring," and "raising the consciousness" of the nation. Usually it was "America" that changed, and the change occurred through public acclamation. The only references to the illegality of King's actions came in Republican representatives' opposition to a bill that toughened penalties for harassment at abortion clinics. Opponents of the bill maintained that it violated prolife demonstrators' freedom of speech and that it would quash the kind of civil disobedience on which King and his supporters had relied.

It was overwhelmingly the early King who appeared on the House and Senate floor. The "I have a dream speech" was the most often quoted of King's speeches and writings. "Letter from a Birmingham Jail," written earlier in 1963, was also prominent in congressional speeches, quoted twenty-four times. King's Nobel Peace Prize acceptance speech, delivered in 1964, was quoted three times. Only 5 (or 4 percent) of the 119 quoted excerpts whose source I was able to identify came from speeches delivered between 1965 and King's death in 1968. Three of those were introduced as coming from King's last speech. In his later speeches King voiced his opposition to American militarism, called for a massive federal financial commitment to the poor, and questioned a capitalist society's capacity to make that commitment. This was not the King who appeared on the House and Senate floor.[8]

Still, there is material even in King's earlier speeches for a forceful challenge to politics as usual. Congressional speakers did not quote the following section of "Letter from a Birmingham Jail": "History is the long and tragic story of the fact that privileged groups seldom give up their privileges voluntarily . . . freedom is never voluntarily given by the oppressor; it must be demanded by the oppressed." Nor did they take the following from the "I have a dream" speech: "The whirlwinds of revolt will continue to shake the foundations of our nation until the bright day of justice emerges." However, these excerpts are not contained in standard quotation dictionaries, nor are King's later speeches. Fully 124 of the 133 quotations from King made by congressional representatives are included in standard compilations of Dr. King's quotations. This suggests that congressional representatives and their speechwriters were reproducing a popular cultural rendition of King rather than deliberately omitting portions of his legacy.[9]

Yet, the King that legislators described was not so obviously the harmless black icon that historian Vincent Harding found in official and popular memory, either. Nor was he the raceless American hero that scholars have found in children's textbooks, public oratory about the King holiday, and television coverage of the holiday. Legislators tended to refer to King in conjunction with other *black* "heroes," "firsts," "greats," or "leaders." These included Frederick Douglass, Sojourner Truth, W. E. B. Du Bois, Harriet Tubman, civil rights activists Rosa Parks and Fannie Lou Hamer, baseball player Jackie Robinson, and former congresswomen Shirley Chisholm and Barbara Jordan. Current or recent congresspeople and federal officials were also invoked along with King: Representatives Maxine Waters and John Lewis, Commerce Secretary Ron Brown, Energy Secretary Hazel O'Leary. This does not suggest an assimilationist, melting-pot narrative of ethnic politics, in which American heroes are stripped of positional identities, honored rather for their individual talents, and claimed universally. Rather, it suggests an ethnic-group, pluralist narrative in which leaders represent the aspirations and accomplishments of their respective groups (so, King for African Americans, César Chávez for Mexican Americans, and Susan B. Anthony for women). In this narrative, King had more in common with Jackie Robinson than with Paul Revere or Vaclav Havel.[10]

Scholars have described an American discourse of public remembering as marked by themes of unity and progress. Yet, analysis of congressional discourse shows interesting differences between black and white speakers in this respect. White speakers tended to imply Americans' universal appreciation for King's message, using "we" and "us" to refer to Americans black and white. "We marvel at the courage of Martin Luther King, Jr. We are humbled by the eloquence of Barbara Jordan," said one. They also sometimes suggested universal appreciation for King during his lifetime: "Let us resolve, in these last few years of the 20th century, to recommit ourselves to the goals with which Martin Luther King inspired us all over a quarter century ago," as one put it; and, "It really was not until the late 1950s that we began to rally in support of the work of Martin Luther King, by businessmen, by laborers, by church leaders, by all Americans, and said 'Let's finally get serious and free ourselves from discrimination.'" The last statement also represented white Americans as the ones doing the liberating (of themselves). At least one speaker suggested oddly that racial unity preceded the movement, describing the "great dream of Martin Luther King's that blacks and whites *can once again* walk together in this country blessed by God in a land of freedom" (emphasis added).[11]

White speakers occasionally suggested that King's dream had been realized, his battle won. Thus one described recent church burnings as "hearken[ing] back to a time when, to paraphrase Dr. King, people were judged not on the content of their character but on the color of their skin," implying that this was no longer the case. Another described King's struggle and concluded that "in the end, the American ideal of equality won, and hate lost." More often, however, white speakers argued that although there were still problems, great progress had been made. As one put it, "We have a long way to go in making our Constitutional principles realities for everyone, but we have accomplished very significant progress." The formulaic quality of the statement undercut its force. Since the comments preceding it emphasized the accomplishments of the movement, and the comments following it rarely gave equal emphasis to the problems remaining, the message was one of measured success and continuing progress.[12]

Black speakers, like white ones, tended to rely on the "we've made progress, but . . ." formulation while emphasizing the "but . . ." clause. Only two speakers drew attention to something like failure. King had "moved to correct the evil, to shed not only light but to bring those evils to the forefront and to terminate them and eradicate them for our society," one observed, but, "during his lifetime he [King] was only partially successful in doing this." Other speakers claimed that King had achieved a measured success: "Martin would want us to raise our sights to the work yet to be done" said one. Another simply posed the question, "If we stop and reflect on where we have gone since the marches and the sit-ins and boycotts of the 1960s, have we really gone that far?" Black congresspeople thus accepted the progress narrative less readily than their white colleagues did. But they were nowhere near as critical of the contemporary state of race relations as were the speakers at the local celebrations of Martin Luther King, Jr., Day that Richard Merelman studied. The King Day celebrations were oriented to black audiences, and their most frequent substantive theme, according to Merelman, was the continuing practice of racial discrimination against blacks. Indeed, references to the distance that blacks still had to go to achieve equality were four times more frequent than references to the distance that blacks had come. Celebrants emphasized conflict rather than unity and continued inequality rather than progress in eradicating it.[13]

These contrasts suggest that in order to understand how King was represented on the House and Senate floors, we need to know more about African American legislators' distinctive political position vis-à-vis both their colleagues and their constituents. In what follows, I argue that in a majority white Congress, black legislators' ability to deliver to their constituents depended on persuading more conservative legislators to approve substantial government intervention. How black congresspeople recounted their relationship to the movement and to King's legacy was important to their own credibility and that of their agenda. At the same time, however, the institutional context in which they operated constrained their efforts to use King's memory to call for broadly redistributive policies. The fact that they memorialized King in Congress rather than, say, a King Day celebration in a predominately black church, limited what they could say and when they could say it.[14]

Protest, Politics, and King's Heirs

The passage of the Voting Rights Act in 1965 began what civil rights activist Bayard Rustin celebrated as a shift "from protest to politics." In many areas of the South, white citizens and authorities kept up intimidation efforts. In the case of Mississippi, they legislated a series of vote-dilution measures to minimize black electoral gains. Still, the number of black officials at local and state levels of government began to grow. There were 1,100 black elected officials by 1969, 3,600 by 1983, and 8,000 by 1993. Championed as evidence of the civil rights movement's success, entry into electoral politics did not fulfill the highest aspirations of the activists who fought for it. Those who made the shift from protest to politics were sobered by the difficulty they encountered in effecting substantive change. A member of the first Washington, D.C., City Council under home rule remembers some of his colleagues who were former activists "still damning the power structure and the system. I had to remind them that they *were* the power structure and the system." Civil rights movement veterans and protest organizations, for their part, found themselves increasingly marginalized by the black officialdom they had fought to create.[15]

The postmovement era has accordingly been marked by persistent tensions between protest and electoral elites and by skirmishes over the guardianship of the civil rights past. For instance, political scientist Adolph Reed, Jr., describes black elected officials' initial coolness to Jesse Jackson's 1984 campaign as reflecting a turf battle between electoral and protest elites. Detroit mayor Coleman Young was blunt when Jackson threw his hat in the ring: Jackson "should continue to preach," Young declared, for "as a politician, he's out of his league." The fact that most black elected officials came around to supporting Jackson, Reed argues, had to do in part with his success in associating himself with King. As an envious strategist for the eventual Democratic nominee, Walter Mondale, put it, Jackson's clout came from his success in "equating this presidential crusade with the civil rights movement." Another example comes from the 1993 March on Washington. According to historian Manning Marable, the march was an effort by remnants of the civil rights elite both to publicize President Bill Clinton's failures on health care and jobs, *and* to regain the mantle of black political leadership from black elected officials. The latter was evident in march organizer Joseph Lowery's declaration that the march was intended to "spark a renaissance in social activism and pass the torch so the struggle will continue." It was underscored by the failure of the march organizers to invite any voting members of Congress to serve on the planning committee.[16]

The ways in which congressional speakers talked about King and the movement similarly reflected tensions both between black aspirations and a centrist political regime and between the leadership claims of officials and activists. Insofar as black legislators in the 103rd, 104th, and 105th Congresses saw themselves as advancing black interests, they represented a constituency 70 percent of which favored "more laws to reduce discrimination" (barely a third of whites polled agreed), and 51 percent of which believed that "the USA is moving toward two separate and unequal societies—one black, one white" (one third of whites agreed). As minority representatives, black legislators had a mandate to secure far-reaching change from an often intransigent political establishment. The task was made more difficult by their lack of long-standing ties to the establishment. Yet in the eyes of black activists, legislators were always in danger of giving up an agenda of progressive change in favor of personal political ambitions. They sought legitimacy as the bearers of black interests, this in potential or actual competition with civil rights activists. At the same time, they sought a program of progressive legislative change, this in competition with those representing mainstream interests. I argue that African American legislators styled their accounts of the past to further both tasks, but that they were more successful in the first than in the second.[17]

KING AS LEGISLATORS REPRESENTED HIM   Congressional speakers frequently described their own relationship to King. Sometimes the relationship was direct, as in, "I feel privileged to have known King personally"; "I met a man who was a preacher from Montgomery"; "I remember Fannie Lou Hamer, Martin Luther King, and Mary McCloud Bethune"; "I was privileged to be with [King] on that march from Selma to Montgomery." Sometimes, rather, the relationship was indirect: "My own story is a testament to King's dream"; "It is doubtful I would be here today in this Congress if many people in this country who were offended in the 1960s by the remarks of Martin Luther King, Jr., had been able to silence him." Formulations like the latter are interesting because they cast the speaker as the fruit of the movement. This claim was often explicit. "I along with many of my colleagues am here today as a direct result of the struggles of the sixties," one speaker averred. African American legislators were both witness to and evidence of progress. "I have seen progress . . . I have seen a poor black man, denied the right to vote, become a Member of Congress," said one; and another: "had Dr. King and many others not made that historic and dangerous walk from Selma to Montgomery, perhaps I would not be standing before this body today"; "Let us not forget those who toiled in order that we would have a place in this House."[18]

Speakers were becomingly humble in acknowledging that their own careers were made possible by the travails of an earlier generation of movement activists. But they also styled themselves as legitimate heirs to that earlier activism. Their own careers were the next stage in a saga of African American struggle. "I was born, as a matter of African American history," Jesse Jackson, Jr., recounted, "on March 11, 1965. On March 7, 1965, in our history, it is known as bloody Sunday. It is the Sunday that the gentleman from Georgia [John Lewis], Martin Luther King, and Jesse

Jackson and many others in our history walked across the Edmund Pettus Bridge for the right to vote. Because of the struggle that they engaged in 1965, I now stand here as the 91st African American to ever have the privilege of serving in the U.S. Congress." Another speaker aligned himself with King by appropriating a portion of King's last speech to describe his own situation: "It is a far from perfect situation which exists in Alabama, or in America, but if we realize this fact, and continue to progress and grow, we will reach Dr. King's promised land. And just like Dr. King, I may not be with you when you get there, but if this day comes after my work on earth is done, I assure you that I will be there in spirit." [19]

Speakers' frequent grouping of King with recent and current congressional representatives had a similar effect. Thus one representative described former congresswoman Barbara Jordan "in the tradition of Frederick Douglass, Martin Luther King, and Thurgood Marshall." I just quoted Jesse Jackson, Jr., describing King and Congressman John Lewis crossing the Edmund Pettus Bridge in 1965. He then went on to praise Lewis for "making it possible for me to serve in the U.S. House of Representatives." Representative Sheila Jackson-Lee cited her African American colleague Harold Ford's leadership in investigating the King and Kennedy assassinations. The message was one of continuity between a movement past and current mainstream politics.[20]

Representatives did not claim exclusive guardianship of the movement's legacy. They shared it, they said, with people whose work followed in King's footsteps, the "unsung heroes" of the movement. Who were these co-legatees? Although they were sometimes activists—for example, members of the NAACP or the Urban League—they were more often not. Rather, they were teachers, ministers, leaders of a boys' club, president of a city growth association, director of a family care center, and a local high school coach. King's legacy in this narrative was service rather than insurgency. This is apparent in speeches made as part of special orders commemorating Black History Month in 1994 and 1997. Both years' orders commemorated activism, the first under the heading, "Empowering Afro-American Organizations: Present and Future," and the second, "Civil Rights Organizations in History: A Reappraisal." In both years, the organizations that were honored by legislators were civil rights organizations of the 1960s (the NAACP, the Southern Christian Leadership Conference, and the Urban League) and, in the main, *civic* organizations in the 1990s: after-school facilities, rehabilitation centers, a police officers league, a historical preservationist group. Describing Black America as "under siege" and quoting A. Philip Randolph as well as King, Representative Eddie Bernice Johnson called for "work at the grassroots level to protect the hard fought gains of the civil rights movement." She went on to describe a sorority, a fund-raising group for civic causes, and Jack and Jill (a group promoting education and self-esteem among black students). Grassroots mobilizing was thus recast as community service rather than extra-institutional challenge made through petitions, boycotts, strikes, and demonstrations. Representative Millender-Macdonald recounted the activism of a member of her California district: he had marched with King in 1963 and served as local NAACP president in the 1970s; today, she said, he was leading her task force on volunteerism.[21]

A story of the movement that ended with volunteerism rather than protest was also evident in speeches urging continued funding for the federal King Holiday Commission. Established in 1984 to promote the holiday, the commission was intended to be privately funded. However, difficulties in raising adequate sums led to congressional annual appropriations of $300,000 after 1990. In 1993, Harris Wofford and Carol Moseley-Braun in the Senate and Ralph Regula and John Lewis in the House proposed legislation to extend appropriations for five years. In hearings and Senate debate, Wofford gave numerous versions of the following rationale:

> Nothing would have ticked Martin off more than people supposedly honoring him by sitting on their duffs watching the tube or sleeping late. The King holiday should be a day on not a day off. A day of action, not apathy. A day of responding to community needs, not a day of rest and recreation. So my old civil rights colleague of the Selma march, Congressman John Lewis, and I have introduced legislation designed to remember Martin the way he would have liked: a day that reflects his proposition that "everybody can be great because everybody can serve." A day that brings the greatness out in people by bringing them together to make a difference in their communities. Fixing parks, tutoring children, rebuilding schools, feeding the hungry, immunizing children, housing the homeless.[22]

What King "would have liked" was "action"—meaning service. Senator Moseley-Braun noted that "the day could be used to donate blood or volunteer at a hospital, to clean up a park or plant flowers in an inner-city neighborhood, to volunteer for the Boy Scouts or Girl Scouts or the Special Olympics, to tutor children or to work with those who have AIDS." Wofford and Moseley-Braun's brief for the legislation was echoed in remarks by other bill supporters. Certainly service is a worthy endeavor with the potential for far-reaching change. However, its assimilation to King's extra-institutional activism was a rhetorical accomplishment rather than an obvious historical fact.[23]

In some of the speeches made in support of the holiday, King's commitment to nonviolence was restyled as a commitment to ending violence, especially among youths. Thus one representative observed,

One needs only listen to the daily news and read the headlines to know that we need this Commission, now more than ever. Our young people are dying in great numbers on the streets, in their classrooms, and in their homes, Mr. Speaker. That is a fact. And the most frightening thing about that fact is—our children are killing each other. The King Holiday Commission is dedicated to teaching the tenets of nonviolence, and the value of community service to our young people.

Senator Moseley-Braun declared: "If there is no other reason for this Commission, it is that we can provide to young people precisely that kind of epiphany that says to them that nonviolence is important because it is predicated on a respect for the humanity of another person." When Coretta Scott King appeared before a congressional hearing on the bill, she was quizzed on strategies to end teenage crime. At a time when the Clinton administration was promoting volunteerism, piggybacking on that initiative may have made strategic sense—even if it meant playing to a belief that the black community's preeminent problem was teen violence. That no one objected to a characterization of the movement's legacy as one of service or offered an alternative suggests its general acceptance among congressional representatives.[24]

In congressional discourse, then, the civil rights movement was effectively assimilated to a pluralist story line. Change, in that account, is incrementally effected through electoral political channels and intermediate organizations, for example, civic associations, social clubs, and self-help groups, not through disruptive collective action. The latter is unnecessary given the existence of multiple avenues for reform. Congressional black representatives never denigrated extra-institutional activism and activists. To the contrary, they acknowledged repeatedly that they were the beneficiaries of past insurgency. However, by recounting King's activism as part of an earlier phase of struggle, as *past,* they portrayed their own careers as its proper successor. Stories of King thus warranted black legislators' claim to represent black interests better than contemporary protest elites could.[25]

KING AS ACTIVISTS REPRESENTED HIM   Black legislators represented Dr. King in a way that legitimated mainstream politics rather than movements as the real legacy of King's movement. How did black activists outside government talk about King? To answer this question, I examined speeches by leading black political figures who were not serving as elected or appointed officials. These included the president of the Children's Defense Fund, Marian Wright Edelman; longtime activist and Rainbow Coalition head, Jesse Jackson; executive director of the NAACP, Benjamin Chavis; chairman of the NAACP, William Gibson; president of the Southern Christian Leadership Conference, Joseph Lowery, and chairman of the Board of Directors of the SCLC, Walter Fauntroy (Fauntroy was a former congressman).

Like congressional representatives, these speakers told commemorative stories about King. But their stories differed in several respects. First, they cast King as a political strategist who was unafraid to use political disruption to further the cause. Indeed, several speakers criticized the popularity of the "I have a dream speech" precisely for its implication that, as Jesse Jackson put it, King was a "passive, pathetic figure"—"a flower in one ear, a dove on the other, 'if I could help somebody,' on his lips." "That's not the Martin Luther King of history," Jackson insisted. In another speech, he observed, "King was no idle dreamer. He was a practical man of action, a leader who understood that change required challenging the structure of entrenched arrangements."[26]

Moral appeal had never been enough to advance the cause of racial equality, these speakers insisted. As the NAACP's Benjamin Chavis noted,

Thirty years ago, Martin Luther King, Jr., made a great speech. But also 30 years ago [Medgar Evers], two months before the March in Washington, June of 1963, was slain in Jackson, Mississippi in the sight of his wife and the sight of his children solely because he was mobilizing brothers and sisters in Mississippi to vote, to go out to vote, to register and to exercise the right to vote.

Like legislators, Chavis invoked King's "I have a dream" speech, but he did so to puncture any illusion that America had responded to King's appeal with acclamation. Other activists emphasized the mobilizing work that had accompanied the 1963 march. Walter Fauntroy declared,

Those who marched on August the 28th, 1963, went on to make that march a great one because they returned home and they contacted their members of Congress and told them, "Don't let your name show up on my ballot in November of 1964 if you haven't voted for the national changes that we marched for on August 28th, 1963." That's why the civil rights bill was to become law within a year after the march on August the 28th, 1963 and a Voting Rights Act and a fair housing bill were to be passed in 1965 and 1966.[27]

Like congressional representatives, these speakers told stories of their relationship to King and represented themselves as King's modern standard bearers—but as activists, not politicians. They often invoked King to criticize the political establishment. Jesse Jackson said, "[E]very morning I wake up and ask myself, 'What would Dr. King have me do today? What would he have expected of me?' I can tell you I know he would have expected me to be right here, standing with working people." And in another speech, referring to the 1963 march, Jackson observed, "Thirty years ago, there was great tension between the change agents of that time and the White House and a Congress frozen in timid action and money-driven, self-perpetuating politics. This is true in 1993." Where congressional leaders tended to group King with cultural and political African American luminaries, these speakers put King in the company of moral reformers and revolutionaries, both black and white: Mahatma Gandhi, Nelson Mandela, Dorothy Day, Tolstoy, and Jesus Christ. In a number of speeches, Marian Wright Edelman grouped King with contemporary activists Elizabeth Glaser, the wife of a Hollywood actor who became an advocate for AIDS funding, and Sarah and Jim Brady, who organized to press for handgun legislation.[28]

Activist speakers were more likely than congressional representatives to quote from King's later speeches and writings. They also used the "we have made progress, but . . ." formulation, following the "but" with hard statistics about the current economic plight of African Americans or calls for economic power. NAACP chair William Gibson said, "And yes, after 30 years, we have gained a small measure of political democracy. But when the contracts are granted in City Hall and the county courthouse and state government, black folk, and other minorities are normally left out." The answer was to mobilize. Jesse Jackson averred, "We must conduct town hall meetings, use boycotts, monitor our government, engage in voter registration, and examine ballot access. . . . We have the power if we shift our attitude and our behavior and turn to each other and plan a mass, mobilized, disciplined action." Both Edelman and Jackson frequently described King's struggle as one in a succession of progressive movements. The civil rights movement had paved the way for mobilization *now*, the next in the narrative of successful struggles. As Edelman put it,

Before the new millennium, you and I must and can compose the third movement by putting the social and economic underpinnings beneath the millions of African American, Asian American, Latino, White, and Native American children left behind when the promise of the civil rights laws and the significant progress of the 1960s and

'70s in alleviating poverty was eclipsed by the Vietnam war, economic recession, and changing national leadership priorities.[29]

In fact, many of the actions that these speakers called for were decidedly nondisruptive. They urged listeners to write to their congresspeople, to treat each other with respect, to take care of children. Although I call them extra-institutional activists, in fact, most of the speakers I just quoted had long and deep relations with Congress and the Democratic Party. Much of their work involved lobbying congressional representatives for favorable legislation. This suggests that their stories about King and the movement were intended to legitimate their position outside the government, and the importance of a protest elite more generally, rather than to get people into the streets.

King as Challenge

Of course, activists aimed to do more than justify their own existence. So did African American congressional representatives. For that reason, they had a stake in *not* recounting the past as past. This is what made their task in commemorating King difficult. As representatives of a constituency whose aspirations were voiced but not realized by the civil rights movement, they had to convince their congressional colleagues that there was much more to be done. They had to warrant a vision of change, not as inevitable, but as federally enacted and as urgent. If collective remembering in the United States is bound to powerful narratives of unity and progress, then African American legislators faced peculiar dilemmas in telling the story of the civil rights movement. How were they to convey not the accomplishments, the steps taken, and the threat averted, but the promises not made good on, the unresolved, the incomplete? How were they to celebrate change achieved through conflict? And how were they to tie remembering to change *now?* These dilemmas were evident in how congressional speakers explained storytelling's purpose.

Black congressional speakers asserted repeatedly that retelling the African American past of collective struggle, individual accomplishment, and national benefit was essential to changing the present. But additional rationales for remembering were also offered. One affirmed that King's contributions were obvious and unforgettable: "Dr. King's stamp upon American history is profound and indelible," as one speaker put it; and another asserted, "His perseverance and leadership is indelibly etched in the minds of all Americans." Recounting King's story celebrated rather than preserved his memory. In another rationale, natural forget-fulness threatened King's legacy ("the moment of civil rights triumph may be a distant memory to some"; "Too many black Americans don't realize the importance and significance of recalling past struggles and achievements and relating those efforts to present day conditions"). Still another rationale held that it was young people, for whom the move-ment had "become ancient history," who were most in need of remedial storytelling. They had to be shown that "they have a responsibility . . . to not just glorify Dr. King as a hero but learn and practice his teachings and beliefs."[30]

Recounting the past was necessary to close a chapter of the past, speak-ers asserted. By remembering, however, we "make sure that the clock is not turned back . . . make sure that we do not repeat that period of our history" for "if we forget the tragic lessons of our history we are doomed to repeat them." The task was "to revel in our history," and contrarily, to "draw back from our history . . . to not have some of the unfortunate con-sequences of our social development repeated." After one congressman concluded his remarks on the 1960 student sit-ins by urging that "the more we can come to grips with that, the more we can put this, parts of history like the sit-ins, behind us, and we can all become indivisible, un-der God, with liberty and justice for all," another speaker corrected him: "I thank the gentleman. I hope we will never put the spirit of the sit-ins behind us." The rhetorical problem is evident. Black congressional story-tellers had to relive the past without forgetting the present. They had to honor the movement's leaders without omitting the unsung heroes. They had to recognize individual fortitude in the face of adversity with-out minimizing the oppressiveness of past conditions. And they had to expose past (and present) suffering without thereby inflaming those who had suffered.[31]

Pervasive in speakers' statements was anxiety, above all, that memory not become nostalgia, that it inspire government action, not substitute for it. Merely remembering was as dangerous as forgetting. "We must do more than keep a memory of a great man," Representative Kweisi Mfume insisted. "We must push further ahead past the pain, the hate, and most of all, the complacency that settles when we forget there is more to be done." Representative Hilliard noted, "It is not a day just to remember him but is a day to be joyful that a man of his caliber came along and set the record straight and changed America." Representative Eleanor Holmes-Norton said, "We should remember not for memory's sake, or for the sake of nostalgia." And Congressman John Lewis remarked, "We are not nostalgic about the past but there are some parts of the past that

I would like to recall." These excerpts show speakers trying to make recounting the past into a special kind of remembering. One speaker introduced his co-celebrants who would "participate in this special order in memory, not just in memory, but in commemoration, I guess, in celebration, of what happened in that little town of Selma." Another argued that "this is a history that we cannot forget; lest we forget, we will surely allow those enemies of democracy who want to restrict the American people's right to vote to wane." And another pleaded, "[L]et us not ever be so brazen, so commonplace that we forget the struggle." The rhetorical awkwardness of these usually eloquent speakers betrays their struggle to make remembering more than celebration and reveals the limits of the commemorative form within which they had to work.[32]

Commemorative Occasions

Black legislative speakers did often forcefully describe a society marked by racial inequality and injustice. But the solution to such conditions was more storytelling. I noted earlier the speaker who asked, "If we stop and reflect on where we have gone since the marches and the sit-ins and boycotts of the 1960s, have we really gone far?" Her answer was to call for "daily efforts to correct the history that is taught to our children." A speaker who emphasized that, despite the work of the civil rights movement, "conditions of homelessness, joblessness, teenage pregnancy, absent fathers, high infant mortality, kids killing kids, and mental and physical illness abound" urged that "[we] constantly remind ourselves and others of the great contributions blacks have made and continue to make to this nation." Senator Carol Moseley-Braun argued that it was "forgetfulness" about "the lessons [King's] life taught us" that had "contributed to the widening gap that remains between the salaries of white and African American workers, the increasing gap between the incomes of middle and lower income African Americans, the continuing segregation of our cities' schools and communities, and the violence among our youth which has reached heights unimaginable even a few years ago." If forgetting had such destructive consequences, then remembering should have equally transformative effects. In that vein, one speaker promised that legislation to commemorate the 1965 Selma to Montgomery March would teach future generations about "those early steps in the civil rights movement that began the road to making the Constitution of this country extend its rights and protections to all of its citizens. For some this will be freedom at last." Another described movement commemorative activities in a project aimed at reducing teen-age pregnancy as essential to building self-esteem and responsible behavior.[33]

Since most of these statements came in commemorative contexts such as Black History Month, King's birthday, and the anniversary of the Voting Rights Act, or in discussions of provisions for official commemoration such as the extension of the King Holiday Commission, it is unsurprising that they concluded with calls for commemoration. But *the majority of King references were made in such contexts*. I noted earlier that the largest number of speeches referring to Dr. King were delivered as part of tributes and on commemorative occasions. In combination with speeches advocating government sponsorship of commemorative activities, they accounted for 275, or 65 percent, of the 420 speeches. Was this simply because tributes dominated congressional speech making? The *Congressional Record* database does not provide the overall number of entries that were tributes relative to entries that were legislative discussions in a congressional session. I therefore chose a two-day period on which the number of overall entries was close to the average (267 entries for March 15 and 16, 1994) and, after discarding procedural entries of the kind discussed earlier, coded the remaining speeches. Of the 266 speeches, 53 (20 percent) were tributes, 9 (3 percent) anniversary speeches, 43 (16 percent) commentaries, 5 (2 percent) speeches calling for commemorative legislation, and 156 (59 percent) speeches about pending legislation. Thus, whereas 65 percent of the speeches referring to King were delivered on commemorative occasions, only 25 percent of all speeches were delivered on such occasions. (Probably there were more tributes and commemorative speeches on holidays, and March 15 and 16 were not holidays. Still, even taking that into account would not substantially reduce the disparity I have described.)

Moreover, African American representatives did not invoke King more often in legislative debates than did white Democrats or Republicans during the 1993 to 1997 period. African American representatives delivered proportionally fewer speeches referring to King in legislative contexts relative to commemorative ones than did white representatives. The largest number of King speeches in a legislative context called for federal response to the wave of church burnings in the South, a measure which enjoyed bipartisan support. The second largest number came in debate related to abortion, and they were more likely to be made by Republicans espousing pro-life positions than by Democrats, white or black. The *Record* reveals, then, an interesting bifurcation: even as African American House and Senate members asserted the importance of remembering in order to bring about tangible change, they did not often invoke the past in substantive legislative discussions.

What prevented them from doing so? One possibility is that they did not believe that invoking King would serve them well in arguing a position in a legislative debate. However, on commemorative occasions, they did often refer to King in talking about persistent racial disparities in health, wealth, and safety, and since legislative debate between 1993 and 1997 covered health care, welfare, toxic waste cleanup, campaign reform, crime, and education, among other things, it is hard to imagine that King's memory would not be a persuasive resource when talking about those issues.

Another possibility is that talking about King and the movement past was seen as inappropriate. Let me suggest a reason why. Whether anything gets done on the floor of Congress has long been debated. Charges that congressional floor debate was mere talk gained force in the context of two trends in the early 1990s. One was representatives' increased attentiveness to their constituents, in part as a result of the media's expanded coverage of congressional activities. For example, until 1979, commemorative legislation, such as naming public buildings or designating special days, accounted for between 1 percent and 10 percent of all legislation. In the 96th Congress, commemorative legislation increased by more than 70 percent and continued to rise, by 1985 accounting for more than one third of all bills signed into law. Attacked for its diversion of money and attention from substantive to purely symbolic concerns, this increase was attributed to congressional representatives' orientation to constituents. A second trend, longer in the making, was the displacement of legislative decision making from the congressional floor to congressional committees and subcommittees and to sites even further removed from public scrutiny. As the writers of the *Encyclopedia of Congress* put it in 1995, "The business of the House is dominated by its committees, and with few exceptions oratory has little discernible impact in the process of proposing, drafting, and voting upon legislation." In fact, committees' autonomy has been formally circumscribed in the last two decades, and amending activity has increased on the floor, but, in the early 1990s, according to the *Encyclopedia* authors, "conventional wisdom holds that floor debate does not change minds." Instead, legislation was widely perceived to be made through the deal-making and lobbying that took place behind closed doors.[34]

One consequence of these developments may have been pressure among congressional representatives to demarcate legislative floor debate both from back-room maneuvering and constituent-driven pomp. Several procedural rules in Congress appear to be means of protecting legislative debate from activities seen as merely symbolic. For example, limiting the duration of one-minute speeches, scheduling them in the morning and at the discretion of the Speaker, and restricting special orders to the end of the day, after legislative business, all serve that function. But there may also have been less explicit pressures to demarcate activities by keeping their characteristic rhetorical styles separate. Refraining from commemorative storytelling during the deliberative work of legislative policymaking would do that. Of course, deliberative discourse has always invoked heroic figures and hallowed tradition. However, the vulnerability of congressional discourse to charges that it involved scant deliberation at all, that it was ritual drama rather than substantive debate, may have made representatives anxious to distinguish making history from memorializing it.

Institutional pressures to separate commemorative storytelling from other forms of discourse may thus account for representatives' infrequent use of stories about Dr. King to criticize policy rather than to affirm it. On legislative occasions, storytelling was at odds with a deliberative rhetorical style, making it difficult to invoke King in debates about substantive policy issues. And on commemorative occasions, storytelling that ended with a call for legislative action was at odds with the privileged genre. The context of their speeches (that it was Martin Luther King, Jr., Day rather than a debate about the budget) encouraged speakers to call for more storytelling rather than for new legislation, more appropriations, better enforcement of existing laws, or an otherwise interventionist federal stance. And in the discussions of health care, welfare, toxic waste cleanup, campaign reform, military defense, crime, education, foreign policy, and telecommunication that took place between 1993 and 1997, the lessons of the civil rights movement were not told.

Paradoxically, then, conventions of storytelling about past insurgency may strengthen institutional politics in two ways. Memorializing dissent enables politicians to legitimate themselves as heirs to an activist past. And if the work of remembering is restricted to special occasions, on which anyone can be honored, from Martin Luther King, Jr., to the constituent whose claim to fame is his stamp collection, then the rest of congressional discourse must be driven by national interests rather than partisan ones, and have tangible rather than symbolic consequences. Stories about King and the movement may have ended up reproducing the legislative institution by their very marginality.

Conclusion

In the early 1990s, black congressional speakers commemorated King in a way that cast electoral politics and community service rather than extra-institutional activism as the legitimate heirs of King and his movement. The Dr. King of black legislators was different from the Dr. King of black activists. The former stood in the company of other African American greats in the worlds of politics, art, and sports. He was the King of "I have a dream . . ." fame, committed to nonviolence and to change through moral witness. His dream had yet to be fully realized, but it was carried on in the work of African American legislators and community volunteers. The latter stood in the company of rebels and revolutionaries. More than unrealized, his legacy was betrayed by continuing economic inequalities as well as by the conservatism of elected officials.

Now, the elected officials' version of the story may have been more successful than activists' version or vice versa, but the fact that both groups continued to use their versions suggests that that was not the case. Rather, the past was apparently malleable enough to serve both activists and officials in their competing tasks. In other cases, that may not be true. For students of social movements, attempts to define the legacy of protest, the kind of activism it warrants, and the truest spokespeople for its aspirations point up important dynamics in the institutionalization of protest. The stewardship of an insurgent past can be a crucial terrain for fighting out continuing leadership claims between protest elites and electoral ones. The question is how much winning the battle over memory counts in gaining recognition as the accepted broker of the group's interests. And what counts as winning? To answer these questions, we might turn to other groups that have made the shift from protest to politics; for example, African National Congress members in South Africa, Irish elected officials associated with Sinn Fein, former Sandinista rebels in Nicaragua, and Solidarity activists in Poland. One can imagine instances in which state officials have so fully appropriated the story of past insurgency that it becomes unavailable for use by those critical of the state. But one can also imagine that a regime that is the self-proclaimed bearer of an insurgent legacy may be open to charges of hypocrisy for its current conservatism. Sociologist Robert S. Jansen found the latter in his study of how Sandinista rebels in Nicaragua and Zapatistas in Mexico appropriated the historical figures that gave names to their movements. In Nicaragua, the Somoza regime barred discussion of Augusto César Sandino after his assassination in 1934. By contrast, the ruling party in Mexico claimed Emiliano Zapata as a hero after his assassination in 1919. This allowed activists more than a half-century later to attack the Mexican government for its betrayal of Zapata's legacy, a powerful ideological resource that the Sandinistas lacked. Stories of the past were *available* to both groups of activists. However, the fact that the Mexican government had claimed the mantle of Zapata's insurgency made it vulnerable to attack on precisely those grounds. This example only points to the need for a fuller understanding of the conditions in which insurgent legacies are more or less useful for officials and for their critics.[35]

For students of collective memory, the case attests to the multiple and conflicting projects within groups often represented as unitary: officials and African Americans, to name two. But the case also points up the inadequacy of an instrumentalist approach by identifying constraints on speakers' ability to use the past. It is not only what actually happened—history in unmediated form—that limits what speakers can do with it. Familiar plot structures also shape the kinds of stories one can tell and the lessons one can derive from them. In addition, however, institutional rules dictate the occasions on which one can tell certain kinds of stories. Black legislators recounted the triumphs and travails of the civil rights movement strategically, but they did so mainly on commemorative occasions. One possible effect, surely not intended, was that their stories of dissent reproduced a view of Congress's policy deliberations as substantive rather than merely symbolic—since the symbolic work of commemoration only took place on occasions reserved for it. This is different than saying that there are political costs to telling a story on the wrong occasion, something that scholars of collective memory have noted. To put it in the language with which I began the chapter, if states have an interest in commemorating the past, they also have an interest in defining some occasions as *non*-commemorative. Certain stories may be difficult to tell because there is simply no occasion on which to tell them.[36]

SEVEN

Conclusion: Folk Wisdom and Scholarly Tales

Prophets and revolutionaries have always known that tales of threat and vengeance, of exodus and redemption, of old wrongs righted and defilement avenged have mobilizing force. Told well, they can lead people to rise up against authorities, ignore the rational calculi that counsel them to free ride on the efforts of others, and court danger, possibly death, in the cause of a triumphal ending. Of course, kings, presidents, and company managers also tell stories. Their tales of threats to the nation or Horatio Algers meeting tests of individual fortitude can make efforts to change the status quo seem ignoble or unnecessary.

So which is it? Is narrative fundamentally subversive or hegemonic? Both. As a rhetorical form, narrative is equipped to puncture reigning verities and to uphold them. At times, it seems as if most of the stories in circulation are subtly or not so subtly defying authorities; at others, as if the most effective storytelling is done by authorities. To make it more complicated, sometimes authorities unintentionally undercut their own authority when they tell stories. And even more paradoxically, undercutting their authority by way of a titillating but politically inconsequential story may actually strengthen it. Dissenters, for their part, may find their stories misread in ways that support the very institutions they are challenging.

For those interested in the relations between storytelling, protest, and politics, this all suggests two analytical tasks. One is to identify the features of narrative that allow it to achieve certain rhetorical effects. The other is to identify the social conditions in which those rhetorical effects are likely to be politically consequential. The surprise is that scholars of political processes have devoted so little attention to either task. While attesting to narrative's rhetorical force, many scholars have accounted for that force exclusively in terms of a story's capacity to elicit an emotional identification with its protagonists. But that misses several possibilities: that we may identify emotionally with a story but not feel called upon to think or do anything much different than we have done; that effecting real change may require people to identify with experiences that are very far from their own; and that, told badly, stories may discourage an emotional identification rather than foster it. As I noted in chapter 5, perhaps those opposing the antisodomy statute that was upheld in the notorious *Bowers v. Hardwick* case would have done better to tell the story of Michael Hardwick, the man who was prosecuted for having consensual sex with a man in his own home. But told the wrong way, the story of Michael Hardwick, who was an admitted former drug user and an enthusiastic party-giver, might have hardened stereotypes about gay men rather than debunked them. We need to ask what it is about narrative that produces an empathetic understanding of a marginalized group's experiences and needs. We should ask the same thing of the other capacities that analysts have claimed for narrative. What enables personal storytelling to reveal the false universality of supposedly universal standards rather than simply producing competing idiosyncratic claims? When is narrative's reliance on figurative language evocative rather than confusing? Most broadly, what are politically effective narratives effective in doing and how, rhetorically, do they do it?

Stories' political effects are also a function of the social contexts in which they are told. That is true, first, in the sense that configurations of power and resources determine what kind of a hearing particular stories secure. It is also true in the sense that whether a story is told in court, in a movement speak-out, or to a reporter influences not only what is said but also how it is interpreted. In other words, the same words may have different meanings, credibility, and authority depending on their setting. A complainant in small claims court who tells an otherwise credible story of having been bilked by his employer loses his case because his story fails to specify the straightforward chain of causality expected of testimony in court. A woman who tells the story of her rape loses her case because, like many victims of trauma, she has filled in missing parts of the story as she has retold it, and now she violates the jury's expectation that true stories remain identical in their retelling. The small claims complainant is hurt by narrative conventions that are peculiar to American courts. The rape victim is hurt by broader cultural conventions that operate within legal settings but extend beyond them.

Norms of storytelling like these are prime ground for sociological investigation. With important exceptions, however, sociologists have tended to style themselves literary critics in studying storytelling. They have spent more time interpreting texts than studying the distribution of storytelling authority or identifying the social epistemologies of storytelling that guide its use. The latter, in particular, has something valuable to offer students of contentious politics. It focuses on how culture constrains challenges to prevailing relations of power and privilege, but it does so without representing challengers as either mystified or stupid. Instead, it asks, What is narrative's epistemological status relative to other discursive forms in an institutional setting? And how does that status shape what those wanting to effect change can do with stories?

In this chapter, I take up those questions once more and draw together the answers I have given in previous chapters. Then I pose an additional question: Should scholars of contentious politics be telling stories as well as studying them? As I have done in previous chapters, I ask what storytelling is seen as good for and bad at. Predictably, I find the same ambivalence about storytelling among scholars as among the public deliberators, legislators, activists, journalists, and laypeople whom I have talked about in previous chapters. I trace the effects of that ambivalence on analyses of political contention and make some suggestions for how to tell non-canonical stories. Finally, I move from the sociology of storytelling that I have developed here to sketch the outlines of a broader sociology of discursive forms.

Canonicity

In stories, events seem to yield their own meaning. The point of the story is not asserted by an authoritative narrator, nor is it authorized by the presentation of theory and evidence in conformity with an accepted logic of inquiry. Rather, the way in which events unfold reveals insights that seem lodged in the events themselves.

If stories did indeed work this way, we can see why they would be politically powerful, both for authorities and challengers. But narrative's self-authorization is threatened from two directions: what I have referred to as narrative's canonicity and its interpretability. With respect to the first, events in a story seem coherent, true, and normatively salient because they conform to stories we have heard before. Narratives depend on plot, and plot depends on previous plots, on a common, conventional, stock of plots. Narratives never reproduce prior narratives exactly. What would be the point? But to stray too far from the familiar is to risk unintelligibility. Canonicity threatens narrative's self-authorization in the sense that it is not the way events unfold in this story that yields a normative point but rather events' accordance with sequences known to us from prior stories.

In some ways, canonical plots serve those challenging the status quo. Groups can gain moral authority and political capital by linking themselves to celebrated revolutionaries, dissidents, and freedom fighters. Leaders secure followers by recounting their personal transformation from apathy to commitment and blindness to clarity in terms known from other stories. Movement groups withstand setbacks by interpreting them as narratively familiar tests of character on the way to victory. But challengers also chafe against the constraints of familiar stories. The African American legislators I described in chapter 6 should have been able to use the story of the civil rights movement to call for action against the continuing obstacles to racial equality. After all, that movement is now honored by most groups along the political spectrum. But the narratives of progress and unity that are built into American commemorative discourse made it difficult for black legislators to claim that the movement's aims were unfulfilled without seeming to denigrate the movement.

The problem goes further. Insofar as those wanting to effect social change must debunk beliefs that have the status of common sense, familiar stories are more obstacle than resource. Told and retold in different settings and in many versions, they have the rich detail and particularity that seem to capture reality in all its complexity. When they give form to well-known binary oppositions—man/woman, moral/political, victimhood/agency, autonomy/dependence—their power comes in part from their reference to other oppositions, all of which privilege one side over the other. Challengers' claims are heard against the backdrop of those familiar stories. Challengers cannot ignore such stories. Instead, they must show that the canonical story misses crucial aspects of reality. But the stories that they can offer as alternatives are likely to seem abstract and narratively thin by comparison.

For example, as I showed in chapter 5, when feminists brought sex discrimination suits against employers, they struggled to prove that women were underrepresented in higher-status, traditionally male jobs because they were discriminated against and not because they had no interest in those jobs. Arguing that women *wanted* the jobs put them at odds with a familiar story in which girls grow up to want women's work, and men grow up to want men's work. To judges, feminists seemed to be saying that women were just like men, something that flew in the face of good sense. Similarly, the women who appeared in criminal court for having killed their abusive husbands found that their stories of victimization sometimes secured them judges' solicitude but not a recognition that they were rational agents who had struck back at their abusers to save their own lives. Even their own lawyers were reluctant to hear a story in which they were both victims and rational actors. Only two stories seemed to make sense to lawyers, judges, and juries. In one, the defendant was a victim: passive, helpless, and irrational. She might successfully plead temporary insanity but not self-defense since that would require that she was competent to assess the danger she was in. In the other story, the defendant was rational—but was feigning her victimization. With only these two stories available, the plea of self-defense was effectively denied to abused women. Here and elsewhere, canonical stories have often discredited, trumped, or distorted challengers' stories.

For activists, familiar story lines shape not only what they are up against in their interactions with the public and authorities but what they are up against within the movement. As they assess different courses of action, familiar stories about what has worked or failed in the past make some options seem radical, moral, fitting, even feasible, and make others seem conservative, immoral, inappropriate, or beyond the realm of possibility. The challenge for the analyst is to account for why certain stories take on the status of common sense and how they rule out tactical options—but to do so without assuming that those processes occur only in people's heads. In chapter 2, I showed that the stories that students told of the 1960 sit-ins produced a conception of protest that for a time competed with the standard one. The sit-ins were moral *and* political, expressive *and* instrumental. As the sit-in stories circulated in the larger movement, however, they were absorbed into a more familiar storyline, one in which protest was moral *or* political, spontaneous *or* strategic. The result was that for the rest of the decade—and perhaps still—people saw direct action as nonpolitical and as requiring neither discipline nor planning.

In chapter 3, I explored more closely the process by which canonical stories set the terms of strategic action. In the mid-1960s, activists in the Student Nonviolent Coordinating Committee rejected the consensus-based and decentralized organizational form that had made them famous. Contrary to what analysts then and since have said, the problem with participatory democracy was neither that it had become unwieldy in an organization that had grown in size and political stature nor that it was inconsistent with the group's new ideological commitments. Rather, an organizational form that had appeared just a short time earlier as practical, political, and black had come to seem ideological, self-indulgent and—no coincidence—as white. The stories that SNCC workers told of their organizational travails at the time show the emergence of a metonymic structure linking participatory democracy with the excessive role of whites in the organization. No one could say just how abandoning participatory democracy would curb the role of whites and, just as important, no one was really asked to. The metonymic association of whites with the excesses of participatory democracy made it possible for black SNCC workers to talk about the virtues of an all-black organization, something that had been difficult to do in an interracial group of friends. But it also enshrined, for SNCC activists and those who came after them, a view of participatory democracy as morally virtuous but politically impractical. To argue differently would have been to challenge a whole cluster of overlapping stories: ones about blacks and whites, moral protest and strategic protest, and democracy and efficiency. So canonical stories gain force from their resonance with other canonical stories, each lending the others the kind of complexity and variation that seem to approximate real life.

Interpretability

None of this should be taken to mean that challengers can only tell canonical stories and that storytelling inevitably reproduces the status quo. Again, students who participated in the sit-ins were able, for a time, to tell a new story about protest, one that opened up new possibilities for action. The abused women who pressed for legal reform were able to draw attention to the cultural norms that contributed to domestic abuse, even as they told the most personal stories of abuse. In these cases and others, challengers departed from familiar plot lines in ways that unsettled the assumptions on which those plot lines rested.

They did so by using literary tropes such as metaphor, irony, ellipsis, and point of view to capture unfamiliar experiences and limn new political possibilities. Such devices worked because we expect multiple meanings in stories. This is a second way in which narrative's self-authorization is threatened. If the normative point of the story seems given by the events themselves, the givenness is tentative. We expect ambiguity in narrative, that is, that words and events will not mean what at first they seem to. We expect to have to work to interpret what is going on. We know that things could have turned out differently but also that a different moral could be derived from the same events told differently. Stories in that sense convey not only the contingency of social life but its indeterminacy. Of course, we encounter ambiguity in other discursive forms: in arguments, analyses, and instructions as much as stories. But we do not often acknowledge the figurative character of language in these other forms, and we are less open to questioning our own initial interpretations and to recognizing the legitimacy of multiple interpretations.

Narrative's canonicity and its interpretability, then, ramify in opposite directions. Say that a member of a marginalized group recounts her life story to political decision makers in the hope that her experience will expose the inadequacy of a current policy. Her story may be misinterpreted or dismissed because it is heard against the backdrop of familiar stories about her group or her experience, stories that make her story ring untrue, idiosyncratic, or no different from the stories that are already known. Narrative's canonicity militates against a real hearing. Alternatively, the petitioner uses figurative language to tell her story. She uses metaphor to draw attention to unnoticed connections, irony to undercut conventional wisdom, combines a parable with an analysis to subvert the expectations of genre. She leaves a great deal unsaid. Decision makers may hear this story as different from the expected one. They may begin to empathize with experiences remote from their own and recognize the legitimacy of needs they had never acknowledged. They may even begin to see that the values they thought were universal do not in fact apply equally to all.

Effective stories can be ambiguous in several ways. One kind of ambiguity in the stories I have discussed stemmed from narrative's *polysemy*. Words had multiple meanings. Events yielded different sorts of normative conclusions. For example, calling the lunch counter sit-ins "spontaneous" meant not that they were unplanned but that they were local, urgent, and moral (meanings not obviously contained in the word). It also meant that the sit-ins were both willed and unwilled (*contrary* meanings contained in the word). That multiplicity of meanings opened up the possibility of an understanding of protest, and a practice of protest, that was fundamentally different than the conventional one.

Narratives' polysemous character may also help individuals and groups to forge coalitions across difference. As I suggested in chapter 1, high-profile crime stories seem to have galvanized coalitions to press for legislative reform not because the stories' normative conclusions were so clear but because they were unclear. The possibility of interpreting the story in different ways allowed groups with different stakes in the issue to sign on to a common project of reform. Something similar may occur at an individual level. When people deliberated about the future of the World Trade Center site, they sometimes claimed to be corroborating earlier speakers' stories by telling stories of their own. In fact, their stories often made quite another point. "My thoughts, exactly," one participant said in beginning her very different story. But such formulations allowed deliberators to advance contrary positions or compromise positions—all without antagonizing anyone by openly disagreeing with them. Narrative's ambiguity, in these cases, preserved the fiction of agreement long enough for people to work through to areas of agreement.

A second kind of ambiguity was *perspectival*. It was not easy to tell from whose point of view a story was being told. Either the identity of the narrator was unclear, or the privileged point of view shifted among different people and an omniscient narrator, or the point of view was inconsistent with the kind of person the story's narrator seemed to be. Perspectival ambiguity may have created authority where it did not exist before. In the sit-in narratives, students denied agency at precisely the point where it mattered, in accounting for the emergence of protest. A three-dot ellipsis in coming-to-political-consciousness stories similarly represented the experience of becoming an activist without explicitly describing it. The device served both to engage the reader and to protect the narrator's authority from challenge, since he or she was not positing how the shift to political consciousness actually occurred. In the stories told by abused women, the coolly appraising voice of the narrator as she reflected on her experience was evident rather than concealed. Events were thus rendered less immediate—and were therefore, one might imagine, less likely to secure the audience's empathy. But the narrator's active role in the narration countered an impression of her helplessness and passivity.

In their stories of domestic abuse, narrators also took an ironical stance in recounting their susceptibility to the romantic blandishments of the men who would become their abusers. Even as they bemoaned their naïveté, they drew readers' attention to the cultural norms that were in part responsible for their failure to leave an abusive relationship. Finally, the stories told by African American congressional representatives were simultaneously their own stories, Dr. King's story, and the story of African Americans' continued struggle for full citizenship. One representative declared, "[W]e will reach Dr. King's promised land. And just like Dr. King, I may not be with you when you get there, but if this day comes after my work on earth is done, I assure you that I will be there in spirit." He warranted his claim to represent African Americans' interests not only by joining with them in their quest to fulfill Dr. King's dream but by recreating King's relationship to his audience, and indeed, speaking King's words.

A third kind of ambiguity, which I referred to as *semantic dissonance,* stemmed from the combination of words, ideas, or emotions that are not usually combined. If the first, polysemous, form of ambiguity relied on gaps in the text (in which multiple meanings may have been at work) and the second on elisions among perspectives, this one relied on seeming contradictions. Sit-in participants described themselves as "weary with waiting" for the full citizenship rights to which they were constitutionally entitled. Weariness would seem to call for rest, and yet the students demanded action; they would wait no longer. The initial discordance of the phrase invited the reader to read more closely, to make sense of an experience that was not like his or her own. In the stories told by abused women, seemingly contradictory phrases and odd juxtapositions were common. One woman realized that she wanted to live as she was "sliding down [her] refrigerator." Another said, "Many times I said, if he don't kill me, I'm sure I'll kill myself, cause it was that painful. I know I want to live"—with nothing between the statements to explain her complete turnaround. A third (this one fictional) explained, "He demolished me. He destroyed me. And I never stopped loving him," with the "and" connecting two things that should not have been connected. Formulations like these invited the audience to try to figure out how the connections could have seemed self-evident to the narrator. They helped audiences to understand how a woman could have been so abused and so love her abuser or how the cultural expectations of romantic love could be simultaneously so unrealistic and so powerful. They helped the reader to empathize with someone who was very different from her.

The three types of ambiguity I have just described were politically effective in different ways. Ambiguity as polysemy made it possible for people and groups to forge agreement across diverse inerests. Perspectival ambiguity created new foundations for political authority. Semantic dissonance made it possible for audiences to empathize with remote experiences. As I argued above, however, narrative's rhetorical capacities are more likely to be realized in certain contexts than others. We can imagine situations in which the forms of ambiguity I have just described would have different effects. For example, if the people deliberating online about the future of the World Trade Center had been charged with making a decision that was binding and that would affect them all directly, they probably would have been more resistant to rhetorical moves that glossed over differences. A deliberator in that situation would not have let pass so easily a fellow deliberator's claim that a story was corroborating her own opinion when it was not. The groups that coalesced around a reform agenda in response to a high-profile crime story probably would not have allowed a group whose goals were antithetical rather than tangential to their own to sign on to the coalition on the basis of a radically different interpretation of the story. In these instances, narrative's polysemy would not have been a resource. With respect to perspectival ambiguity, we may ask when it is confusing to obscure or multiply points of view and when it undermines rather than strengthens the narrator's authority. And with respect to narrative's reliance on dissonant elements, we may ask, When does the seeming contradiction estrange the audience rather than compel an attempt to understand difference? One could argue that for abused women, oddly juxtaposing disparate ideas and emotions was a risky strategy since the task was to make the narrator seem reasonable. This, like the other questions, only suggests the need for more research on the social and institutional conditions in which narrative's rhetorical capacities are likely to be realized.

Ambivalence

So far, I have argued that if stories' dependence on prior stories predisposes them to reproduce the familiar, their interpretability makes them useful in gaining a hearing for the new. Narrative's capacity to produce multiple meanings, to elide forms of authority, and to hold opposites in productive tension all make it a useful rhetorical tool with which to question the existing distribution of power. Again, narrative has that power because we expect ambiguity in stories. Indeed, we tend to see it as prime discursive expression of the literary as against the logical, the symbolic as against the literal.

But this view may also account for a popular ambivalence about narrative. Stories are seen as authentic but also as artful. They are seen as morally compelling unless they are trumped by political or economic imperatives. To "tell one's story" means to express one's most authentic self; to "tell a story" means to lie; and to say that something is "just a story" means that it has little claim to authority. That we see narrative in different, even contradictory, ways is hardly surprising. We have similarly different ideas of love, thinking about it sometimes in romantic, mythic terms and sometimes in terms of compromise, commitment, and hard work. We think of technology as both progressive and dangerous. I would argue that our views of narrative are even more contradictory because authentic and deceptive truly are opposites. But rather than seeing this divergence as culturally functional, as sociologists like Ann Swidler have done, we can hypothesize that it redounds to the benefit of some groups more than others. If narrative is seen in terms of emotional/rational, female/male, particular/universal, folkloric/scientific, cultural/political oppositions, then when members of lower-status groups tell stories, they are more likely to be tagged with the negative poles of those oppositions. In other words, if a woman or a person of color tells a story, he or she may be questioned about the reasonableness, generalizability, or political seriousness of the story. When a man or a white person tells a story, it may be heard as an analysis or an argument. Even if it is heard as a story, it is less likely to elicit concerns about its credibility.[1]

In my analysis of deliberation about the future of the World Trade Center site in chapter 4, I found something different: that narrative authority was stratified not by *group* but by *setting*. Women were more likely than men to tell stories rather than give reasons in order to back up their opinions. But the fact that men as much as women used stories to back up opinions that they thought might be unpopular suggests that storytelling was not devalued by its association with women. Nor were deliberators any less likely to respond to women's stories seriously than they were to men's. The disparity between reason-giving and storytelling appeared in the kinds of discussions that elicited storytelling. People were much less likely to back up their claims with stories in discussions of transportation, housing, and economic development than they were in discussions of the planned memorial and broad themes in rebuilding. In their comments about storytelling, deliberators made clear why that was the case. Storytelling was seen as normatively powerful when it came to issues of culture and memory; powerless when it came to issues of policy and finance. The restriction of narrative to some topics had indirect but potentially important effects for disadvantaged groups. Storytelling conventions reproduced a view of policy as problem solving rather than politics. That, in turn, may have made it more difficult for groups who were traditionally excluded from policy elites' decision making to register their preferences, even as they were invited to do just that.

A similar restriction of storytelling to certain occasions operated on the House and Senate floors. As I said earlier, when African American legislators told stories of Dr. King and the civil rights movement to argue that the movement's work remained unfinished, they were up against the generic conventions of progress and unity that structure American commemorative discourse. They were also up against the norms that restricted commemorative storytelling to occasions in Congress when legislators celebrated loyal constituents, important political figures, and historic dates. Such occasions were temporally separated from the work of congressional deliberation and were generally seen as having little effect on the legislative process. Moreover, the commemorative context of African American legislators' storytelling led them to end their stories not with calls for legislative reform but with calls for more storytelling. The result was that storytellers themselves helped to curb the impact of the civil rights movement on policymaking. At the same time, they reproduced a view of Congress's policy deliberations as substantive rather than symbolic—since the symbolic work of commemoration only took place on occasions reserved for it.

So institutional conventions of storytelling influence what people can do strategically with stories. In the previous pages, I have described the narrative conventions that operate in legal adjudication, media reporting, television talk shows, congressional debate, and public deliberation. Sociolinguists have documented such conventions in other settings: in medical intake interviews, for example, parole hearings, and jury deliberations. One could certainly generate a catalogue of the institutional conventions of storytelling. To some extent, those conventions reflect the peculiarities of the institution as it has developed historically. They also serve practical functions; some explicit, others less so. I have argued that the lines institutions draw between suitable and unsuitable occasions for storytelling or for certain kinds of stories serve to legitimate the institution. Allowing complainants in small claims court to tell their own stories distinguishes small claims court from higher courts, while penalizing complainants for telling the kinds of stories they tell in everyday conversations distinguishes small claims court from a nonlegal setting. Reserving storytelling in Congress for explicitly symbolic occasions defines other occasions by contrast as nonsymbolic. Discouraging storytelling in policy-oriented discussions in a public deliberative forum casts such discussions as more properly the purview of experts than the public.

As these examples suggest, while institutions have different norms of storytelling, storytelling does some of the same work in many institutions. It does so because of broadly shared assumptions about narrative's epistemological status. Stories are generally thought to be more affecting but less authoritative than analysis, in part because narrative is associated with women rather than men, the private sphere rather than the public one, and custom rather than law. Of course, conventions of storytelling and the symbolic associations behind them are neither unitary nor fixed. Nor are they likely to be uniformly advantageous for those in power and disadvantageous for those without it. Narrative's alignment along the oppositions I noted is complex. For example, as I showed in chapter 5, Americans' skepticism of expert authority gives those telling stories clout. In other words, we may contrast science with folklore (with science seen as much more credible), but we may also contrast it with common sense (with science seen as less credible). Contrary to the lamentation of some media critics and activists, when disadvantaged groups have told personal stories to the press and on television talk shows, they have been able to draw attention not only to their own victimization but to the social forces responsible for it.

Leverage also comes from the fact that popular beliefs about how stories operate and what they are good for change over time. Indeed, effective political strategy may come from working the line between what is currently appropriate and inappropriate. In that vein, activists have sometimes challenged not only institutionalized narratives but institutionalized ways of evaluating narrative. For example, the AIDS activists who secured representation for people with HIV/AIDS on research review panels were not just ensuring the recognition of their collective interests by those making funding decisions. Challenging the opposition between science and story, they argued successfully that the science would be better if it attended to the accounts of those suffering from the disease.[2]

Should disadvantaged groups tell stories? Yes. They should not be afraid to tell stories that are accomplished in a literary sense. Such stories can mobilize support and participation, elicit empathy and understanding on the part of authorities and potential allies, forge coalitions across difference, and begin to limn political possibilities beyond our current political idiom. Just as the best novelists both hew to generic conventions and transcend them, so political challengers can break the hold of canonical stories on common sense by telling stories in new ways. To do so is not an exercise in spin or bad faith. It does not require that disadvantaged groups stop themselves from recounting their experiences honestly and authentically. To the contrary, speaking from the heart probably means speaking in a more literary fashion than challengers have often done when they have concentrated instead on generating a simple, single message.

At the same time, in their efforts to develop good strategy, activists should be aware of the ways in which their own reliance on familiar stories may unnecessarily circumscribe their strategic options. Familiar stories about the organization's past, as well as about the movement's past and about contention generally, may make some options seem unnecessarily unrealistic or inappropriate. In particular, metonymic associations may operate to rule out options not because there is any evidence of a particular tactic's inefficiency or ideological inconsistency but because it has become identified with a group that is unpopular for other reasons. Finally, activists should work not only on revising canonical stories but on revising conventions of storytelling. They should debunk popular assumptions about what makes a narrative credible, should reveal that justifications for the status quo that pose as expert opinion or natural fact are "just stories," and should push for a redistribution of storytelling authority.

Scholars Telling Stories

If groups challenging the status quo should tell stories, should the scholars who study those groups? Academics have been no more immune to the recent enthusiasm for storytelling than the managers, journalists, and politicians described in chapter 1. In fields ranging from anthropology to law, neuroscience, and urban planning, scholars have taken up narrative as a method as well as an object of analysis. Within sociology, the call for narrative by comparative historical scholars has been especially interesting since scholars in that field have long sought to distinguish their methods from those of historians, sometimes by denigrating narrative relative to methods of multiple case comparison. I want to consider briefly the arguments for narrative that historical sociologists have made in order to broach the possibility that popular epistemologies of storytelling may operate in their analyses just as much as those of lay people and activists. Again, my interest is in how those epistemologies may limit options—here, analytical rather than tactical ones.

For a number of historical sociologists writing today, narrative analysis of historical episodes such as revolutions or civil wars can provide the historical detail and texture lacking in non-narrative analyses. It can also capture the contingency of historical developments, the intersection of multiple causal paths, the importance of temporal sequencing, and the power of agency and events to transform structures. Embracing narrative does not mean renouncing the project of generalizable causal explanation, historical sociologists now say. To the contrary, it can assist in that project: Narrative analysis can show that a detailed historical account of a set of events in all their idiosyncrasy is nevertheless consistent with a macrocausal argument; it can rule out rival explanations; and it can generate new and better questions. Narrative can be combined with other strategies of causal analysis, for example, with a Millsean method of agreement and difference and/or with ordinal methods for grasping partial causation. Told in the right way, narratives can avoid becoming, as James Mahoney puts it, "mere description" or "story telling."[3]

The last statement is curious. If narrative is better than story, then what is story? Let me consider the claims made for methodological narrativism by Andrew Abbott, Ronald Aminzade, Kevin Fox Gotham and William G. Staples; Larry Griffin; James Mahoney; Jill Quadagno and Stan Knapp; and Robin Stryker. Strikingly, none of the authors I have mentioned ever define "story." They do frequently contrast narrative and story in defining *narrative* but in ways that make it difficult to identify just what the difference between the two is. For example, both Larry Griffin and Robin Stryker use historian Lawrence Stone's definition of narrative: "the organization of material in a chronologically sequential order and the focusing of the content into a single coherent story, albeit with subplots" (Stryker paraphrases the same statement as follows: "Narratives . . . organize material into chronological order to tell stories about what happened"). Stone himself actually uses *story* and *narrative* interchangeably. But narrative's champions in historical sociology do not seem to use the terms interchangeably. Abbott does do so, referring to narrative "in the generic sense of process, or story." But the other authors I mentioned distinguish between the two terms. For example, Stryker observes that a "narrative is a story of what happened"—a statement that would be tautological if the two words meant the same thing. Narratives "do more than tell a story," Quadagno and Knapp write.[4]

So what is the difference between story and narrative? It is not obviously that story refers to events as they happened and narrative to the representation of those events. Nor is it that story refers to a bare-bones, unembellished representation of events, along the lines of the *fabula/sjuzhet* distinction of Russian formalists. The difference is not that story is descriptive and narrative explanatory. To the contrary, Griffin writes, stories present "an artful blend of explanation and interpretation," and both Stryker and Quadagno and Knapp refer to narrative's explanatory dimension without implying that story lacks such a dimension. The difference is not that narrative provides a certain *kind* of explanation. Aminzade describes "analytic narratives" as "theoretically structured stories about coherent sequences of motivated actions," but he is not clear on whether the theoretical structure defines a narrative or an "analytic narrative," since in the previous sentence he refers to "narrative"—without the qualifier "analytic"—as what historians use to "capture the unfolding of social action over time in a manner sensitive to the order in which events occur." The distinction between narrative and story is not that narrative is the structure of events and story is the point they yield. This is something that Griffin at one point suggests in commenting that narratives are marked by "the consistency of the theme, or story," but then seems to deny in the next sentence, when he refers to "the telling of the central theme as a story," as if story is one way to convey the central theme, not the theme itself.[5]

The difference, finally, is not even that narrative is good and story bad. Certainly *narrative* is the privileged term in these authors' discussions. But in at least two ways narrative seems to aspire to story. To tell a story is to capture events in their full immediacy, close to the way things really happened, albeit with excessive detail. Stories here are implicitly contrasted to the theoretical abstraction characteristic of case comparison. Even as scholars deny the possibility of a pretheorized historical reality, then, their use of *story* seems to point to such a reality. Narrative aspires to story, second, in the sense that stories both recount events and convey their larger cultural significance. Historian Lawrence Stone, approvingly cited by several of the authors I mentioned, describes stories as organized by a "pregnant principle." The examples he gives indicate the grand scope of such stories: "Thucydides' theme was the Peloponnesian wars and their disastrous effects upon Greek society and politics; Gibbon's the decline and fall of the Roman empire; Macaulay's the rise of a liberal participatory constitution in the stresses of revolutionary politics." Even as narrativists bemoan stories' lack of explanatory rigor, they are drawn to its capacity to make a point, a big point. So, story is something more than narrative since it conveys the significance of recounted events, or better, it turns incidents into events. And story is something less than narrative: close to a description of events that does not go beyond the particular. In historical sociologists' brief, story is the kind of unnamed background, both positive and negative, in relation to which narrative has value.[6]

Of what consequence is this ambivalent view of storytelling? That it may underestimate the extent to which historical accounts are shaped by fidelity to good storytelling. Each of the things that narrative is supposed to be good at illuminating—temporal sequence, causal complexity, the power of agency against structure, people's historical experience of social processes—are more influenced by the narrative form of the analysis than these analysts recognize. Take narrative's reliance on a clear beginning, middle, and end. Since we take the beginning of the story as the beginning of when things start to matter ("once upon a time"), we may not question the chronological starting point of an analysis, even though a different starting point would yield a different analysis. Or take narrative's dependence on characters whose actions drive events and whose fates tender normative conclusions. The protagonists of stories stand in for larger groups or identities, yet stories often do not specify the criteria for their representativeness. Difference within groups or in experiences may be obscured as a result. In analyses of past contention, we may talk about "challengers," that is, the story's protagonists, without fully exploring their internally differentiated, tenuously unified, and emergent character. Or we may confuse movements with the formal organizations that compose them. Organizations become characters with goals and motives; the story of their birth and metamorphosis becomes the movement; their demise becomes the end of the movement.[7]

Champions of narrative have recognized some of the dangers that come along with narrative's capacity to convey causal complexity. Complexity may be had at the expense of theoretical parsimony, they have pointed out. Narrative therefore should be integrated with other techniques of causal analysis, especially case comparison, they argue. Another danger stems from the fact that narratives smuggle explanation into description, thus obscuring the fact that what came before a particular development may not be responsible for it. Narratives relax the demands of causal explanation. "Following, not verifying, the story is essential to successful narrative," Griffin observes. He recommends that analysts pose counterfactuals at critical causal junctures to determine whether a particular event would have occurred had certain antecedent conditions not been present.[8]

However, that analytical strategy does not deal adequately with the possibility that familiar narratives are built into the very concepts that analysts use simply to recount events. This is to say more than that concepts have theoretical underpinnings and that to choose a concept is to adopt a hypothesis. Narrative is distinctive as a rhetorical form not only in its synthesis of description and explanation but in its synthesis of explanation with normative prescription. The story's end both makes sense of events that preceded it and tenders a moral conclusion, one that is familiar from prior stories. If histories of interpretation are built into the concepts that analysts use, what does that mean for historical analysis? A concept may gain its power less from its capacity to illuminate particulars of the case than to find in the case familiar moral lessons. Analysts may neglect questions and lines of analysis not because they are incongruous with a particular theoretical framework but because they are normatively awkward.[9]

In that vein, sociologist Margaret Somers argues that sociological conceptions of agency reflect a story that goes back to sociology's founding about the liberation of modern society from the shackles of traditionalism. For early sociologists, agency was defined as "freedom from . . ." with the dots signaling all that characterized traditional society. But since society was understood through a naturalism that posited universal laws of social development, agency was understood in terms of the lone individual confronting all the forces of society. That made it difficult even to consider the social construction of agency since it seemed to suggest one more way in which the individual was constrained by the power of society. Here is another story built into an analytic concept: as political scientist Lisa Disch tells it, feminists over the last thirty years have championed personal storytelling as a counter to the false universality of abstract argument. To privilege *voice* against abstraction has been to acknowledge that all perspectives are partial. But it has also meant giving up any ground from which to probe how voice is authorized in historical accounts. As Disch's experience with a Holocaust survivor attests, to talk about the narrative conventions shaping people's personal stories is tantamount to saying that the storyteller is lying. Joan Scott tells a similar story about "experience," which has come to be seen as the bedrock of historical analysis (by orthodox historiographers as much as by their opponents). With experience conceptualized as possessed by individual selves, it has been difficult to examine the historical constitution of the selves who are doing the experiencing. In sum, historical sociologists have claimed narrative's superior capacity to represent temporal sequence, causal complexity, people's lived experience, and their agency. But each one of these concepts has a history that has naturalized certain questions and rendered others difficult to pose. The specifically narrative dimension of these histories suggests that the difficulty is as much normative as conceptual.[10]

What is the alternative? Is there a way to do narrative analysis without reproducing narrative's conventional and normative character? One way is to tell stories in less literary fashion; the other is to tell them in more literary fashion. The first requires that we recognize how stories' form drives our questions and conclusions. So, we should scrutinize the points at which we choose to begin and end our accounts, and consider whether our analysis might be different if the story started or ended at a different point. We should ask whether the entities that act in our accounts are as distinct and coherent as characters in a story. We can scrutinize the operation of metaphor, metonymy, and ellipsis in the texts we write, asking what explanatory and, possibly, normative work is being done by the particular trope.

We might also join stories with nonstoried representations of historical processes. Historical sociologists' call to integrate narrative with other methods of causal inference is in this vein. As I noted, Larry Griffin goes further in urging an "interrogation and cross-examination" of narrative sequences aimed at making explicit the causal linkages that are being posited among events. Other analysts, too, have sought to exploit narrative's capacity to capture eventfulness while refusing its mode of demonstrating causality. For example, Peter Bearman and his colleagues have used network methods to model connections among events as a way to specify the relevant beginnings and endings of historical episodes. Andrew Abbott has used optimal matching techniques to account for the structure of professional careers and the history of welfare states.[11]

Rather than representing temporal sequences in ways that are less literary, we might also do so in ways that are more literary. Just as metaphors can hint at possibilities that lie beyond our current political repertoire, they can hint at possibilities that lie beyond our current analytical repertoire. This is what Griffin's proposal for a "cross-examination and interrogation" of narrative does: interrogation and cross-examination are effective metaphors for very different modes of causal inference. Other scholars have used the metaphor of psychoanalysis to describe the researcher's relationship with her subjects and a "disciplined dialogue" to describe the relationship between theory and methods. We might consider still other metaphors: for example, conversation or deliberation. Another strategy is to multiply points of view in the stories we tell. The object is not to suggest that if we could represent all people's perspectives, they would add up to one complete picture. Nor is it to substitute authenticity for evidence as the basis for textual authority. It is, however, the first step to questioning how supposedly irreducible vantage points and the identities that are attached to them are constructed in the first place. We might exploit the literary tradition of the story-within-the-story in order to historicize the concepts and conventions that guide historical analysis. Exposing the normative commitments that undergird our own concepts of agency, interest, voice, and experience may help to historicize those concepts in the lives of the people we study by opening up analytical possibilities that have dropped out of our own conceptual lexicons.[12]

Finally, we can explore the institutional work done by our disciplinary conventions of narrative, that is, our expectations about when narrative is appropriate and what relation it is thought to bear to logic, experience, voice, and other foundational principles. We should explore the legitimating work that is done for a discipline or an approach by the boundary drawn between narrative and non-narrative, or between different sorts of narrative, or, as in the example I gave before, between narrative and story.

Toward a Sociology of Discursive Forms

Sociologists can learn a great deal about narrative from literary critics. But they also have something valuable to offer of their own. Where literary analyses of narrative texts give us access to meaning, sociological analyses of storytelling performances give us access to the social organization of meaning, or better, the social organization of the capacity to mean credibly and authoritatively. That, in turn, can help us to understand how, most of the time, institutions reproduce themselves and why, sometimes, they become vulnerable to challenge.

Why stop with stories? Just as there is a folk wisdom about what narrative is good for and when it is appropriate and what relation it has to truth, so there is a folk wisdom about other discursive forms. Speeches, confessions, interviews, and testimony are the subjects of popular beliefs about their epistemological status and proper uses. Some beliefs about narrative are distinctive to particular institutions, and some extend beyond institutional boundaries. The same is true of beliefs about these other forms. Take the interview as an example: interview styles are very different in a medical setting, where the object is to diagnose an illness, than in a job setting, where the object is to determine whether a candidate should be hired. Interview styles are different for journalists, lawyers, sociologists, and social workers, all of whom conduct interviews as part of their routine work. (I should say their routine work *now,* since journalists only began using interviews regularly in the mid-1800s.)[13]

Conventions of interviewing reflect a combination of technical demands for certain kinds of information, legal requirements governing how information can be elicited from people, norms distinctive to each institution about how to conduct a legally unassailable or interpretively rich interview, and popular assumptions about the way a good interview looks. For example, when corporate recruiters interview job candidates, they often ask them questions that are not likely to yield the kind of information they need to decide whether to hire the person. But those questions do protect the employer against anti-discrimination lawsuits. That is an example of how legal requirements shape the content of interviews. Veteran journalists counsel neophytes that they will often get the best information from interview subjects after they put away their notebooks, but that they should then take out their notebooks again to signal that "I'm still a reporter, I'm still doing my job." That is an example of how institutional traditions shape the content of interviews. Perhaps as a result of the savvy that public figures now have about effective presentations of self, interviews by journalists that rattle a subject's composure are often thought to be better, to be truer, than those that do not. But public figures can exploit that belief. By showing emotion in interviews, they may seem more revealing, more emotionally authentic, less ingenuous, and more honest. That is an example of how a popular epistemology of the interview shapes the content of interviews.[14]

Our expectations about what makes for truthfulness in interviews come in part from what we know about comparable discursive forms. The closer a particular interview is to what we think of as a confession, the more likely we are to believe it. The closer it is to a conversation, the more we expect that the information it yields will depart from the party line, both in the sense of being less dogmatic and being less authoritative. The closer an interview is to interrogation, the more we may worry about the ethics of the method. The lines that organizations draw between interviews and these and other forms of gathering information (deliberation, canvassing, deposition, formal inquiry, and so on) surely serve to legitimate practices, organizations, and institutions. For example, an executive recruitment firm will advertise its professional interview method—not the conversations it conducts, which would hardly seem worth paying for. On the other hand, the touted method of the firm may be an interview that styles itself a conversation, allowing recruiters to exploit a more informal and less anxiety-producing form of information-gathering. In legal proceedings, people are "interviewed" and "deposed" at different stages of the process. The distinction helps to define not only the kind of information that is sought but its role in the process.

Like the celebrity who loses her composure strategically, people try to capitalize on conventions of interviewing. At the same time, just as is true of storytelling, breaching the conventions of interviewing may carry penalties. And conforming to the conventions may serve some groups better than others. What can be asked of interview subjects and what subjects can be required to reveal probably differ depending on the status of those interviewed and interviewing. Just as conventions of interviewing help to sustain institutions, they probably also reproduce existing inequalities.

These are just some of the hunches that one might pursue through a sociology of discursive forms. What animates them, as well as the broader approach to culture that I have in mind, is the recognition that people use culture practically and that culture sets the terms of practical action. Studying the conventions governing people's use of cultural forms can help to flesh out that insight empirically. People know what the conventions are. They know when it is inappropriate to give a speech and why analysis is more trustworthy than storytelling. If they do not know personally, they can turn to any number of practical guides, formal injunctions, and informal tips. The researcher, too, can draw on these materials to piece together a cultural common sense about the interview or storytelling, and in particular, an epistemology of the form: a set of assumptions about its relation to truth and knowing. What may be less obvious to culture's users are the ways in which conventions of cultural expression work to reproduce existing distributions of power and inequality. Certain discursive forms seem less credible or authoritative when used by certain groups. Certain discursive forms are open to all groups but are restricted to particular settings and occasions. The boundaries that institutions enforce between one discursive form and another may operate to legitimate the institution—and to insulate it from attack. In these and other ways, the conventions of culture's practical use may operate to reproduce the current state of things. By the same token, however, challenging those conventions may have transformative political effect.

Notes

1. Figures on Democratic and Republican campaign spending are from Thomas B. Edsall and James V. Grimaldi, "On Nov. 2, GOP Got More Bang for Its Billion, Analysis Shows," *Washington Post*, 30 December 2004.
2. Greenberg and Carville are quoted in Adam Nagourney, "Kerry Advisers Point Fingers at Iraq and Social Issues," *New York Times*, 9 November 2004; Carville's comments on *Meet the Press* are quoted in William Safire, "The Way We Live Now: Narrative," *New York Times Magazine*, 5 December 2004, 34.
3. On "Ashley's Story," see Scott Simmie, "A Hug That Resonates," *Toronto Star*, 28 October 2004. Thanks to Richard Reiss for drawing my attention to the commercial.
4. Bob Garfield, "10 Ads I Loved," *Advertising Age*, 20 December 2004, 14; see also Adam Green, "The Talk of the Town: The Pollies," *New Yorker*, 7 March 2005, 30.
5. Safire, "The Way We Live Now," 34.
6. Joseph Perkins, "Al Gore's Campaign of Dishonesty," *San Diego Union-Tribune*, 6 October 2000; on the Bush campaign's focus on Gore's credibility, see, for example, Edward Walsh, "Cheney Rips Gore's 'Problem' with Credibility," *Washington Post*, 7 October 2000. For a comparison of Bush's campaign promises on spending with his proposed budget, see Paul Krugman, "Bush's Funny Numbers: The Saga Continues," *Pittsburgh Post-Gazette*, 4 October 2000. For a discussion of Bush's misleading statements about his proposed tax cuts, see Richard W. Stevenson, "The 2000 Campaign: Checking the Facts," *New York Times*, 19 October 2000; Krugman, "Bush's Funny Numbers"; and Paul Krugman, "Reckonings: We're Not Responsible," *New York Times*, 18 October 2000.

1.   On storytelling for managers, see Stephen Denning, *The Springboard: How Storytelling Ignites Action in Knowledge-Era Organizations* (Boston: Butterworth-Heinemann, 2000); on "narrative medicine," see Dinitia Smith, "Diagnosis Goes Low Tech," *New York Times*, 11 October 2003, sec. B. On the International Storytelling Center and storytelling festivals, see Jill Jordan Sieder, "Time for Once Upon a Time," *U.S. News and World Report*, 27 October 2003, 14.

2.   On the Enola Gay controversy, see Edward T. Linenthal and Tom Engelhardt, eds., *History Wars: The Enola Gay and Other Battles for the American Past* (New York: Henry Holt, 1996); on the controversy over the commemorations of Columbus, see Timothy Kubal and Rhys Williams, "Political Process and the Puzzle of Cultural Change: Opportunities, Repertoires, and Reception" (Unpublished ms., University of Cincinnati, Dept. of Sociology, 2005).

3.   The quotation is from the Listening to the City online dialogues, New York, 30 July–12 August 2002, http://www.listeningtothecity.org. Here and in the following, I have not listed the location of the quotation in the dialogues so as to preserve the privacy of participants.

4.   For the postmodernist argument about the exhaustion of master narratives, see Jean-Francois Lyotard, *The Postmodern Condition* (Minneapolis: University of Minnesota Press, 1984). I draw substantially on scholarship in sociolinguistics, conversational analysis, anthropology, folklore, and sociology on the conventions of narrative use. As I discuss in note 33, some of this literature addresses specifically institutional conventions of narrative, especially in legal settings. However, it devotes little attention to popular beliefs about how storytelling operates and popular estimations of storytelling's value relative to other discursive forms. Nor does this literature fully explore the consequences of narrative conventions for the political use of stories.

5.   The literature on storytelling is now vast. Some of the works that proved seminal to the rediscovery of the form in the social sciences include, in psychology, Jerome Bruner, *Actual Minds, Possible Worlds* (Cambridge, MA: Harvard University Press, 1986), and Kenneth J. Gergen and Mary M. Gergen, "Narratives of the Self," in *Studies in Social Identity*, ed. Theodore R. Sarbin and Karl E. Scheibe (New York: Praeger, 1983); in law, Derrick Bell, *And We Are Not Saved: The Elusive Quest for Racial Justice* (New York: Basic Books, 1989); Richard Delgado, "Legal Storytelling for Oppositionists and Others: A Plea for Narrative," *Michigan Law Review* 87 (1989): 2411–41; and Mari J. Matsuda, "Looking to the Bottom: Critical Legal Studies and Reparations," *Harvard Civil Rights–Civil Liberties Law Review* 22 (1987): 323–99; and in history, the work of Hayden White, especially "The Value of Narrativity in the Representation of Reality," *Critical Inquiry* 7 (1980): 5–27. Interest in storytelling in the fields of folklore, sociolinguistics, and conversational

analysis is long-standing, much of it following the pioneering work of William Labov and of Harvey Sacks. See, for example, William Labov and Joshua Waletsky, "Narrative Analysis: Oral Versions of Personal Experience," in *Essays on the Verbal and Visual Arts,* ed. June Helm (Seattle: University of Washington Press, 1967); William Labov, *Language in the Inner City: Studies in the Black English Vernacular* (Philadelphia: University of Pennsylvania Press, 1972); Harvey Sacks, *Lectures on Conversation,* ed. Gail Jefferson (Oxford: Blackwell, 1992). Students of social movements have also become interested in narrative. For early formulations, see Robert A. Benford, "'You Could Be the Hundredth Monkey': Collective Action Frames and Vocabularies of Motive within the Nuclear Disarmament Movement," *Sociological Quarterly* 34 (1993): 195–216; Scott Hunt and Robert Benford, "Identity Talk in the Peace and Justice Movements," *Journal of Contemporary Ethnography* 22 (1994): 488–517; and Gary A. Fine, "Public Narration and Group Culture: Discerning Discourse in Social Movements," in *Social Movements and Culture,* ed. Hank Johnston and Bert Klandermans (Minneapolis: University of Minnesota Press, 1995). For more recent work, see the essays in Joseph E. Davis, ed., *Stories of Change: Narrative and Social Movements* (Albany: State University of New York Press, 2002).

6. I discuss this conundrum in my "Culture In and Outside Institutions," *Research in Social Movements, Conflicts, and Change* 25 (2004): 161–83.

7. On how culture mediates political opportunity, see Doug McAdam, John D. McCarthy, and Mayer N. Zald, "Introduction: Opportunities, Mobilizing Strategies, and Framing Processes," in *Comparative Perspectives on Social Movements: Political Opportunities, Mobilizing Structures, and Cultural Framings,* ed. Doug McAdam, John D. McCarthy, and Mayer N. Zald (New York: Cambridge University Press, 1996); Doug McAdam, Sidney Tarrow, and Charles Tilly, *Dynamics of Contention* (New York: Cambridge University Press, 2001); and Sidney Tarrow, *Power in Movement: Social Movements, Collective Action, and Politics,* 2nd ed. (New York: Cambridge University Press, 1998). On how ideology shapes tactical choice, see Gary L. Downey, "Ideology and the Clamshell Identity: Organizational Dilemmas in the Anti-Nuclear Power Movement," *Social Problems* 33 (1986): 357–71; David A. Snow and Robert D. Benford, "Master Frames and Cycles of Protest," in *Frontiers in Social Movement Theory,* ed. Aldon D. Morris and Carol McClurg Mueller (New Haven, CT: Yale University Press, 1992); David S. Meyer, "Opportunities and Identities: Bridge-Building in the Study of Social Movements," in *Social Movements: Identity, Culture, and the State,* ed. David S. Meyer, Nancy Whittier, and Belinda Robnett (New York: Oxford University Press, 2002); and Pamela E. Oliver and Hank Johnston, "What a Good Idea! Ideologies and Frames in Social Movement Research," *Mobilization* 5 (2000): 37–54. For discussions of cultural change as a kind of movement outcome, see Doug McAdam, "Culture and Social Movements," in *New Social Movements: From Ideology to Identity,* ed. Enrique Laraña, Hank Johnston, and

Joseph R. Gusfield (Philadelphia: Temple University Press, 1994); and Nancy Whittier, "Meaning and Structure in Social Movements," in *Social Movements* (see above, this note). I expand on the gaps I have described in my "Culture Is Not Just in Your Head," in *Rethinking Social Movements: Structure, Meaning, and Emotion,* ed. Jeff Goodwin and James M. Jasper (Lanham, MD: Rowman and Littlefield, 2004).

8. Patricia Ewick and Susan Silbey, in "Narrating Social Structure: Stories of Resistance to Legal Authority," *American Journal of Sociology* 108 (2003): 1328–72, ask in a related vein, "[A]t what point do the schemas embedded in the individual narratives [of resistance] convert into collective frames [of mobilization]?" (1365–66). See their valuable discussion of the ways in which narratives may diffuse and with what effects. See also Gary Alan Fine's study of the diffusion of urban legends in his *Manufacturing Tales: Sex and Money in Contemporary Legends* (Knoxville: University of Tennessee Press, 1992).

9. On shifts in classical approaches to rhetoric, see James Jasinski, *Sourcebook on Rhetoric: Key Concepts in Contemporary Rhetorical Studies* (Thousand Oaks, CA: Sage, 2001), introduction. Note that the stories I treat here are not those studied by literary critics. Where writers may play with our expectations by beginning a story midway through instead of with some version of "once upon a time," most people tell stories with beginnings, middles, and ends in chronological order. Where literary critics may see characters simply as reflections of other operations in the text, characters are vitally important in the stories most people tell. In my treatment of the formal features of narrative, I am less concerned with whether plot, point of view, and so on are characteristic of all narratives than with whether they figure in the stories that are most prominent in everyday life. Charles Tilly refers to "standard stories," "sequential, explanatory accounts of self-motivated human action," in much the same way as I refer to everyday stories. See his *Stories, Identities, and Social Change* (New York: Rowman and Littlefield, 2002); see also Hayden White's discussion in *Metahistory: The Historical Imagination in Nineteenth-Century Europe* (Baltimore: Johns Hopkins University Press, 1973), 8. For different definitions of narrative than the one I am using, see Lewis P. Hinchman and Sandra K. Hinchman, "Introduction," in *Memory, Identity, Community: The Idea of Narrative in the Human Sciences* (Albany: State University of New York Press, 1997). Some writers distinguish "narrative" from "story" by restricting the latter to compositions of fictional events (for example, see Donald Polkinghorne, *Narrative Knowing and the Human Sciences* [Albany: State University of New York Press, 1988]). Structuralist literary perspectives instead treat narrative as the interrelation between story (the temporal sequence of events) and discourse (how those events are represented); for a good discussion, see Mieke Bal, *Narratology: Introduction to the Theory of Narrative,* trans. Christine van Boheemen (Toronto: University of Toronto Press, 1985).

10. Peter Brooks, *Reading for the Plot: Design and Intention in Narrative* (Cambridge, MA: Harvard University Press, 1984), 4; "Well, we were having our dinner once at me Mum's" is from J. Ashkam, "Telling Stories," *Sociological Review* 30 (1982): 555–73. Communications scholar Charlotte Linde refers to narrative's creation of a "storyworld" in *Life Stories: The Creation of Coherence* (New York: Oxford University Press, 1993). See also William Labov's seminal work on the "orientation" component of narrative in Labov and Waletsky, "Narrative Analysis"; see also Labov, *Language in the Inner City,* chap. 9. Conversational analysts describe the "entrance" and "exit" talk that people use to introduce and end stories. See, for example, Gail Jefferson, "Sequential Aspects of Storytelling in Conversation," in *Studies in the Organization of Conversational Interaction,* ed. Jim Schenkein (New York: Academic Press, 1978).

11. Leo Tolstoy, *War and Peace* (New York: Simon and Schuster, 1942). For good discussions of point of view, see Gérard Genette, *Narrative Discourse: An Essay in Method,* trans. Jane E. Lewin (Ithaca, NY: Cornell University Press, 1980); Shlomith Rimmon-Kenan, *Narrative Fiction: Contemporary Poetics* (London: Methuen, 1983); Robert E. Scholes and Robert Kellogg, *The Nature of Narrative* (New York: Oxford University Press, 1968); and Bal, *Narratology.* See also the discussion of point of view in storytelling in small claims court in John M. Conley and William O'Barr, *Rules versus Relationships: The Ethnography of Legal Discourse* (Chicago: University of Chicago Press, 1990); and Peter Brooks's discussion of point of view in victim impact statements in "Illicit Stories," *Diacritics* 25 (1995): 41–51.

12. The king and queen example is from E. M. Forster, *Aspects of the Novel* (Harmondsworth, UK: Penguin, 1962), 87. J. Hillis Miller writes that plot consists of "an initial situation, a sequence leading to a change or reversal of that situation, and a revelation made possible by the reversal of situation" in his "Narrative," in *Critical Terms for Literary Study,* ed. Frank Lentricchia and Tom McLaughlin (Chicago: University of Chicago Press, 1990), 75. On plot's relation to unfolding events, see Polkinghorne, *Narrative Knowing;* and Miller, "Narrative." On reversal or inversion, see chapter 2 of Rimmon-Kenan, *Narrative Fiction;* and Gerald Prince, *A Grammar of Stories: An Introduction* (The Hague: Mouton, 1973).

13. White, "Value of Narrativity"; Labov and Waletzy, "Narrative Analysis"; Labov, *Language in the Inner City,* chap. 9.

14. Ewick and Silbey, "Narrating Social Structure," 1343.

15. Wolfgang Iser, "The Reading Process: A Phenomenological Approach," *New Literary History* 3 (1972): 285. On narrative's resistance to interpretive closure, see, from very different perspectives, Paul Ricoeur, "Hermeneutics and the Critique of Ideology," chap. 2 in *Hermeneutics and the Human Sciences: Essays on Language, Action, and Interpretation,* trans. John B. Thompson (New York: Cambridge University Press, 1981), and Miller, "Narrative." Martha S. Feldman and Kaj Skoldberg make a different argument about a particular

kind of gap common in narrative: the *enthymeme*. An enthymeme in classical rhetoric is a syllogism from which a major or minor premise is missing. The audience is expected to fill in the missing logic based on commonly held beliefs. To make the premise explicit would be to open it to challenge. Enthymemes are thus effective in mobilizing ideological assumptions in order to persuade. See their "Stories and the Rhetoric of Contrariety: Subtexts of Organizing (Change)," *Culture and Organization* 8 (2002): 275-92.

16. For a useful comparison of narrative and explanation, see Larry J. Griffin, "Temporality, Events, and Explanation in Historical Sociology: An Introduction," *Sociological Methods and Research* 20 (1992): 403-27. Livia Polanyi, in *Telling the American Story: A Structural and Cultural Analysis of Conversational Storytelling* (Norwood, NJ: Ablex, 1985), 13, notes that a report is either elicited by the recipient or is told to fulfill a requirement to recount a series of events. That context determines how the different elements of the account are evaluated. Polanyi points out that the recipient may treat as relevant parts of the account that the narrator sees as unimportant (as in a report by a witness given to police).

17. Bruner, *Actual Minds, Possible Worlds*. Hayden White discusses the etymology of narrative in *The Content of the Form: Narrative Discourse and Historical Representation* (Baltimore: Johns Hopkins University Press, 1987), 215n.

18. Quotations from the Michotte study appear in Theodore R. Sarbin, *Narrative Psychology: The Storied Nature of Human Conduct* (New York: Praeger, 1986), 13. On our tendency to turn to narrative to make sense of the anomalous, see also Polkinghorne, *Narrative Knowing;* Bruner, *Actual Minds;* Peter Bearman and Katherine Stovel, "Becoming a Nazi: Models for Narrative Networks," *Poetics* 27 (2000): 69-90; and Charles Tilly, *Why?* (Princeton: Princeton University Press, 2006), chap. 3. On the use of narrative to cope with stressful events, see Norman K. Denzin, *The Alcoholic Self* (Newbury Park, CA: Sage, 1987); Faye D. Ginsburg, *Contested Lives: The Abortion Debate in an American Community* (Berkeley and Los Angeles: University of California Press, 1989); Gareth Williams, "The Genesis of Chronic Illness: Narrative Reconstruction," in *Memory, Identity, Community: The Idea of Narrative in the Human Sciences*, ed. Lewis P. Hinchman and Sandra K. Hinchman (Albany: State University of New York Press, 1997); and Terry L. Orbuch, "People's Accounts Count: The Sociology of Accounts," *Annual Review of Sociology* 23 (1997): 455-78. I argue later that many stories we tell in everyday life also have a broken-off quality. Indeed, storytelling in conversation tends to be more collaborative than we often recognize. Stories of trauma may be simply at one end of continuum of narratives that range from the complete to the incomplete.

19. On the relations between narrative, self, and identity, see Polkinghorne, *Narrative Knowing;* and David Carr, "Narrative and the Real World: An Argument for Continuity," in *Memory, Identity, Community* (see note 18). For a fascinating account of the shaping of selves in relation to legal rights, see

David M. Engel and Frank W. Munger, *Rights of Inclusion: Law and Identity in the Life Stories of Americans with Disabilities* (Chicago: University of Chicago Press, 2003). On narrative and collective identity, see William H. Sewell, "Introduction: Narratives and Social Identities," *Social Science History* 16 (1992): 479–88; Margaret Somers, "Narrativity, Narrative Identity, and Social Action: Rethinking English Working-Class Formation," *Social Science History* 16 (1992): 591–630; and Ginsburg, *Contested Lives.*

20. Some psychologists go further: emotions may *be* narrative. When someone slights us, we feel like the scrawny man having sand kicked in his face. We know that anger calls for revenge, shame for redemption, and embarrassment for action to restore one's dignity because of the stories we have heard over and over again in which those responses are thematized. Emotions are thus configured by canonical plots, plots that we glean from novels, films, advertisements, songs, and so on. Stories provide a guide to our own feelings. On emotions as narrative, see Theodore R. Sarbin, "Emotional Life, Rhetoric, and Roles," *Journal of Narrative and Life History* 5 (1995): 213–20. On the cultural scripts from which emotions are learned, see Arlie Hochschild, "Emotion Work, Feeling Rules, and Social Structure," *American Journal of Sociology* 85 (1979): 551–75; James M. Jasper, *The Art of Moral Protest: Culture, Biography, and Creativity in Social Movements* (Chicago: University of Chicago Press, 1997); Cheshire Calhoun, "Making Up Emotional People: The Case of Romantic Love," in *The Passions of Law,* ed. Susan A. Bandes (New York: New York University Press, 1999); and Martha Craven Nussbaum, "Narrative Emotions: Beckett's Genealogy of Love," in *Love's Knowledge: Essays on Philosophy and Literature,* ed. Martha Craven Nussbaum (New York: Oxford University Press, 1990).

21. Julian E. Orr, *Talking about Machines: An Ethnography of a Modern Job* (Ithaca, NY: ILR Press, 1996). On storytelling in a midwestern insurance firm, see Charlotte Linde, "Narrative in Institutions," in *The Handbook of Discourse Analysis,* ed. Deborah Schiffrin, Deborah Tannen, and Heidi Hamilton (Malden, MA: Blackwell, 2001); on storytelling in families, see Elizabeth Stone, *Black Sheep and Kissing Cousins: How Our Family Stories Shape Us* (New York: Times Books, 1988); on storytelling and fatherhood, see "The 'Father Knows Best' Dynamic in Dinnertime Narratives," in *Gender Articulated: Language and the Socially Constructed Self,* ed. Kira Hall and Mary Bucholtz (London: Routledge, 1995).

22. I define institutions as routinized sets of practices around a defined purpose that are accompanied by rewards for conformity and penalties for deviation. Structures, by contrast, are patterns of durable relations. The concept of structure tells us nothing more than that: where a capitalist market structure refers only to the system by which goods are exchanged, the market as a capitalist institution comprises also the justifications that are attached to the form and the normative codes that operate within it. See Ronald L. Jepperson, "Institutions, Institutional Effects, and Institutionalism," in *The New*

Insitutionalism in Organizational Analysis, ed. Paul DiMaggio and Walter K. Powell (Chicago: University of Chicago Press, 1991); and Ann Swidler, *Talk of Love: How Culture Matters* (Chicago: University of Chicago Press, 2001). For valuable discussions of culture as schemas, see William H. Sewell, "A Theory of Structure: Duality, Agency, and Transformation," *American Journal of Sociology* 98 (1992): 1-29; and Elisabeth Clemens and James M. Cook, "Politics and Institutionalism: Explaining Durability and Change," *Annual Review of Sociology* 25 (1999): 441-66. I expand on this argument in my "Culture In and Outside Institutions" (see note 6 above), 161-83. Robin Wagner-Pacifici, *Theorizing the Standoff: Contingency in Action* (Cambridge: Cambridge University Press, 2000).

23. Claude Lévi-Strauss, "The Structural Analysis of Myth," in *Structural Anthropology*, trans. Clarie Jacobson and Brooke Grundfest Schoepf (New York: Basic Books, 1963), 216. For an approach to political culture that draws on Lévi-Strauss, see Jeffrey C. Alexander and Philip Smith, "The Discourse of American Civil Society: A New Proposal for Cultural Studies," *Theory and Society* 22 (1993): 151-207; and Jeffrey C. Alexander, *The Meanings of Social Life: A Cultural Sociology* (New York: Oxford University Press, 2003).

24. See, for example, Jacques Derrida, "Structure, Sign, and Play in the Discourse of the Human Sciences," in *Writing and Difference*, trans. Alan Bass (Chicago: University of Chicago Press, 1978). On binary oppositions in policy and legal discourse, see Joan W. Scott, "Deconstructing Equality-versus-Difference: Or, the Uses of Poststructuralist Theory for Feminism," in *The Postmodern Turn: New Perspectives on Social Theory*, ed. Steven Seidman (New York: Cambridge University Press, 1994).

25. On network television's use of recombination, see Todd Gitlin, *Inside Prime Time* (New York: Pantheon, 1985). On the legal system's adversarialism and its ideological effects, see Lynn Chancer, *High-Profile Crimes: When Legal Cases Become Social Causes* (Chicago: University of Chicago Press, 2005).

26. Chancer, *High-Profile Crimes*, chap. 2.

27. Kristin Luker, *Abortion and the Politics of Motherhood* (Berkeley and Los Angeles: University of California Press, 1984).

28. Joseph E. Davis, "Social Movements and Strategic Narratives: Creating the Sexual Abuse Survivor Account," in *Strategic Narrative: New Perspectives on the Power of Personal and Cultural Stories*, ed. Wendy Patterson (Lanham, MD: Lexington Books, 2002). On coming-out stories in the women's movement and the gay and lesbian movement, see Kenneth Plummer, *Telling Sexual Stories: Power, Change, and Social Worlds* (London: Routledge, 1995).

29. On the Megan Kanka case, see Matthew Purdy, "Wave of New Laws Seeks to Confine Sexual Offenders," *New York Times*, 29 June 1997, sec. 1. On the Kendra Webdale case, see Marc Santora, "Court Upholds Law for Forced Treatment," *New York Times*, 18 February 2004, sec. B1. "Moral shock" is discussed in Jasper, *Art of Moral Protest*, 106.

30. Luker, *Abortion*.

31. On kernel stories, see Susan Kalcik, ". . . like Ann's gynecologist or the time I was almost raped," in *Women and Folklore,* ed. Claire R. Farrer (Austin: University of Texas Press, 1975); and Shonna L. Trinch and Susan Berk-Seligson, "Narrating in Protective Order Interviews: A Source of Interactional Trouble," *Language in Society* 31 (2002): 383–418. On the narrative/paradigmatic narrative distinction, see Linde, "Narrative in Institutions"; on the story/narrative distinction, see David R. Maines, *The Faultline of Consciousness: A View of Interactionism in Sociology* (New York: Aldine de Gruyter, 2001), chap. 8.

32. Shoshana Blum-Kulka, *Dinner Talk: Cultural Patterns of Sociality and Socialization in Family Discourse* (Mahwah, NJ: Lawrence Erlbaum, 1997). On storytelling in working-class American families, see Shirley Brice Heath, *Ways with Words: Language, Life, and Work in Communities and Classrooms* (Cambridge: Cambridge University Press, 1983). On Christian conversion narratives, which became the model for the slave narratives published by abolitionists, see Kimberly K. Smith, "Storytelling, Sympathy, and Moral Judgment in American Abolitionism," *Journal of Political Philosophy* 6 (1998): 356–77. Paying attention to the conventions of narrative's use points to slippage between narrative's formal features and its conventional ones. For example, although all stories have beginnings, middles, and ends, in everyday conversation a story's end is often arrived at collaboratively. I begin to tell a story, and you finish it. Or I tell a story, and you attach the moral— and then revise the story in line with the moral you have just identified. Anthropologists of non-Western societies remind us that stories may not always render events in temporal order, moving from distant to less-distant past. On the collaborative character of storytelling, see Douglas Maynard, "Narratives and Narrative Structure in Plea Bargaining," *Law and Society Review* 22 (1988): 449–81; John F. Manzo, "Jurors' Narratives of Personal Experience in Deliberation Talk," *Text* 13 (1993): 267–90; John A. Robinson, "Personal Narratives Reconsidered," *Journal of American Folklore* 94 (1981): 58–85; and Livia Polanyi, "So What's the Point?" *Semiotica* 25 (1979): 207–41, in which she notes differences in non-Indo-European narrative structure.

33. On storytelling in small claims court, see Conley and O'Barr, *Rules versus Relationships;* on storytelling in 911 calls, see Jack Whalen, "A Technology of Order Production: Computer-Aided Dispatch in Public Safety Communications," in *Situated Order: Studies in the Social Organization of Talk and Embodied Activities,* ed. Paul Ten Have and George Psathas (Washington, DC: University Press of America, 1995); on storytelling in Protestant churches, see Robert Wuthnow, "Fundamentalism and Liberalism in Public Religious Discourse," in *The New American Cultural Sociology,* ed. Philip Smith (New York: Cambridge University Press, 1998). For a fascinating account of how stories of the self differ across institutional settings, see Robert Zussman, "Autobiographical Occasions, Introduction to the Special Issue," *Qualitative*

Sociology 23 (2000): 5-8; see also Jaber F. Gubrium and James A. Holstein, *The Self We Live By: Narrative Identity in a Postmodern World* (New York: Oxford University Press, 2000). For an excellent overview of the performance of first-person narrative generally, with special attention to the institutional conventions of narrative, see Kristin M. Langellier, "Personal Narratives: Perspectives on Theory and Research," *Text and Performance Quarterly* 9 (1989): 243-76, and for a sociological perspective on how legal contexts shape storytelling, see Patricia Ewick and Susan Silbey, "Subversive Stories and Hegemonic Tales: Toward a Sociology of Narrative," *Law and Society Review* 29 (1995): 197-226.

34. On 911 calls, see Whalen, "A Technology of Order Production"; on scientific investigation, see Bruno Latour and Steve Woolgar, *Laboratory Life: The Social Construction of Scientific Facts* (Beverly Hills, CA: Sage, 1979). On the law/narrative distinction, see Kim Lane Scheppele, "Foreword: Telling Stories," *Michigan Law Review* 87 (1989): 2073-98; Ruth Wodak, "The Interaction between Judge and Defendant," in *Handbook of Discourse Analysis,* ed. Teun Adrianus van Dijk (London: Academic Press, 1985), vol. 4.

35. Liz Hoggard, "Love Story; Ann Shore Runs the Ultimate Anti-Shop, Selling Anything That Takes Her Fancy," *Independent* (London), 29 September 2002.

36. The newspaper search was done on LexisNexis (Reed Elsevier Group, Orlando, Fl.) using Boolean search terms.

37. On narrative journalism, see the collection of essays in *Nieman Reports* 54 (fall 2000), published by the Nieman Foundation for Journalism, Harvard University.

38. Listening to the City online dialogue, 30 July-12 August 2002, http://www.listeningtothecity.org.

39. William A. Gamson, "Political Discourse and Collective Action," *International Social Movement Research* 1 (1988): 219-44; Swidler, *Talk of Love.* Conley and O'Barr, *Rules versus Relationships.*

40. Edwin Hollander, "Confidential Status and Idiosyncrasy Credit," *Psychological Review* 65 (1985): 117-27, describes the kind of acceptable breach of the rules that I am referring to as "idiosyncrasy credit." This is similar to what Pierre Bourdieu captures in his discussion of linguistic capital. In his famous example of what he calls a "strategy of condescension," the mayor of a town in the province of Béarn in France gives a speech celebrating a local poet and is praised by the local newspaper because his speech is given in "good quality Béarnais." The mayor's native tongue is Béarnais, but the fact that French is usually used on such occasions *and* the fact that the mayor, who is a professor, is obviously fully competent in French, together make the mayor's breach of the rules admirable rather than a faux-pas. Pierre Bourdieu, "Price Formation and the Anticipation of Profits," in *Language and Symbolic Power,* ed. John B. Thompson, trans. Gino Raymond and Matthew Adamson (Cambridge, MA: Harvard University Press, 1991), 68.

41. See especially Pierre Bourdieu, "Price Formation and the Anticipation of Profits," and *Distinction: A Social Critique of the Judgment of Taste*, trans. Richard Nice (Cambridge, MA: Harvard University Press, 1984); see also his *Outline of a Theory of Practice*, trans. Richard Nice (New York: Cambridge University Press, 1977).

42. Julian McAllister Groves, "Learning To Feel: The Neglected Sociology of Social Movements," *Sociological Review* (1995): 435–61. James M. Jasper makes a case for compassion in his "Sentiments, Ideas, and Animals: Rights Talk and Animal Protection," in *Ideas, Ideologies, and Social Movements*, ed. Peter A. Coclanis and Stuart Weems Bruchey (Columbia: University of South Carolina Press, 1999).

43. On AIDS activists' institutional gains, see Steven Epstein, *Impure Science: AIDS, Activism, and the Politics of Knowledge* (Berkeley and Los Angeles: University of California Press, 1996).

CHAPTER TWO

1. Franklin McCain is quoted in Howell Raines, *My Soul Is Rested: Movement Days in the Deep South Remembered* (New York: Putnam, 1977), 84. On the Greensboro sit-in and the spread of the movement, see William H. Chafe, *Civilities and Civil Rights: Greensboro, North Carolina, and the Black Struggle for Freedom* (New York: Oxford University Press, 1980); and Clayborne Carson, *In Struggle: SNCC and the Black Awakening of the 1960s* (Cambridge, MA: Harvard University Press, 1981).

2. Michael Walzer, "A Cup of Coffee and a Seat," *Dissent* 7 (spring 1960): 114. On the sit-ins as spontaneous, see Carson, *In Struggle;* Howard Zinn, *SNCC, the New Abolitionists* (Boston: Beacon, 1964); Frances Fox Piven and Richard A. Cloward, *Poor People's Movements: Why They Succeed, How They Fail* (New York: Pantheon, 1977); and Donald R. Matthews and James W. Prothro, *Negroes and the New Southern Politics* (New York: Harcourt, Brace and World, 1966). Martin Oppenheimer described the sit-ins spreading "like a grass fire" in *The Sit-In Movement of 1960* (Brooklyn, NY: Carlson, 1989), 40. On the role of older activists and ministers in the protests, see Aldon D. Morris, *Origins of the Civil Rights Movement: Black Communities Organizing for Change* (New York: Free Press, 1984).

3. On the Montgomery bus boycott, see David J. Garrow, *Bearing the Cross: Martin Luther King, Jr., and the Southern Christian Leadership Conference* (New York: Vintage, 1988); Jo Ann Gibson Robinson and David J. Garrow, *The Montgomery Bus Boycott and the Women Who Started It: The Memoir of Jo Ann Gibson Robinson* (Knoxville: University of Tennessee Press, 1987). On Claudette Colvin, see Juan Williams, *Eyes on the Prize: America's Civil Rights Years, 1954–1965* (New York: Viking, 1987), 62.

4. Betty Friedan is quoted in David Horowitz, "Rethinking Betty Friedan and *The Feminine Mystique:* Labor Union Radicalism and Feminism in Cold War

America," *American Quarterly* 48 (1996): 1–42, which recounts Friedan's early career. See also Ruth Rosen, *The World Split Open: How the Modern Women's Movement Changed America* (New York: Viking, 2000).

5. On the Tallahassee sit-in movement, see Lewis Killian, "Organization, Rationality and Spontaneity in the Civil Rights Movement," *American Sociological Review* 49 (1984): 770–83. On Parks, see Frank Adams, *Unearthing Seeds of Fire: The Idea of Highlander* (Winston-Salem, NC: John F. Blair, 1975). On Friedan, see Horowitz, "Rethinking Betty Friedan"; and Rosen, *The World Split Open*. Vincent Boudreau notes a similar rationale for describing protest as spontaneous on the part of Burmese insurgents in his *Resisting Dictatorship: Repression and Protest in Southeast Asia* (New York: Cambridge University Press, 2004), chap. 9.

6. "Call for Unity in Struggle for Freedom," *Howard University Hilltop*, 7 March 1960.

7. On stories of "being born" during protest, see Lawrence Weschler, *The Passion of Poland, from Solidarity through the State of War* (New York: Pantheon, 1984); and on having been "blind" and coming to "see," see Robert D. Benford and Scott A. Hunt, "Dramaturgy and Social Movements: The Social Construction and Communication of Power," *Sociological Inquiry* 62 (1992): 36–55.

8. Mancur Olson, *The Logic of Collective Action: Public Goods and the Theory of Groups* (Cambridge, MA: Harvard University Press, 1998). On preexisting bonds of solidarity as the basis for participation, see, for example, David A. Snow, Louis A. Zurcher, and Sheldon Ekland-Olson, "Social Networks and Social Movements: A Microstructural Approach to Differential Recruitment," *American Sociological Review* 45 (1980): 787–801; Gerald Marwell and Pamela Oliver, *The Critical Mass in Collective Action: A Micro-Social Theory* (New York: Cambridge University Press, 1993); Doug McAdam and Ronelle Paulsen, "Specifying the Relationship between Social Ties and Activism," *American Journal of Sociology* 99 (1993): 640–67; and Roger V. Gould, *Insurgent Identities: Class, Community, and Protest In Paris From 1848 to the Commune* (Chicago: University of Chicago Press, 1995). On collective responsibility as the basis for participation, see Pamela Oliver, "'If You Don't Do it, Nobody Else Will': Active and Token Contributors to Local Collective Action," *American Sociological Review* 49 (1984): 601–10. On moral shock as the basis for participation, see James M. Jasper, *The Art of Moral Protest: Culture, Biography, and Creativity in Social Movements* (Chicago: University of Chicago Press, 1997). On identity as the basis for participation, see Nathan Teske, *Political Activists in America: The Identity Construction Model of Political Participation* (New York: Cambridge University Press, 1997); and Francesca Polletta and James M. Jasper, "Collective Identity and Social Movements," *Annual Review of Sociology* 27 (2001): 283–305.

9. For overviews of the scholarship on framing, see David A. Snow, "Framing Processes, Ideology, and Discursive Fields," in *The Blackwell Companion to*

Social Movements, ed. David A. Snow, Sarah Anne Soule, and Hanspeter Kriesi (Malden, MA: Blackwell, 2004); Francesca Polletta and M. K. Ho, "Frames and Their Consequences," in *The Oxford Handbook of Contextual Political Studies*, ed. Robert E. Goodin and Charles Tilly (Oxford: Oxford University Press, forthcoming 2006). William Gamson identifies "injustice," "identity," and "agency" components of frames in *Talking Politics* (New York: Cambridge University Press, 1992). He also suggests that although the identity of the "they" in an adversarial ("us and them") frame may be elusive ("In the pursuit of cultural change, the target is often diffused throughout the whole civil society and the 'they' being pursued is structurally elusive" [85]), the "we" must be clearly specified ("In sum, frames with a clear 'we' and an elusive 'they' are quite capable of being fully collective and adversarial" [85]). On the importance of specifying activists and antagonists, see also Randy Stoecker, "Community, Movement, Organization: The Problem of Identity Convergence in Collective Action," *Sociological Quarterly* 36 (1995): 111–30.

10. Morris, *Origins of the Civil Rights Movement*, 72.
11. Debra Friedman and Doug McAdam, "Collective Identity and Activism: Networks, Choices, and the Life of a Social Movement," in *Frontiers in Social Movement Theory*, ed. Aldon D. Morris and Carol McClurg Mueller (New Haven, CT: Yale University Press, 1992). Charles Smith is quoted in Killian, "Organization, Rationality and Spontaneity in the Civil Rights Movement," 781; Wehr is quoted in Anthony Oberschall, "The 1960s Sit-Ins: Protest Diffusion and Movement Take-Off," *Research in Social Movements, Conflict and Change* 11 (1989): 35. James H. Laue, *Direct Action and Desegregation, 1960–1962: Toward a Theory of the Rationalization of Protest* (Brooklyn, NY: Carlson, 1989); Gomillion is quoted in Laue, *Direct Action and Desegregation*, 82.
12. Friedman and McAdam, "Collective Identity and Activism," 162–63 (emphasis added). Survey in John M. Orbell, "Protest Participation among Southern Negro College Students," in *The Seeds of Politics: Youth and Politics in America*, ed. Anthony M. Orum (Englewood Cliffs, NJ: Prentice-Hall, 1972). Expulsions are discussed in Laue, *Direct Action and Desegregation*, 77. SNCC reported that nearly two hundred students had been expelled during that period ("From You Know Who . . . ," n.d. [July 1960], Student Nonviolent Coordinating Committee Papers, 1959–1972, microfilm [hereafter, SNCC Papers], reel 1, frame 291). Michael Walzer wrote that the sit-ins had galvanized a surge of church-based adult movement organizations. But, he pointed out, "the students, for the most part, do not attend the weekly meetings in the churches. Embarrassing moments often follow suggestions that students present rise and be applauded. They turn out to have stayed on campus for a meeting of their own" ("The Politics of the New Negro," *Dissent* 8 [1961]: 241).
13. Interview with Ella Baker in Emily Stoper, *The Student Nonviolent Coordinating Committee: The Growth of Radicalism in a Civil Rights Organization* (Brooklyn,

NY: Carlson, 1989), 265–72. On the 1960 National Student Association meeting, see "Theopolis Fair, John Baker, Jerry Byrd, Henrietta Eppse Represent Fisk," *Fisk University Forum,* 30 September 1960. John Lewis is quoted in Milton Viorst, *Fire in the Streets: America in the 1960s* (New York: Simon and Schuster, 1979), 116. On African students and representatives at Southern colleges, see "Cameroun's Foreign Minister Visits Xavier U. Campus," *Xavier University Herald,* October 1960. SNCC invited the brother of Tom Mboya to be keynote speaker at its first conference, addressing the "relationship of the African freedom movement to our own fight" (Marion S. Barry, Chairman, to Dear Friend, 10 October 1960, SNCC Papers, reel 4, frame 920). Joan Burt to the Editor, "The Time Is Now, We Have to Use it Well," *Howard University Hilltop,* 31 May 1960; *Fisk University Forum,* 28 October 1960; "Retreat Best in History of School, Declares Dean Green," *Fisk University Forum,* 30 September 1960. On student protest worldwide, see Richard Flacks, *Youth and Social Change* (Chicago: Markham, 1971).

14. "Campus Politics," *Xavier University Herald,* January 1960; "Student Sloth," *Xavier University Herald,* October 1960; Theopolis Fair, "Theopolis Fair, John Baker, Jerry Byrd, Henrietta Epse Represent Fisk," *Fisk University Forum,* 30 September 1960. On the "beatniks," see Rev. Carroll Feltum, Jr., "Like— Being Way Out," *Knoxville College Aurora,* March 1960. The fact that some of these characterizations appeared when the sit-ins were well underway and at the same time as some were referring to 1960 as "the year of the student" ("Retreat Best in History of School," *Fisk University Forum,* 30 September 1960) suggests that accusations of student apathy continued to be a powerful challenge.

15. "Students Stage Sitdown Demand," *North Carolina Agricultural and Technical College Register,* 5 February 1960.

16. "Humane aspects of the American dream" is from Glen Mitchell, "Sitdown Protest in Pictorial Retrospect," *Shaw University Journal,* May 1960; "shackles of immorality, archaic traditions, and complacency" from H. Julian Bond and Melvin A. McCaw, "Special Report: Atlanta Story," *Student Voice,* June 1960, reprinted in *Student Voice 1960–1965: Periodical of the Student Nonviolent Coordinating Committee,* ed. Clayborne Carson (Westport, CT: Meckler, 1990), 4; the sit-ins are described as a challenge to apathy in Mitchell, "Sitdown Protest in Historical Retrospect." For the argument that the injustices described in successful frames are "situational" rather than "individual," see Bert Klandermans, "The Formation and Mobilization of Consensus," *International Social Movement Research* 1 (1988): 179. The sit-ins are described as a "surprise (and shock)" in "A Report on the Student Direct Action Movement at Penn State as of March 31, 1960," SNCC Papers, reel 44, frame 2.

17. The sit-ins are described as the result of "spontaneous combustion" in "A Report on the Student Direct Action Movement at Penn State as of March 31, 1960," SNCC Papers, reel 44, frame 22; "[t]he fact that the protest broke out overnight . . ." appears in Jane Stembridge, Speech to National Student

Association, SNCC Papers, reel 44, frames 1280–83; "[i]t is really strange— to do things alone" appears in SNCC Newsletter Entry, 1960, SNCC Papers, reel 5, frame 190. Protest is described as "burst[ing]" in Jane Stembridge to Lillian Lipsen, 18 August 1960, SNCC Papers, reel 4, frame 207; "breaking" in Sample Fund-Raising Letter for Student Nonviolent Coordinating Committee, SNCC Papers, reel 3, frame 785; "exploding" in Lerone Bennett, "What Sit-Downs Mean to America," *Ebony* 15 (1960): 35; "sweeping" in "Focus on Jackson, Tenn.," *Student Voice,* November 1960, reprinted in Carson, *Student Voice 1960–1965,* 23; "surging" in "Across the Editor's Desk," *Student Voice,* November 1960, reprinted in Carson, *Student Voice 1960– 1965,* 22; "rip[ping] through the city like an epidemic" in "Drama of the Sitdown," *Shaw University Journal,* March–April 1960; as involving students "fired" by "the spark of the sit-ins" in "Students March for Civil Rights" in *Student Voice,* special supplementary issue, November 1960, reprinted in Carson, *Student Voice 1960–1965,* 20; and like a "chain-reaction" in Walt DeLegall, "Students Continue Woolworth Picket," *Howard University Hilltop,* 8 April 1960. Philander Smith College students are quoted in "Up Against the Obstacles," n.d., SNCC Papers, reel 4, frame 980; Vanderbilt students are quoted in "This Is Important," n.d., SNCC Papers, reel 44, frame 113.

18. "Statement Submitted by SNCC to the Platform Committee of the National Democratic Convention," 7 July 1960, SNCC Papers, reel 1, frames 243– 48; The Student Nonviolent Coordinating Committee to Mr. Bill Strong, 31 July 1960, SNCC Papers, reel 1, frame 207.

19. "Only prayer" appears in Sandra Battis to Editor, *Fisk University Forum,* 30 September 1960; "spirit of love" in "Newsletter to Congressmen," August 1960, SNCC Papers, reel 1, frame 291; "[h]ere were two harmless young people" in "Column from Cambridge Correspondent," n.d., SNCC Papers, reel 62, frame 130; Robert Booker, "Ode to a Lunch Counter," *Knoxville College Aurora,* June 1960.

20. Reference to being tired "of waiting for the American dream to materialize" appears in Edward King to Dear Friend, 12 September 1960, SNCC Papers, reel 4, frame 920; "tired of un-American discrimination" in H. David Hammond to Editor, *Howard University Hilltop,* 8 April 1960; "tired of moving at an ox-cart pace" in Walzer, "Cup of Coffee"; tired of "wait[ing] for the course of time . . ." in Frank Smith and Olin Grant, n.t. (memo to SNCC), Philander Smith College, Little Rock, Ark., 12 March 1960, SNCC Papers, reel 4, frame 977. "[t]aken it" appears in Joan Burt, letter to the editor, *Howard University Hilltop,* 31 May 1960; "95 years of discussions" in R. A. Ward, letter to the editor, *Knoxville College Aurora,* April 1960; "[a]fter hundreds of years" in "Justifiable Recalcitrance," *Shaw University Journal,* March–April 1960; "[o]ur biggest influence" in Wilma Dykeman and James Stokely, "Sit Down Chillun, Sit Down!" *Progressive,* 24 June 1960, 10; and "stifle" your "feelings" in "Congratulations Sit-Inners," *Howard University Hilltop,* 30 September 1960.

21. "The myth of student apathy" appears in Michael Thelwell, "Students Picket in Spontaneous Move," *Howard University Hilltop*, 7 March 1960; "a death blow to apathy" in The Student Nonviolent Coordinating Committee to Mr. Bill Strong, 31 July 1960, SNCC Papers, reel 1, frame 207; "false robe of sophistication and unconcern" in "This Is Important," n.d. (memo), SNCC Papers, reel 44, frame 113; "no longer may students be called the 'Silent Generation'" in "The New Freedom," SNCC Papers, reel 4, frame 108; "tired of waiting" in Marion S. Barry to Honorable Byron L. Johnson, 22 August 1960, SNCC Papers, reel 1, frame 285; "weary with waiting" in Walzer, "Cup of Coffee," 114; "we had been ready" and "we have been planning" in Fuller, "We Are All So Very Happy," 13. The block quotation is from Mitchell, "Sitdown Protest in Pictorial Retrospect."

22. Henry Thomas Report, n.d. [July 1960], SNCC Papers, reel 5, frame 170; Walzer, "Cup of Coffee," 119.

23. Charles McDew, "Spiritual and Moral Aspects of the Student Nonviolent Struggle in the South," in *The New Student Left: An Anthology*, ed. Mitchell Cohen and Dennis Hale (Boston: Beacon, 1966), 57.

24. J. Hillis Miller, "Narrative," in *Critical Terms for Literary Study*, ed. Frank Lentricchia and Tom McLaughlin (Chicago: University of Chicago Press, 1990), 72.

25. James C. Scott, *Domination and the Arts of Resistance: Hidden Transcripts* (New Haven, CT: Yale University Press, 1990). ·

26. Quoted in Robert D. Benford, "'You Could Be the Hundredth Monkey': Collective Action Frames and Vocabularies of Motive within the Nuclear Disarmament Movement," *Sociological Quarterly* 34 (1993): 196.

27. Ibid. On the importance of a "clear" specification of activists, antagonists, and targets, see Randy Stoecker, "Community, Movement, Organization: The Problem of Identity Convergence in Collective Action," *Sociological Quarterly* 36 (1995): 113. On the importance of a "clearly interpretable" rationale for action, see David A. Snow and Robert D. Benford, "Ideology, Frame Resonance, and Participant Mobilization," *International Social Movement Research* 1 (1988): 203.

28. "Boom—It Happened" appears in "Call for Unity in Struggle for Freedom," *Howard University Hilltop*, 7 March 1960.

29. Figures on sit-in participation appear in Anthony Oberschall, "The 1960s Sit-Ins," 31–53. Quotations from the Highlander workshop appear in Aimee Isgrig Horton, *The Highlander Folk School: A History of Its Major Programs, 1932–1961* (Brooklyn, NY: Carlson, 1989), 242; and "Excerpts from Tape of College Workshop—April 1–2, 1960," State Historical Society of Wisconsin, Highlander Research and Education Center Records, 1917–1987, box 78, folder 9. Minutes of SNCC Meeting, 25–27 November 1960, SNCC Papers, reel 1, frame 780.

30. Jane Stembridge to Mrs. Schreiber, 18 July 1960, SNCC Papers, reel 4, frame 189; Marion Barry and Jane Stembridge to Mr. Lawrence Gundiff, 7 July 1960, SNCC Papers, reel 1, frame 29.

31. Horton is quoted in Selma Workshop, 13–16 December 1963, SNCC Papers, reel 9, frame 382. Many of the SNCC staffers interviewed by sociologist Emily Stoper in 1965 said they joined SNCC because they "did not want to be held back by the bureaucratic slowness or mature restraint of the NAACP or even SCLC" (*Student Nonviolent Coordinating Committee*, 92). On the SNCC debate over direct action, see Carson, *In Struggle*.

32. Christopher Lasch, *The New Radicalism in America, 1889–1963: The Intellectual as a Social Type* (New York: Knopf, 1965), 289. Hayden is quoted on the sit-ins in Jim Miller, *Democracy Is in the Streets: From Port Huron to the Siege of Chicago* (New York: Simon and Schuster, 1987), 52; Hayden on the "moral clarity of the movement" in To SDS, From Hayden Re: Race and Politics Conference, n.d. [1961], SNCC Papers, reel 9, frame 42; Robert Alan Haber, "From Protest to Radicalism: An Appraisal of the Student Movement," in Cohen and Hale, *The New Student Left*, 40; Robb Burlage, "For Dixie with Love and Squalor," n.d. [1962], SNCC Papers, reel 9, frame 1144.

33. Staughton Lynd, "On White Power," *New Left Notes*, 24 August 1966; on direct action in the new left and antiwar movements, see Stewart Burns, *Social Movements of the 1960s: Searching for Democracy* (Boston: Twayne, 1990), 181.

34. Saul David Alinsky, *Rules for Radicals: A Practical Primer for Realistic Radicals* (New York: Random House, 1971), 103–4.

35. Jane O'Reilly, "The Housewife's Moment of Truth," *Ms.* (spring 1972): 54.

36. Ibid.

37. Letters, *Ms.*, July 1972, 44–45; Mary Thom, *Inside Ms.: Twenty-Five Years of the Magazine and the Feminist Movement* (New York: Henry Holt, 1997), 24–25. Amy Farrell notes that there were twenty thousand letters in response to the three hundred thousand copies of the preview issue that had been distributed. With a circulation of seven million, a typical issue drew two hundred letters; see "'Like a Tarantula on a Banana Boat': Ms. Magazine, 1972–1989," in *Feminist Organizations: Harvest of the New Women's Movement*, ed. Myra Marx Ferree and Patricia Yancey Martin (Philadelphia: Temple University Press, 1995), 24.

38. Natalie Zemon Davis, *Fiction in the Archives: Pardon Tales and Their Tellers in Sixteenth-Century France* (Stanford, CA: Stanford University Press, 1987), 20.

39. Ibid., 29–30, 30–31.

CHAPTER THREE

1. On the impact of open and closed political systems in shaping activists' tactical choices, see Herbert Kitschelt, "Political Opportunity Structures and Political Protest: Anti-Nuclear Movements in Four Democracies," *British Journal of Political Science* 16 (1986): 57–85; for the impact of administrative bureaucracies' degree of support, see Edwin Amenta, Drew Halfmann, and Michael P. Young, "The Strategies and Contexts of Social Protest: Political Mediation and the Impact of the Townsend Movement," *Mobilization* 4

(1999): 1–24 (the authors note that they seek to identify the tactics most likely to be effective, not necessarily those likely to be chosen); on movement groups' differentiating strategies and tactics for funding, see Mayer N. Zald and John D. McCarthy, "Social Movement Industries: Competition and Cooperation among Movement Organizations," *Research in Social Movements, Conflicts and Change* 3 (1980): 1–20.

2. On the influence of activists' ideological commitments, or "master frames," see David A. Snow and Robert D. Benford, "Master Frames and Cycles of Protest," in *Frontiers in Social Movement Theory,* ed. Aldon D. Morris and Carol McClurg Mueller (New Haven, CT: Yale University Press, 1992), 146. On the effects of activists' prefigurative commitments, see Wini Breines, *Community and Organization in the New Left, 1962–1968: The Great Refusal* (New Brunswick, NJ: Rutgers University Press, 1989); Barbara Epstein, *Political Protest and Cultural Revolution: Nonviolent Direct Action in the 1970s and 1980s* (Berkeley and Los Angeles: University of California Press, 1991); Gary L. Downey, "Ideology and the Clamshell Identity: Organizational Dilemmas in the Anti–Nuclear Power Movement," *Social Problems* 33 (1986): 357–71.

3. Charles Tilly, "Now Where?" in *State/Culture: State-Formation after the Cultural Turn,* ed. George Steinmetz (Ithaca, NY: Cornell University Press, 1999), 419. Elisabeth Clemens uses the notion of repertoires to show how activists' choice of organizational form is shaped by prevalent standards of appropriateness. See her "Organizational Form as Frame," in *Comparative Perspectives on Social Movements,* ed. Doug McAdam, John D. McCarthy, and Mayer N. Zald (New York: Cambridge University Press, 1996), 208. James Jasper's concept of "tastes in tactics" is closer to what I have in mind than the notion of ideological commitment since it connotes something less elaborated. See his *The Art of Moral Protest: Culture, Biography, and Creativity in Social Movements* (Chicago: University of Chicago Press, 1997).

4. For an exception to the neglect of the constraining dimensions of repertoires, see Carol Conell and Kim Voss, "Formal Organizations and the Fate of Social Movements: Craft Association and Class Alliance in the Knights of Labor," *American Sociological Review* 55 (1990): 255–69.

5. Sherryl Kleinman, *Opposing Ambitions: Gender and Identity in an Alternative Organization* (Chicago: University of Chicago Press, 1996), 38–39. For an interesting study of how activists' views of what is appropriate are shaped by kindred groups, see also Sarah Soule, "The Diffusion of an Unsuccessful Innovation," *Annals of the American Academy of Political and Social Science* 566 (1999): 120–31.

6. The union official is quoted in Marshall Ganz, "Resources and Resourcefulness: Strategic Capacity in the Unionization of California Agriculture, 1959–1966," *American Journal of Sociology* 105 (2000): 1039, 1041.

7. On participatory democracy in the 1960s, see Breines, *Community and Organization in the New Left;* Jane Mansbridge, *Beyond Adversary Democracy* (Chicago: University of Chicago Press, 1983); and Joyce Rothschild and J. Allen

Whitt, *The Cooperative Workplace: Potentials and Dilemmas of Organizational Democracy and Participation* (New York: Cambridge University Press, 1986).

8. On the debate over decision making in SNCC and its causes, see Clayborne Carson, *In Struggle: SNCC and the Black Awakening of the 1960s* (Cambridge, MA: Harvard University Press, 1981); Doug McAdam, *Freedom Summer* (New York: Oxford University Press, 1988); Nicolaus Mills, *Like a Holy Crusade: Mississippi, 1964—The Turning of the Civil Rights Movement in America* (Chicago: I. R. Dee, 1992); Emily Stoper, *The Student Nonviolent Coordinating Committee* (Brooklyn, NY: Carlson, 1989); Todd Gitlin, *The Sixties: Years of Hope, Days of Rage* (New York: Bantam, 1987); Sara Evans, *Personal Politics: The Roots of Women's Liberation in the Civil Rights Movement and the New Left* (New York: Knopf, 1979); Cleveland Sellers with Robert Terrell, *The River of No Return: The Autobiography of a Black Militant and the Life and Death of SNCC* (Jackson: University Press of Mississippi, 1990); Richard H. King, *Civil Rights and the Idea of Freedom* (New York: Oxford University Press, 1992); Belinda Robnett, *How Long? How Long? African American Women in the Struggle for Civil Rights* (New York: Oxford University Press, 1997); and Edward Morgen, *The 60's Experience: Hard Lessons about Modern America* (Philadelphia: Temple University Press, 1991).

9. Roman Jakobson, "The Metaphoric and Metonymic Poles," in *Critical Theory Since Plato*, ed. Hazard Adams (New York: Harcourt, Brace, Jovanovich, 1971); for a good discussion of Jakobson's use of metonymy, see David Lodge, *The Modes of Modern Writing: Metaphor, Metonymy, and the Typology of Modern Literature* (Ithaca, NY: Cornell University Press, 1977), 76. For a discussion of metonymy in terms of a web or cluster of terms, see Groupe Mu (J. Dubois, F. Edeline, J. M. Kinkenberg, P. Minguet, F. Pire, and H. Trinon), *A General Rhetoric*, trans. Paul B. Burrell and Edgar M. Slotkin (Baltimore: Johns Hopkins University Press, 1981); on metonymy generally, see also, George Lakoff and Mark Johnson, *Metaphors We Live By* (Chicago: University of Chicago Press, 1980).

10. David Lodge discusses metonymy's condensation of a series of events in *The Modes of Modern Writing*, 85–86. Hugh Bredin, "Metonymy," *Poetics Today* 5 (1984): 57; Lodge, *Modes of Modern Writing*.

11. Leo Tolstoy, *Anna Karenina* (New York: W. W. Norton, 1970). In his discussion of how, in the postwar period, legal notions of responsibility for Nazi atrocities were gradually replaced by guilt by association with the Holocaust, Jeffrey C. Alexander also emphasizes metonymy's establishment of broad-grained causal relations. See his *The Meanings of Social Life: A Cultural Sociology* (New York: Oxford University Press, 2003), chap. 2.

12. On anti–corporate globalization activists' view of "Californian" protest, see Francesca Polletta, *Freedom Is an Endless Meeting: Democracy in American Social Movements* (Chicago: University of Chicago Press, 2002), 176–201.

13. On SNCC's formation, see David Halberstam, *The Children* (New York: Random House, 1998); Carson, *In Struggle;* and David Garrow, *Bearing the Cross* (New York: Vintage, 1988).

14. Bob Moses, interview by author, Boston, 9 December 1992. On participatory decision making as a means of building local leadership, see Polletta, *Freedom Is an Endless Meeting;* and Charles Payne, *I've Got the Light of Freedom: The Organizing Tradition and the Mississippi Freedom Struggle* (Berkeley and Los Angeles: University of California Press, 1995).

15. On SNCC's ability to mobilize national support, see Polletta, *Freedom Is an Endless Meeting;* Payne, *I've Got the Light of Freedom;* and Carson, *In Struggle.*

16. On the growth of SNCC's staff, see McAdam, *Freedom Summer;* and Carson, *In Struggle.* See James Forman, *The Making of Black Revolutionaries* (1972; repr., Seattle: University of Washington Press, 1997), 413.

17. For objections to centralization, SNCC Staff Meeting, 10 October 1964, handwritten notes taken by Mary E. King, State Historical Society of Wisconsin, Madison (hereafter, SHSW), Mary E. King Papers. "White, college-educated Northerners" appears in Viki and Martin to Dear ——, 9 December 1964, SHSW, Martin and Viki Nicolaus Papers.

18. Proposal for decentralized structure in [Casey Hayden], "Memorandum on Structure," [November 1964], Casey Hayden Papers, private collection.

19. Discussion of the two proposals appears in "Ivanhoe opened the session . . ." [notes of staff retreat, Waveland, MS, 7–12 November 1964], Betty Garman Robinson Papers, private collection; the MFDP letter is quoted in Mike Miller, "The Mississippi Freedom Democratic Party," in *The New Left: A Documentary History,* ed. Massimo Teodori (Indianapolis, IN: Bobbs-Merrill, 1969), 110; "That is, the people, residents of Shaw decided . . ." in Mary Sue Gellatly to Mrs. Franz, 6 April 1965, SHSW, COFO-Shaw Papers.

20. "So far I've been using the SNCC technique" appears in Nancy and Gene Turvitz to Dear Friends, 10–14 July 1965, SNCC Papers, reel 61, frames 1071–72; "[t]here has been a stopping of all projects" in "Report for Monroe County," 3 March 1965, SNCC Papers, reel 65, frame 976; "[a]pathy stems from problems of program" in Staff Meeting, 1 April 1965, SHSW, Jo Ann Robinson Papers; "[w]hat we've had so far is discussion" in Sandra Watts, "Meridian Report," 23 November 1964, SNCC Papers, reel 66, frames 1259–60; "[t]here is no plan" in Mary Brumder Report, [fall 1964], SNCC Papers, reel 66, frame 1265.

21. "Too many damn nursery schools" appears in "Hattiesburg Report from Barbara Schwartzbaum," [November 1964], SNCC Papers, reel 66, frame 1270; "[m]any of us do not see the relationship" in Dick Kelley, "I would like to get rid of a few gripes," 28 November 1964, SNCC Papers, reel 66, frame 1268; "[q]uestion of whether we are a social service agency" in "Ivanhoe opened the session . . . ," [notes of staff retreat, Waveland, MS, 7–12 November 1964], Betty Garman Robinson Papers, private collection.

22. On vacillating leadership, see "To: Richard Haley, From: Jo Ann Ooiman," 6 June 1965, SHSW, Jo Ann Robinson Papers; "Why don't people speak?" and "Who decided that?" from Mike [Kenney] to Brun, 3 February 1965, SNCC Papers, reel 71, frame 387; "I asked someone to deal with two personnel problems . . ." in Minutes of Staff Meeting in Hattiesburg, 22 December 1964, Elaine DeLott Baker Papers, private collection.

23. "Southern staff workers favor strong leadership and structure," in Minutes of Steering Committee Meeting, 23 February 1965, SNCC Papers, reel 34, frames 395–96; Judy Richardson, interview by author, Boston, 10 December 1992.

24. For example, halfway through a staff meeting in early 1965, one staffer complained that "a lot of people got up and began to discuss their [programmatic] needs . . . and we cut them off to talk of structure." In spite of this intervention, the discussion remained on structure (Meeting Notes, [February 1965], SHSW, Mary E. King Papers). "People here are incapable of dealing with the real problem" appears in Executive Committee Meeting Minutes, 12–14 April 1965, SNCC Papers, reel 3, frames 410–26; Dorothy Zellner, interview by author, New York, 4 March 1992.

25. Mike to Gordon, 18 January 1965, SNCC Papers, reel 71, frames 348–49.

26. [Mike Thelwell], "Mississippi's Metaphysical Mystics—A Sect Wrapped Up in a Clique within a Cult," [November 1964], SHSW, Mary E. King Papers.

27. *River of No Return*, 131 (see note 8). "More concerned with their own liberation" appears in "Mississippi's Metaphysical Mystics" (see note 26); "local-people-itis" in New York SNCC Meeting, June 1966, King Library and Archives, Martin Luther King, Jr., Center for Nonviolent Social Change, Atlanta, James Forman Collection, audiotape 199.

28. "The 'freedom highs' are essentially white intellectuals" appears in [Charles] Cobb, "On Snick/Revolution/and Freedom," [April 1965], SNCC Papers, reel 33, frames 269–72; Executive Committee Meeting Minutes, 12–14 April 1965, SNCC Papers, reel 3, frames 410–26.

29. "They didn't know who the hell you were" appears in Donald Harris, interview, in Stoper, *Student Nonviolent Coordinating Committee*, 145–72; "[i]t used to be a band of brothers" in "Tougaloo Mtg., Aug. 64," SNCC Papers, reel 39, frame 877. On SNCC workers' concerns about volunteers and the media coverage of the summer project, see Julian Bond, interview by author, Washington, DC, 23 March 1992; Betty Garman Robinson, interview by author, Baltimore, MD, 19 June 1996; Fred Mangrum, interview by Robert Wright, 8 July 1969, Moorland-Spingarn Research Center, Howard University, Ralph Bunche Oral History Collection; and Minutes, Fifth District Meeting, 25 November 1964, SHSW, Mary E. King Papers.

30. "Problem is that people can't trust [the] project director" and following quotations are from Minutes, Fifth District Meeting, 25 November 1964, SHSW, Mary E. King Papers; "[u]nless you forget yourself" and following

quotations are from Canton Valley View Staff Meeting, 2 December 1964, SHSW, Jo Ann Robinson Papers, box 2.

31. Minutes, Fifth District Meeting, 25 November 1964, SHSW, Mary E. King Papers; *River of No Return,* 157 (see note 8); Bob Moses, interview by Clayborne Carson, Martin Luther King Papers Project, Stanford University, Clayborne Carson Papers; Minutes, Fifth District Meeting, 25 November 1964, SHSW, Mary E. King Papers.

32. Bond quoted in Stoper, *Student Nonviolent Coordinating Committee,* 276. An example of a reference to the black-white problem appears in SNCC Staff Meeting, [fall 1964], notes taken by Mike Miller, Mike Miller Papers, private collection.

33. "Anarchist" appears in Mary King to Julian Bond, [spring 1965], SNCC Papers, reel 36, frame 14; "obstructionist" in "Personal. M. to Jim Forman," [spring 1965], SNCC Papers, reel 12, frames 512-13; "Look at the people at Waveland" in Mary King, *Freedom Song: A Personal Story of the 1960s Civil Rights Movement* (New York: W. Morrow, 1987), 484; defender of loose structure in Staff Meeting, 2 February 1965, transcription of handwritten notes taken by Mary E. King, SHSW, Mary E. King Papers; "conspiracy theories" in King, *Freedom Song,* 484.

34. Meeting Fragment, [February 1965], SHSW, Mary E. King Papers.

35. Review of SNCC staffers in Executive Committee Meeting Minutes, 12–14 April 1965, SNCC Papers, reel 3, frames 410–26. Complaints about SNCC's efforts at "tightening up" appear in Mike [Miller] to Cyn[thia Washington], October 1965, SNCC Papers, reel 24, frames 116–17; "[w]e're not individuals anymore" in "Personal. M. to Jim Forman," [spring 1965], ibid., reel 12, frames 512–13.

36. [Charles] Cobb, "On Snick/Revolution/and Freedom" (see note 28); *River of No Return,* 132 (see note 8).

37. "People really have no ideas for programs" appears in Nancy and Gene Turvitz to Dear Friends, 10–14 July 1965, SNCC Papers, reel 61, frames 1071–72; "[p]eople came because of frustration on their projects" in Executive Committee Meeting Minutes, 12–14 April 1965, SNCC Papers, reel 3, frames 410–26; see also Mike to Gordo, 6 March 1965, ibid., reel 71, frame 469 ("Stokely left for Alabama to recapture the old days and keep from facing the new problems").

38. Quotations are from SNCC Staff Conference, "Assumptions Made by SNCC," 11 May 1966, SNCC Papers, reel 3, frames 1053–58. See also Staff Conference, 8–13 May 1966, King Library and Archives, James Forman Collection, audiotapes 151, 153, 180.

39. On the impact of the Black Power controversy, see Ruby Doris S. Robinson, "To: SNCC Central Committee, Organizational Report," 21 October 1966, Martin Luther King Papers Project, Clayborne Carson Papers; Julian Bond, interview by author, Washington, DC, 23 March 1992; Jennifer Lawson, phone interview by author, 9 June 1992. Stanley Wise, interview by author, Atlanta, GA, 9 June 1992.

40. Stokely Carmichael, "Integration Is Completely Irrelevant to Us: What We Want Is Power for People Who Don't Have It," *The Movement* (June 1966): 127. Also Kwame Ture (Stokely Carmichael), interview by author, Williamstown, MA, 6 February 1995.

41. "Speaking 'in the tone'" appears in "Black Power: The Widening Dialogue" (discussion between Carmichael and Randolph Blackwell of the SCLC), *New South* (summer 1966): 74; "[b]reak open the chains" and "awaken . . . the black community" in "Motions, Recommendations, Mandates of Central Committee Meeting, May 14–17, 1966," SNCC Papers, reel 3, frames 585–89; "educate black people" in Stokely Carmichael, "Report from the Chairman," 7 May 1967, ibid., reel 3, frames 1129–32; Forman in Central Committee Meeting Notes, 22 September 1967, ibid., reel 72, frames 173–205.

42. On this rendering of leadership, see Adolph Reed, Jr., "The 'Black Revolution' and the Reconstitution of Domination" in *Race, Politics and Culture: Critical Essays on the Radicalism of the 1960s*, ed. Adolph Reed, Jr. (Westport, CT: Greenwood Press, 1986). As Robnett (*How Long? How Long?*) points out, it was also a distinctively masculine notion of leadership.

43. On SNCC's final years, see Carson, *In Struggle*; and Forman, *Making of Black Revolutionaries*. On participatory democracy's use in the new left, see Francesca Polletta, "Strategy and Democracy in the New Left," in *The New Left Revisited*, ed. Paul Buhle and John McMillian (Philadelphia: Temple University Press, 2003).

44. Norm Fruchter, "Mississippi: Notes on SNCC," *Studies on the Left* 5 (1965): 74–80.

45. Victor Rabinowitz, "An Exchange on SNCC," *Studies on the Left* 5 (1965): 83–91; "To the Editors . . ." by Mike Miller, 20 August 1965, Mike Miller papers, private collection.

46. Richard Rothstein, "A Short History of ERAP," Students for a Democratic Society Papers, Series 2b, no. 21.

47. "When labor people" in John Tarleton, "After Quebec, What Next," *New York Indypendent*, May 2001; "the reality is that certain individuals play roles . . ." in Colin Rajah, "Harsh Reality: Confronting Race on the Student Left," *The Activist* (online journal, fall 2000); "white activist . . . norms" in Daraka Larimore-Hall, "Race, Structure, and Vegan Food: A Look at the USAS Conference," *The Activist* (online journal, fall 2000); "cultural trappings" in Tarleton, "After Quebec."

CHAPTER FOUR

1. For representative elaborations of deliberative democratic theory, see Benjamin Barber, *The Conquest of Politics: Liberal Philosophy in Democratic Times* (Princeton, NJ: Princeton University Press, 1988); James Bohman, *Public Deliberation: Plurality, Complexity, and Democracy* (Cambridge, MA: MIT Press,

1996); John S. Dryzek, *Discursive Democracy: Politics, Policy, and Political Science* (Cambridge: Cambridge University Press, 1990); Joshua Cohen, "Deliberation and Democratic Legitimacy," in *The Good Polity: Normative Analysis of the State,* ed. Alan Hamlin and Philip Pettit (New York: Blackwell, 1989); Amy Guttman and Dennis F. Thompson, *Democracy and Disagreement* (Cambridge, MA: Harvard University Press, 1996); James S. Fishkin, *Democracy and Deliberation: New Directions for Democratic Reform* (New Haven, CT: Yale University Press, 1991); and James S. Fishkin, *The Voice of the People: Public Opinion and Democracy* (New Haven, CT: Yale University Press, 1995).

2. For discussions of storytelling as an aid to or substitute for classical reasoned discourse, see Iris Marion Young, "Communication and the Other: Beyond Deliberative Democracy," in *Democracy and Difference: Contesting the Boundaries of the Political,* ed. Seyla Benhabib (Princeton, NJ: Princeton University Press, 1996); Iris Marion Young, *Inclusion and Democracy* (Oxford: Oxford University Press, 2000); Lynn M. Sanders, "Against Deliberation," *Political Theory* 25 (1997): 347–76; and Kimberly K. Smith, "Storytelling, Sympathy, and Moral Judgment in American Abolitionism," *Journal of Political Philosophy* 6 (1998): 356–77. For a critique of classical deliberation's exclusive character, see Susan Bickford, *The Dissonance of Democracy: Listening, Conflict, and Citizenship* (Ithaca, NY: Cornell University Press, 1996).

3. For recent overviews of exercises in deliberative democracy, as well as the kinds of research typical in the field, see Michael X. Delli Carpini, Fay Lomax Cook, and Lawrence R. Jacobs, "Public Deliberation, Discursive Participation, and Citizen Engagement: A Review of the Empirical Literature," *Annual Review of Political Science* 7 (2004): 315–44; Mark Button and Kevin Mattson, "Deliberative Democracy in Practice: Challenges and Prospects for Civic Deliberation," *Polity* 31 (1999): 609–39; Archon Fung, "Recipes for Public Spheres: Eight Institutional Design Choices and their Consequences," *Journal of Political Philosophy* 11 (2003): 338–67; and John Gastil and James P. Dillard, "Increasing Political Sophistication Through Public Deliberation," *Political Communication* 16 (1999): 3–23. For a review of recent literature on online deliberation, see Lincoln Dahlberg, "The Internet and Democratic Discourse: Exploring the Prospects of Online Deliberative Forums Extending the Public Sphere," *Information, Communication and Society* 4 (2001): 615–33. The exception to the dearth of research on the role of alternative discursive forms in deliberation is empirical work on jury deliberation, where analysts have distinguished between "verdict-driven" and "evidence-driven" deliberation. See Valerie P. Hans and Neil J. Vidmar, *Judging the Jury* (New York: Plenum, 1986); see also Sanders, "Against Deliberation."

4. On the online dialogues, see Cliff Figallo, Jed Miller, and Marc Weiss, "Listening to the City," *Group Facilitation* 6 (2004): 25–31; and Francesca Polletta and Lesley Wood, "Deliberation after 9/11," in *Wounded City: The Social Effects of the 9/11 Disaster,* ed. Nancy Foner (New York: Russell Sage Foundation, 2005).

5. On voter turnout for the 2000 election, see R. Claire Snyder, "Democratic Theory and the Case for Public Deliberation," in *Democracy's Moment: Reforming the American Political System for the Twenty-First Century*, ed. Ronald Hayduck and Kevin Mattson (Lanham, MD: Rowman and Littlefield, 2002). Stephen Earl Bennett and Linda L. M. Bennett discuss the survey in "What Political Scientists Should Know about the Survey of First-Year Students in 2000," *Political Science and Politics* 34 (2001): 296. Snyder cites polls attesting to Americans' distrust of their political institutions ("Democratic Theory," 79). On contemporaty political discourse as polarized, see Fishkin, *Voice of the People*.

6. On deliberation as uncoerced, see John S. Dryzek, *Deliberative Democracy and Beyond: Liberals, Critics, Contestations* (New York: Oxford University Press, 2000), 17. Participants make arguments that all can accept as persuasive in Cohen, "Deliberation"; discussion of "universal standards" appears in Dryzek, *Deliberative Democracy*, 69; "common good" in Cohen, "Deliberation"; "impartial values" in Jon Elster, "Introduction," in *Deliberative Democracy*, ed. Jon Elster (New York: Cambridge University Press, 1998), 6. As an example of theoretical difference here, Elster talks about the requirement that deliberators be committed to "values of rationality and impartiality" ("Introduction," 8), while Benjamin Barber rejects the idea of grounding deliberation in universalist principles: "In a democracy, living will is always trump" ("Foundationalism and Democracy," in *Democracy and Difference* [see note 2], 356).

7. The argument that people will accept a decision that does not match their preferences is made by Joshua Cohen and Charles Sabel, "Directly-Deliberative Polyarchy," *European Law Journal* 3 (1997): 313–42; see also Ian Shapiro, "Optimal Deliberation?" *Journal of Political Philosophy* 10 (2002): 196–211. On the integration of public deliberation with existing processes, see Cohen, "Deliberation"; Fishkin, *Voice of the People*; and Guttman and Thompson, *Democracy and Disagreement*. For discussion of the way public deliberation avoids polarizing public discourse, see Fishkin, *Voice of the People*; Cohen discusses how it makes for a more informed citizenry and greater trust in government in "Deliberation"; Fishkin, *Voice of the People*; and Guttman and Thompson, *Democracy and Disagreement*.

8. On deliberation working better for those skilled in its discursive requirements, see Bickford, *Dissonance of Democracy*; Young, "Communication and the Other"; Young, *Inclusion and Democracy*; Sanders, "Against Deliberation"; and Jane Mansbridge, "Everyday Talk in the Deliberative System," in *Deliberative Politics: Essays on Democracy and Disagreement*, ed. Stephen Macedo (New York: Oxford University Press, 1999); on some groups not being seen as rational deliberators, see Bickford, *Dissonance of Democracy*.

9. Martha Minow, *Making All the Difference: Inclusion, Exclusion, and American Law* (Ithaca, NY: Cornell University Press, 1990).

10. On the need for diverse forms of discourse, see Young, "Communication and the Other," and *Inclusion and Democracy;* see also Mansbridge, "Everyday Talk." On stories as equalizing, see Young, *Inclusion and Democracy;* and Sanders, "Against Deliberation"; on the way stories can gain a hearing for minority values, see Jane C. Murphy, "Lawyering for Social Change: The Power of the Narrative in Domestic Violence Law Reform," *Hofstra Law Review* 21 (1993): 1243–93; that stories can get new issues on the agenda is affirmed in Murphy, "Lawyering for Social Change," and Young, "Communication and the Other."

11. On stories making real the consequences of abstract governmental action, see Young, *Inclusion and Democracy;* how stories counter stereotypes is discussed in Murphy, "Lawyering for Social Change"; Smith describes how stories reveal the particularist character of ostensibly universal standards in "Storytelling"; see also Sanders, "Against Deliberation"; and Iris Marion Young, "Activist Challenges to Deliberative Democracy," *Political Theory* 29 (2002): 670–90.

12. For the argument that claims should "connect the particular to the general," see Dryzek, *Discursive Democracy,* 68; on personal stories as too particularistic, see Dryzek, *Discursive Democracy,* 69; as unrepresentative of the group, see David Miller, "Is Deliberative Democracy Unfair to Disadvantaged Groups?" in *Democracy as Public Deliberation: New Perspectives,* ed. Maurizio Passerin D'Entrèves (Manchester: Manchester University Press, 2002), 217; as dangerously widening perceptions of difference, see Miller, "Is Deliberative Democracy Unfair?" 210; as provoking vengeance, see Dryzek, *Discursive Democracy,* 69; for "appeal to universal standards," see Dryzek, *Discursive Democracy,* 69; for "invoke reasons," see Miller, "Is Deliberative Democracy Unfair?" 221.

13. Guttmann and Thompson discuss how personal storytelling can precede an appeal to values in *Democracy and Disagreement,* 137; the claim that values can be integrated into the story itself is made by Dryzek, *Discursive Democracy,* 69, and Miller, "Is Deliberative Democracy Unfair?"; Guttman and Thompson describe a "politics of futile gesture" in *Democracy and Disagreement,* 137. There is some confusion among deliberative democrats about whether the problem is storytelling or "testimony." The latter term is used by Lynn Sanders, who emphasizes how groups recount their experiences in their own distinctive idioms. Sometimes, deliberative democrats seem to fault simply that. But they also tend to use storytelling and testimony interchangeably. For example, Dryzek argues that "testimony is similar to one of Young's three alternative forms of communication, storytelling" (*Discursive Demcoracy,* 66) before going on to criticize both writers—especially Young. Miller writes that Sanders's "testimony . . . corresponds roughly to what Young means by storytelling" ("Is Deliberative Democracy Unfair?" 207–8) and defines storytelling as "speech in which someone presents a personal narrative—their life story, so to speak—as a way of explaining what it

means to occupy a certain place in society and/or to dramatize the injustice suffered by a certain group" (208). His definition does not indicate that the speech is unique to the group. Gutmann and Thompson refer to "testimony" rather than storytelling, defining it as "a statement or narrative that gives public voice to a critical stance of some individual or group, but does not seek a perspective that can be justifiable to other individuals or groups" (*Democracy and Disagreement*, 136).

14. On storytelling and reason-giving as separate political discourses, even for storytelling's champions, see, see Young, *Inclusion and Democracy*, 74. Guttman and Thompson argue that deliberators must "reach out" to their audiences (*Democracy and Disagreement*, 137).

15. On the devices used in ordinary conversation to create a storyworld, see Charlotte Linde, *Life Stories: The Creation of Coherence* (New York: Oxford University Press, 1993); Deborah Schiffrin, "The Management of a Co-Operative Self During Argument: The Role of Opinions and Stories," in *Conflict Talk: Sociolinguistic Investigations of Arguments in Conversations*, ed. Allen D. Grimshaw (Cambridge: Cambridge University Press, 1990).

16. On audiences' reformulation of a story's point, see Douglas Maynard, "Narratives and Narrative Structure in Plea Bargaining," *Law and Society Review* 22 (1988): 449–81; John F. Manzo, "Jurors' Narratives of Personal Experience in Deliberation Talk," *Text* 13 (1993): 267–90; John A. Robinson, "Personal Narratives Reconsidered," *Journal of American Folklore* 94 (1981): 58–85; Livia Polanyi, "So What's the Point?" *Semiotica* 25 (1979): 207–41.

17. On deliberation as involving an effort of imagination, see Robert E. Goodin, "Democratic Deliberation Within," *Philosophy and Public Affairs* 29 (2000): 81–110.

18. Polletta and Wood, "Deliberation after 9/11." On current models of deliberation, see Delli Carpini, Cook, and Jacobs, "Public Deliberation."

19. On substitutes for verbal and visual cues in online communication, see Susan C. Herring, "Computer-Mediated Discourse," in *The Handbook of Discourse Analysis*, ed. Deborah Schiffrin, Deborah Tannen, and Heidi E. Hamilton (Malden, MA: Blackwell, 2001); Joseph B. Walther and Malcolm R. Parks, "Cues Filtered Out, Cues Filtered In: Computer-Mediated Communication and Relationships," in *Handbook of Interpersonal Communication*, ed. I. M. L. Knapp and J. A. Daly (Thousand Oaks, CA: Sage, 2002). On opinion shift in online and face-to-face deliberation, see Shanto Iyengar, Robert C. Luskin, and James S. Fishkin, "Facilitating Informed Public Opinion: Evidence from Face-to-Face and On-Line Deliberative Polls," paper presented at the annual meeting of the American Political Science Association, Philadelphia, 2003. On online dialogues as the public commons of the future, see J. Woody Stanley, Christopher Weare, and Juliet Musso, "Participation, Deliberative Democracy, and the Internet: Lessons from a National Forum on Commercial Vehicle Safety," paper presented at the Conference on Prospects for Electronic Democracy, Pittsburgh, PA, September 2002; and M. Poster,

"Cyberdemocracy: The Internet and the Public Sphere," in *Reading Digital Culture*, ed. David Trend (Malden, MA: Blackwell, 2001), 265.

20. William Labov and Joshua Waletsky, "Narrative Analysis: Oral Versions of Personal Experience," in *Essays on the Verbal and Visual Arts*, ed. June Helm (Seattle: University of Washington Press, 1967); William Labov, *Language in the Inner City: Studies in the Black English Vernacular* (Philadelphia: University of Pennsylvania Press, 1972), chap. 9. Numerous scholars have proposed revisions to the original Labovian schema; see, for example, Charlotte Linde, *Life Stories: The Creation of Coherence* (New York: Oxford University Press, 1993); Michael J. Toolan, *Narrative: A Critical Linguistic Introduction* (New York: Routledge, 1988). We suspended one Labovian requirement—that an account refer to a specific past-time event—in order to include what we called "habitual narratives," in which events were recurrent but still had a narrative arc. These were common in the online dialogues. Livia Polanyi refers to something similar as *generic past-time narratives*. Such narratives are "structured around indefinite past time events encoded in event clauses with generic modals such as *would* or *used to*." See Livia Polanyi, *Telling the American Story: A Structural and Cultural Analysis of Conversational Storytelling* (Norwood, NJ: Ablex, 1985), 11. A note on our methodology: We chose twelve groups from the twenty-six that were formed. Although the sampling unit in this study is a forum group, the unit of analysis is the claim. For each group, coders analyzed all narrative and non-narrative claims in the threads for that group, with one exception. All groups had an "introductions" thread (sometimes called something else) in which participants were asked to give their names, say something about their backgrounds, say why it was important for them to participate in the dialogue, and describe their reactions to 9/11 ("What was your immediate reaction to the events of 9/11? How have your feelings changed since then if at all?"). Because participants were invited by organizers to tell personal stories in this thread, we decided to eliminate it from our analysis. We read 5,345 messages. Coders could record more than one claim for each message and could code both narrative and non-narrative claims in the same message. A single message, therefore, could potentially contribute a number of narrative claims and non-narrative claims. For more information on the methodology of the study, see Francesca Polletta and John Lee, "Is Storytelling Good for Democracy?" unpublished paper, Department of Sociology, Columbia University, March 2005.

21. To protect the anonymity of participants, I have provided pseudonyms for all names used in the messages that I quote. I have not corrected messages for grammar or spelling, and have inserted text only where the meaning might otherwise be unclear. Bracketed ellipses [. . .] indicate text that I deleted; unbracketed ones were in the original.

22. On the introduction of a story into ongoing talk, see Gail Jefferson, "Sequential Aspects of Storytelling in Conversation," in *Studies in the Organization*

of Conversational Interaction, ed. Jim Schenkein (New York: Academic Press, 1978).

23. The comparisons of observed and expected proportions of claims and odds ratios are based on chi-square comparisons and logistic regression analyses presented in Polletta and Lee, "Is Storytelling Good for Democracy?"

24. On storytelling as occasioned, see Harvey Sacks, *Lectures on Conversation*, ed. Gail Jefferson (Oxford: Blackwell, 1992); and Jefferson, "Sequential Aspects of Storytelling."

25. On the necessity for different forms of deliberation and deliberative talk in settings characterized by mutual distrust, see Jane Mansbridge, "Should Blacks Represent Blacks and Women Represent Women? A Contingent 'Yes,'" *Journal of Politics* 61 (1999): 628–57.

26. To ensure comparability across groups, in this part of the analysis we considered only claims that appeared in threads introduced by the organizers.

27. Martha L. McCoy and Patrick L. Scully argue that personal storytelling can build trust among deliberators in, "Deliberative Dialogue to Expand Civic Engagement: What Kind of Talk Does Democracy Need?" *National Civic Review* 92 (2002): 117–35.

CHAPTER FIVE

1. Katie Roiphe, *The Morning After: Sex, Fear, and Feminism on Campus* (Boston: Little, Brown, 1993), 109.

2. For factual inaccuracies in Roiphe's account, see Katha Pollitt's review of Roiphe's *Morning After*, "Not Just Bad Sex," *New Yorker*, 4 October 1993, 220. See also Kathryn Abrams's sophisticated critique of the book in the context of feminist debates, "Songs of Innocence and Experience: Dominance Feminism in the University," *Yale Law Journal* 103 (1994): 1533–60. "Culture of complaint" is from Robert Hughes, *Culture of Complaint: The Fraying of America* (New York: Oxford University Press, 1993). Naomi Wolf, *Fire with Fire: The New Female Power and How It Will Change the Twenty-First Century* (New York: Random House, 1993), 136.

3. Martha Minow, "Surviving Victim Talk," *University of California Los Angeles Law Review* 20 (1993): 1411–45; Wendy Kaminer, *I'm Dysfunctional, You're Dysfunctional: The Recovery Movement and other Self-Help Fashions* (New York: Vintage, 1993); Elayne Rapping, *The Culture of Recovery: Making Sense of the Self-Help Movement in Women's Lives* (Boston: Beacon, 1996). Betty Friedan is quoted in Sarah Crichton, "Sexual Correctness: Has It Gone Too Far?" *Newsweek*, 25 October 1993, 52.

4. Wolf, *Fire with Fire*; Rapping, *Culture of Recovery*.

5. On the mid-1980s debates over pornography, see Carole S. Vance, "More Pleasure, More Danger: A Decade after the Barnard Sexuality Conference," in *Pleasure and Danger: Exploring Female Sexuality*, 2nd ed., ed. Carole S. Vance (New York: Pandora, 1992). Naomi Wolf's article was "The Silent

Treatment," *New York Magazine*, 1 March 2004, 22–29. For responses to the article, see Laura Barton, "Who's Crying Wolf?" *Guardian* (London), 26 February 2004; Anne Applebaum, "I Am Victim," *Washington Post*, 25 February 2004. On similar debates among gay and lesbian activists, see John D'Emilio, "Making and Unmaking Minorities: The Tensions between Gay History and Politics," chap. 13 of *Making Trouble: Essays on Gay History, Politics, and the University* (New York: Routledge, 1992), 181–90; and Steven Epstein, "Gay Politics, Ethnic Identity: The Limits of Social Constructionism," *Socialist Review* 17 (1987): 9–54.

6. Kristin Bumiller, *The Civil Rights Society: The Social Construction of Victims* (Baltimore: Johns Hopkins University Press, 1988). A reluctance to appear as a victim has appeared in other studies of how people use the law. See Carol J. Greenhouse, Barbara Yngvesson, and David M. Engel, *Law and Community in Three American Towns* (Ithaca, NY: Cornell University Press, 1994) on the "narratives of avoidance" of the law, told with satisfaction and pride, that were common in the communities they studied.

7. Quotation from *American and Commercial Daily Advertiser*, 26 March 1841, in Michael P. Young, "Confessional Protest: The Evangelical Origins of Social Movements in the United States, 1800–1840" (PhD diss., New York University, 2000), 206–7.

8. Young, "Confessional Protest," 267.

9. Kimberly K. Smith, "Storytelling, Sympathy, and Moral Judgment in American Abolitionism," *Journal of Political Philosophy* 6 (1998): 356–77.

10. Ibid., 373.

11. On public speak-outs against rape, see Marcy Rein, "Softspoken Speakout," *Off Our Backs*, 30 November 1977. On public speak-outs for abortion rights, see Katha Pollitt, "Abortion History 101," *Nation*, 1 May 2000, 10.

12. On the connections between women's liberationist personal storytelling and the coming-out stories of the gay and lesbian movements, see Kenneth Plummer, *Telling Sexual Stories: Power, Change, and Social Worlds* (New York: Routledge, 1995). For a critical discussion of the evolution of the "survivor" label, see Liz Kelly, Sheila Burton, and Linda Regan, "Beyond Victim or Survivor: Sexual Violence, Identity and Feminist Theory and Practice," in *Sexualizing the Social: Power and the Organization of Sexuality*, ed. Lisa Adkins and Vicki Merchant (New York: St. Martin's, 1996).

13. On the development of consciousness-raising in the women's liberationist movement, see Alice Echols, *Daring to Be Bad: Radical Feminism in America, 1967–1975* (Minneapolis: University of Minnesota Press, 1989); Kathie Sarachild, "Consciousness-Raising: A Radical Weapon," in *Feminist Revolution*, abridged ed., ed. Kathie Sarachild (New York: Random House, 1978); and Maren Lockwood Carden, *The New Feminist Movement* (New York: Sage, 1974).

14. Steven Epstein, *Impure Science: AIDS, Activism, and the Politics of Knowledge* (Berkeley and Los Angeles: University of California Press, 1996).

15. Nancy Whittier, "Emotional Strategies: The Collective Reconstruction and Display of Oppositional Emotions in the Movement against Child Sexual Abuse," in *Passionate Politics: Emotions and Social Movements,* ed. Jeff Goodwin, James M. Jasper, and Francesca Polletta (Chicago: University of Chicago Press, 2001).

16. Martha Mahoney argues similarly that press accounts of battered women have tended to highlight the sensational cases, in which abuse was so grotesque as to seem aberrant. One result has been a failure to take full account of the prevalence of domestic abuse. See Martha R. Mahoney, "Victimization or Oppression? Women's Lives, Violence, and Agency," in *The Public Nature of Private Violence: The Discovery of Domestic Abuse,* ed. Martha Albertson Fineman and Roxanne Mykitiuk (New York: Routledge, 1994).

17. Vicki Schultz, "Telling Stories about Women and Work: Judicial Interpretations of Sex Segregation in the Workplace in Title VII Cases Raising the Lack of Interest Argument," *Harvard Law Review* 103 (1990): 1749-1843.

18. Ibid.

19. Ibid., 1801.

20. Ibid., 1809.

21. Ibid.

22. For accounts of legal advocates' efforts to win the admission of such testimony, see Elizabeth M. Schneider, *Battered Women and Feminist Lawmaking* (New Haven, CT: Yale University Press, 2000).

23. For the figure on acquittals, see Abigail Trafford, "Why Battered Women Kill: Self-Defense, Not Revenge, Is Often the Motive," *Washington Post,* 26 February 1991; on convictions overturned on appeal, see Holly Maguigan, "Battered Women and Self-Defense: Myths and Misconceptions in Current Reform Proposals," *University of Pennsylvania Law Review* 140 (1991): 379-486. On judges' failure to give instructions to juries, see Maguigan, "Battered Women and Self-Defense," 435; on attorneys' failure to see the case for self-defense, see Schneider, *Battered Women and Feminist Lawmaking,* 122. See also Janet Parrish, *Trend Analysis: Expert Testimony on Battering and Its Effects in Criminal Cases* (Philadelphia: Clearinghouse, 1995).

24. Schneider, *Battered Women and Feminist Lawmaking,* 122; Maguigan, "Battered Women and Self-Defense," 385.

25. Mahoney, "Victimization," 64.

26. Schneider, *Battered Women and Feminist Lawmaking,* 80; Kim Lane Scheppele, "Just the Facts, Ma'am: Sexualized Violence, Evidentiary Habits, and the Revision of Truth," *New York Law School Law Review* 37 (1992): 123-72.

27. On battered women in custody disputes, see Schneider, *Battered Women and Feminist Lawmaking.* On dichotomized conceptions of autonomy and dependence and how they affect divorce law and welfare reform, see Martha Albertson Fineman, "Masking Dependency: The Political Role of Family Rhetoric," *Virginia Law Review* 81 (1995): 2181-2216; and Martha Albertson

Fineman, "Fatherhood, Feminism and Family Law," *McGeorge School of Law, University of the Pacific, McGeorge Law Review* 32 (2001): 1031–49.

28. Judge Dubé is quoted in Schneider, *Battered Women and Feminist Lawmaking,* 142.

29. Lynne N. Henderson, "Legality and Empathy," *Michigan Law Review* 85 (1987): 1574–1653. For a critique of the claimed virtue of narrative that is somewhat different from mine, see Toni M. Massaro, "Empathy, Legal Storytelling, and the Rule of Law: New Words, Old Wounds?" *Michigan Law Review* 87 (1989): 2099–2127.

30. Henderson, "Legality and Empathy," 1639.

31. Ibid., 1643, 1618, 1615–16. *Shapiro v. Thompson* 394 U.S. 618 (1969).

32. Jane C. Murphy, "Lawyering for Social Change: The Power of the Narrative in Domestic Violence Law Reform," *Hofstra Law Review* 21 (1993): 1243–93.

33. Kathryn Abrams, "Unity, Narrative and Law," *Studies in Law, Politics, and Society* 13 (1993): 3–35.

34. The story is quoted in Schneider, *Battered Women and Feminist Lawmaking,* 10.

35. Roddy Doyle, *The Woman Who Walked into Doors* (New York: Viking, 1996), 175.

36. For good discussions of point of view, see Gérard Genette, *Narrative Discourse: An Essay in Method,* trans. Jane E. Lewin (Ithaca, NY: Cornell University Press, 1980); Shlomith Rimmon-Kenan, *Narrative Fiction: Contemporary Poetics* (London and New York: Routledge, 2002); Robert Scholes and Robert Kellogg, *The Nature of Narrative* (New York: Oxford University Press, 1968); and Mieke Bal, *Narratology: Introduction to the Theory of Narrative* (Toronto: University of Toronto Press, 1998). For a good discussion of point of view in victim impact statements, see Peter Brooks, "Illicit Stories," *Diacritics* 25 (1995): 41–51.

37. Murphy, "Lawyering for Social Change."

38. Ibid., 1281, 1283, 1283–84.

39. Ibid., 1280.

40. On the use of the conversational historical present to signal a new event, see Nessa Wolfson, "Conversational Historical Present Alternation," *Language* 55 (1979): 168–82.

41. Murphy, "Lawyering for Social Change," 1283.

42. Ibid., 1279, 1280.

43. Ibid., 1282.

44. Ibid., 1281, 1283, 1280.

45. Howard Schneider, "Md. to Free Abused Women: Schaefer Commutes 8 Terms, Citing Violence," *Washington Post,* 20 February 1991.

46. Tamar Lewin, "More States Study Clemency for Women Who Killed Abusers," *New York Times,* 21 February 1991, sec. A; Tamar Lewin, "Criticism of Clemency May Affect Efforts to Free Battered Women," *New York Times,* 2 April 1991, sec. A.

47. Northrop Frye, *Anatomy of Criticism: Four Essays* (Princeton, NJ: Princeton University Press, 1957), 41.

48. W. Lance Bennett, *News: The Politics of Illusion*, 3rd ed. (White Plains, NY: Longman, 1996), 39.

49. For an overview of research findings related to exemplar use, see Dolf Zillmann and Hans-Bernd Brosius, *Exemplification in Communication: The Influence of Case Reports on the Perception of Issues* (Mahwah, NJ: Lawrence Erlbaum, 2000). On exemplar use in relation to controversial issues, see Stephen D. Perry and William J. Gonzenbach, "Effects of News Exemplification Extended: Considerations of Controversiality and Perceived Future Opinion," *Journal of Broadcasting and Electronic Media* 41 (1997): 229–45. On exemplars' value as informational shortcuts, see Zillmann and Brosius, *Exemplification in Communication*.

50. Jason Salzman, phone interview by author, 21 April 2004; see also Jason Salzman, *Making the News: A Guide for Activists and Nonprofits*, rev. ed. (Boulder, CO: Westview, 2003); Kimberly Blanton, interview by author, New York, 26 May 2004.

51. Myra Marx Ferree, William Anthony Gamson, Jürgen Gerhards, and Dieter Rucht, *Shaping Abortion Discourse: Democracy and the Public Sphere in Germany and the United States* (New York: Cambridge University Press, 2002), 245; Herbert Gans, *Deciding What's News: A Study of CBS Evening News, NBC Nightly News, Newsweek, and Time* (New York: Vintage Books, 1980), 44.

52. Rapping, *Culture of Recovery*.

53. Laura Grindstaff, *Money Shot: Trash, Class, and the Making of TV Talk Shows* (Chicago: University of Chicago Press, 2002).

54. Joshua Gamson, *Freaks Talk Back: Tabloid Talk Shows and Sexual Nonconformity* (Chicago: University of Chicago Press, 1998); see also Whittier, "Emotional Strategies."

CHAPTER SIX

1. For work on states' representations of the past, see, for example, the essays in Eric J. Hobsbawm and Terence Ranger, eds., *The Invention of Tradition* (New York: Cambridge University Press, 1983); the essays in Jeffrey K. Olick, ed., *States of Memory: Continuities, Conflicts, and Transformations in National Retrospection* (Durham, NC: Duke University Press, 2003); and David I. Kertzer, *Ritual, Politics, and Power* (New Haven, CT: Yale University Press, 1988).

2. On South Africa's Truth and Reconciliation Commission and other truth commissions, see Martha Minow, *Between Vengeance and Forgiveness: Facing History after Genocide and Mass Violence* (Boston: Beacon, 1998). On the effects of authorities being forced to tell their stories, see Francesca Polletta, "The Structural Context of Novel Rights Claims: Rights Innovation in the Southern Civil Rights Movement, 1961–1966," *Law and Society Review*

34 (2000): 367–406. On governments' efforts to control access to historical archives, see Keith M. Wilson, ed., *Forging the Collective Memory: Government and International Historians through Two World Wars* (Providence, RI: Berghahn Books, 1996); for an example of a political career destroyed by an awkward telling of the past, see Jeffrey K. Olick and Daniel Levy's discussion of the forced resignation of German Bundestag President Philipp Jenninger in 1988 following a speech given about ordinary Germans' views of Jews in 1933, a speech given on the eve of the anniversary of Kristallnacht, in "Collective Memory and Cultural Constraint: Holocaust Myth and Rationality in German Politics," *American Sociological Review* 62 (1997): 921–36. On battles over government-sponsored memorials and exhibitions, see, for example, Edward T. Linenthal and Tom Engelhardt, eds., *History Wars: The Enola Gay and Other Battles for the American Past* (New York: Henry Holt, 1996).

3. On the commemorative interests of "political structures and ordinary people" see John Bodnar, *Remaking America: Public Memory, Commemoration, and Patriotism in the Twentieth Century* (Princeton, NJ: Princeton University Press, 1994), 18; on those of "dominants and subordinates," see Richard Merelman, "Challenge and Resistance: Two Cases of Cultural Conflict in the United States," in *Language, Symbolism, and Politics,* ed. Richard Merelman (Boulder, CO: Westview, 1992), 248; and on "official" and "popular" memory, see Shaunna L. Scott, "Dead Work: The Construction and Reconstruction of the Harlan Miners Memorial," *Qualitative Sociology* 19 (1996): 388. On the risks of commemorating past insurgency, see Stephen Greenblatt, "Murdering Peasants: Status, Genre and the Representation of Rebellion," *Representations* 1 (1983): 1–29.

4. An initiative by Representative Newt Gingrich made the *Congressional Record* accessible by Internet beginning in 1993. I used this source in conjunction with published transcripts of congressional hearings, some text from earlier printed issues of the *Congressional Record,* and newspaper accounts and analyses. On special orders and one-minute speeches, see Charles Tiefer, *Congressional Practice and Procedure: A Reference, Research, and Legislative Guide* (New York: Greenwood, 1989).

5. Entries in the *Congressional Record* may consist of a single speech, the extension of remarks by one congressperson, or an extended debate. By "speech," I mean a statement that was either a single entry or part of one (but I counted numerous speaking turns by one representative in the entry as a single speech). When I refer to the number of "references to King," I mean the number of speeches in which King was mentioned at least once.

6. Figures on African American representatives' invocations of King include the nonvoting representative from the District of Columbia but not the delegates from the Virgin Islands. J. C. Watts of Oklahoma, one of the two African American Republican representatives, made two speeches referring to

King (Watts's term began in 1995); the other, Gary Franks of Connecticut, made no speeches citing King during his two terms of office (surprising, since he was on the King Holiday Commission).

7. House, Rep. Martini of New Jersey speaking on Black History Month, 104th Cong., 1st sess., 141 *Cong. Rec.* (28 February 1995): E460. On presidential, congressional, and popular constructions of the "American dream," see John Kenneth White, "Storyteller in Chief: Why Presidents Like to Tell Tales," in *Tales of the State: Narrative in Contemporary U.S. Politics and Public Policy,* ed. Sanford Schram and Philip T. Neisser (Lanham, MD: Rowman and Littlefield, 1997); and Miriam B. Rosenthal and Sanford Schram, "Pluralizing the American Dream," in *Tales of the State.* The fact that 1993 was the thirtieth anniversary of the "I have a dream" speech may account in part for its high profile in the 103rd congressional session (1993–94), when it appeared in twenty-six speeches by congressional representatives. In the next two-year period, it appeared in thirteen speeches. However, it appeared in nine speeches between January and May of 1997, which is only one-quarter of the 105th Congress.

8. "I Have a Dream" (speech given at the March on Washington for Jobs and Freedom, Washington, DC, 28 August 1963); "Letter from Birmingham City Jail," in Martin Luther King, Jr., *A Testament of Hope: The Essential Writings of Martin Luther King, Jr.,* ed. James Melvin Washington (San Francisco: Harper and Row, 1986); Nobel Peace Prize acceptance speech (Oslo, Norway, 10 December 1964); "I've Been to the Mountaintop" (speech delivered in support of striking sanitation workers, Mason Temple, Memphis, TN, 3 April 1968).

9. King, *Testament of Hope,* 87, 103.

10. Vincent Harding, *Martin Luther King: The Inconvenient Hero* (Maryknoll, NY: Orbis, 1996), 469. On the representation of King in children's textbooks, see Herbert R. Kohl, *Should We Burn Babar? Essays on Children's Literature and the Power of Stories* (New York: New Press, 1995); on King in public oratory about the King holiday, see Eyal J. Naveh, *Crown of Thorns: Political Martyrdom in America from Abraham Lincoln to Martin Luther King, Jr.* (New York: New York University Press, 1990); Harding, *Martin Luther King;* Scott A. Sandage, "A Marble House Divided: The Lincoln Memorial, the Civil Rights Movement, and the Politics of Memory, 1939–1963," *Journal of American History* 24 (1993): 135–67. On television coverage of the King holiday, see Christopher P. Campbell, *Race, Myth and the News* (Thousand Oaks, CA: Sage, 1995). On assimilationist and pluralist models, see Michael Omi and Howard Winant, *Racial Formation in the United States: From the 1960s to the 1980s* (New York: Routledge, 1986). Following the ethnic-group model, King was rarely linked with revolutionaries or dissidents: once with American revolutionaries (the Minutemen and Paul Revere) and once with Nobel Prize–winning dissidents (Vaclav Havel, Andrei Sakharov, Desmond Tutu, Aung San Suu Kyi, and Lech Walesa).

11. House, Rep. Boyd of Florida speaking on Black History Month, 105th Cong., 1st sess., 143 *Cong. Rec.* (11 February 1997): H434; House, Rep. Gilman of New York, "In Honor of Martin Luther King, Jr.," 105th Cong., 1st sess., 143 *Cong. Rec.* (7 January 1997): E22; Senate, Senator Kennedy of Massachusetts speaking on Employment Nondiscrimination Act of 1996, 104th Cong., 2nd sess., 142 *Cong. Rec.* (10 September 1996): S10134; House, Rep. McIntosh of Indiana speaking on the Church Arson Prevention Act, 104th Cong., 2nd sess., 142 *Cong. Rec.* (18 June 1996): H6457. On themes of unity and progress in American commemoration, see Michael G. Kammen, *Mystic Chords of Memory: The Transformation of Tradition in American Culture* (New York: Knopf, 1991).

12. Senate, Senator Biden of Delaware speaking on Church Arson Prevention Act of 1996, 104th Cong., 2nd sess., 142 *Cong. Rec.* (26 June 1996): S6941; House, Rep. Reed of Rhode Island, speaking on Church Arson Prevention Act of 1996, 104th Cong., 2nd sess., 142 *Cong. Rec.* (18 June 1996): H6462. House, Rep. Frank of Massachusetts speaking on Freedom Summer Remembered, 103rd Cong., 2nd sess., 140 *Cong. Rec.* (21 June 1994): H4759.

13. House, Rep. Hilliard of Alabama speaking on King Holiday and Service Act of 1994, 103rd Cong., 2nd sess., 140 *Cong. Rec.* (15 March 1994): H1332; Senate, Senator Moseley-Braun of Illinois speaking on King Holiday and Service Act of 1994, 103rd Cong., 2nd sess., 140 *Cong. Rec.* (23 May 1994): S6163; House, Rep. Johnson of Texas speaking on Black History Month, 105th Cong., 1st sess., 143 *Cong. Rec.* (11 February 1997): H430. Richard M. Merelman, *Representing Black Culture: Racial Conflict and Cultural Politics in the United States* (New York: Routledge, 1995), 87–89.

14. On the position of black legislators in a majority-white Congress, see Carol M. Swain, *Black Faces, Black Interests: The Representation of African Americans in Congress* (Cambridge, MA: Harvard University Press, 1993).

15. Bayard Rustin, "From Protest to Politics: The Future of the Civil Rights Movement," *Commentary* 39 (1965): 25–31. On vote dilution, see Frank R. Parker, *Black Votes Count: Political Empowerment in Mississippi after 1965* (Chapel Hill: University of North Carolina Press, 1990). Figures on black elected officials in Manning Marable, *Beyond Black and White: Transforming African American Politics* (London: Verso, 1995), 145. Quotation from D.C. councilperson in Eric Pianin, "The March and the Dream," *Washington Post*, 27 August 1983. On post-1960s tensions between black protest elites and political ones, see Adolph L. Reed, *The Jesse Jackson Phenomenon: The Crisis of Purpose in Afro-American Politics* (New Haven, CT: Yale University Press, 1986); Marable, *Beyond Black and White;* Robert Charles Smith, *We Have No Leaders: African Americans in the Post–Civil Rights Era* (Albany: State University of New York Press, 1996); Swain, *Black Faces, Black Interests;* Clarence Lusane, *African Americans at the Crossroads: The Restructuring of Black Leadership and the 1992 Elections* (Boston: South End, 1994); and

William L. Clay, *Just Permanent Interests: Black Americans in Congress, 1870–1991* (New York: Amistad, 1992).

16. Reed, *Jesse Jackson,* 8; Young is quoted in Martin Schram and Dan Balz, "Jackson's Run Poses Dilemma for Black Leaders," *Washington Post,* 27 November 1983; Reed, *Jesse Jackson,* 28; Mondale strategist quoted in Schram and Balz, "Jackson's Run"; Marable, *Beyond Black and White;* Lowery quoted in ibid., 145.

17. Figures in Marable, *Beyond Black and White,* 146.

18. House, Rep. Payne of New Jersey speaking on King Holiday and Service Act of 1994, 103rd Cong., 2nd sess., 140 *Cong. Rec.* (15 March 1994): H1332; House, Rep. Hilliard of Alabama, "Dr. M. L. King Holiday Commission," 103rd Cong., 2nd sess., 140 *Cong. Rec.* (15 March 1994): H1330; House, Rep. Meek of Florida speaking on 1965 Voting Rights Under Attack, 103rd Cong., 2nd sess., 140 *Cong. Rec.* (22 March 1994): H1874; House, Rep. Rangel of New York, "Tribute to the Late Justice Thurgood Marshall," 103rd Cong., 1st sess., 139 *Cong. Rec.* (15 September 1993): H6762; Senate, Senator Moseley-Braun of Illinois, "The 25th Anniversary of the Assassination of Martin Luther King, Jr.," 103rd Cong., 1st sess., 139 *Cong. Rec.* (3 April 1993): S4498; House, Rep. Mfume of Maryland, "Expressing the Sense of Congress on the Senior Representative of the Nation of Islam," 103rd Cong., 2nd sess., 140 *Cong. Rec.* (23 February 1994): H572; House, Rep. Thompson of Mississippi, "Freedom Summer Remembered," 103rd Cong., 2nd sess., 140 *Cong. Rec.* (21 June 1994): H4760; House, Rep. Collins of Illinois, "Selma to Montgomery National Historic Trail," 104th Cong., 2nd sess., 142 *Cong. Rec.* (14 May 1996): H4916; House, Rep. Millender-McDonald of California, "Commemorating Black History Month," 105th Cong., 1st sess., 143 *Cong. Rec.* (13 February 1997): H581.

19. House, Rep. Jackson of Illinois speaking on Black History Month, 105th Cong., 1st sess., 143 *Cong. Rec.* (11 February 1997): H428; House, Rep. Hilliard of Alabama, "Church Burnings," 104th Cong., 2nd sess., 142 *Cong. Rec.* (10 June 1996): H6114.

20. House, Rep. Jackson-Lee of Texas, "Tribute to the Late Hon. Barbara Jordan," 104th Cong., 2nd sess., 142 *Cong. Rec.* (24 January 1996): H822; House, Rep. Jackson of Illinois speaking on Black History Month, 105th Cong., 1st sess., 143 *Cong. Rec.* (11 February 1997): H427; House, Rep. Jackson-Lee, "Tribute to Harold Ford, Sr.," 104th Cong., 2nd sess., 142 *Cong. Rec.* (26 September 1996): H11364.

21. House, Rep. Payne of New Jersey, speaking on Black History Month, 103rd Cong., 2nd sess., 140 *Cong. Rec.* (23 February 1994): H661; House, Rep. Johnson of Texas speaking on Black History Month, 103rd Cong., 2nd sess., 140 *Cong. Rec.* (23 February 1994): H659; House, Rep. Millender-McDonald, speaking on Black History Month, 105th Cong., 1st sess., 143 *Cong. Rec.* (13 February 1997): H581.

22. Senate, Senator Wofford of Pennsylvania speaking on the King Holiday and Service Act of 1994, 103rd Cong., 1st sess., 139 *Cong. Rec.* (3 April 1993): S4508.

23. Senate, Senator Moseley-Braun, speaking on the King Holiday and Service Act of 1994, 103rd Cong., 2nd sess., 140 *Cong. Rec.* (23 May 1994): S6164.

24. House, Rep. Clayton of North Carolina speaking on the King Holiday and Service Act of 1994, 103rd Cong., 2nd sess., 140 *Cong. Rec.* (15 March 1994): H1333; Senate, Senator Moseley-Braun, speaking on the King Holiday and Service Act of 1994, 103rd Cong., 2nd sess., 140 *Cong. Rec.* (23 May 1994): S6172. The testimony of Coretta Scott King appears in The King Holiday and Service Act of 1993, Hearing Before the Committee on the Judiciary, Senate, 103rd Cong., 2nd sess., 13 April 1994 (Washington, DC: Government Printing Office, 1995). Campbell, in *Race, Myth and the News,* describes a similar framing in the media's coverage of the King Holiday in 1993.

25. On pluralism, see William A. Gamson, *The Strategy of Social Protest,* 2nd ed. (Belmont, CA: Wadsworth, 1990); and Doug McAdam, *Political Process and the Development of Black Insurgency, 1930–1970* (Chicago: University of Chicago Press, 1982).

26. Jesse L. Jackson, Sr., remarks made at Martin Luther King Memorial Breakfast, Washington, DC, 15 January 1996; Jesse L. Jackson, Sr., "Expanding the Marketplace: Inclusion, the Key to Economic Growth," speech given at Windows on the World, New York, NY, 15 January 1998.

27. Benjamin Chavis quoted in "News Conference with Organizers of the upcoming 30th Anniversary March on Washington," transcript, Federal News Service, 19 August 1993; Reverend Walter Fauntroy, ibid. I secured transcripts of all the speeches I could during the period from 1 January 1993 to 31 December 1998, mainly through news services, and, in the case of Marian Wright Edelman, from her office. Of the 26 speeches given by Jesse Jackson during this period for which I obtained transcripts, 22 (or 85 percent) referred to King; of the 29 speeches given by Marian Wright Edelman, for which I obtained transcripts, 19 (66 percent) referred to King. I was able to obtain only a few transcribed speeches by Joseph Lowery, Walter Fauntroy, William Gibson, and Benjamin Chavis, leaders of the SCLC and the NAACP. Chavis was the only one whose speeches tended not to refer to King (only one of five did so).

28. Jesse L. Jackson, Sr., "Draft Remarks," speech delivered to the United Food and Commercial Workers National Convention, Chicago, IL, 28 July 1998; Jesse L. Jackson, Sr., quoted in "News Conference with Organizers of the Upcoming 30th Anniversary March on Washington," transcript, Federal News Service, 19 August 1993. King is grouped with Nelson Mandela and Jesus Christ in Jesse L. Jackson, "Remarks at the National Rainbow Coalition Violence Summit," transcript, Federal News Service, 7 January 1994; with Christ, Tolstoy, and Gandhi in Marian Wright Edelman, speech delivered at the State of the World Forum, San Francisco, CA, 4 November 1997;

with Christ, Tolstoy, Gandhi, and Dorothy Day in Marian Wright Edelman, "The Measure of Our Success," commencement address given to Southern Methodist University, Dallas, TX, 22 May 1993; and with Elizabeth Glaser and Sarah and Jim Brady in Marian Wright Edelman, "Address to Harvard Medical School" (Cambridge, MA, 9 June 1994) and "Address to Milton Academy" (Milton, MA, 10 June 1994).

29. On the "we've made progress but . . ." formulation using statistics, see the speeches by Marian Wright Edelman cited in note 28 above. William Gibson is quoted in "News Conference with Organizers of the Upcoming 30th Anniversary March on Washington," transcript, Federal News Service, 19 August 1993; Jackson, "Rainbow Coalition Violence Summit"; Marian Wright Edelman, "Progress or Peril? Community or Chaos? America's Unfinished Symphony," speech delivered at the National Cathedral, Washington, DC, 16 January 1995. A similar formulation appears in Marian Wright Edelman, "Toward the Development of African American Children," speech delivered to the annual conference of the National Urban League, Washington, DC, 2 August 1993. Jesse L. Jackson, Sr., recounts King's movement as one of four movements in "Draft Remarks," speech delivered to the annual conference of the National Urban League, Philadelphia, PA, 5 August 1998.

30. House, Rep. Dixon of California speaking on Martin Luther King, Jr., Memorial Bill Extension of Remarks, 103rd Cong., 1st sess., 139 *Cong. Rec.* (7 April 1993): E922; House, Rep. Stokes of Ohio speaking on Black History Month, 103rd Cong., 1st sess., 139 *Cong. Rec.* (24 February 1993): H846; House, Rep. Norton of the District of Columbia, "Tribute to James Farmer, Civil Rights Freedom Fighter," 105th Cong., 1st sess., 143 *Cong. Rec.* (24 April 1997): H1870; Senate, Senator Moseley-Braun, speaking on the King Holiday and Service Act of 1994, 103rd Cong., 2nd sess., 140 *Cong. Rec.* (23 May 1994): S6166; House, Rep Johnson of Texas, speaking on Black History Month, 103rd Cong., 1st sess., 139 *Cong. Rec.* (24 February 1993): H854. Kirk Savage, in his study of civil war monuments entitled "The Politics of Memory: Black Emancipation and the Civil War Monument," in *Commemorations: The Politics of National Identity,* ed. John R. Gillis (Princeton, NJ: Princeton University Press, 1994), found that movement sponsors offered several rationales for such monuments, "occasionally advancing the argument that people are forgetful and need their social memory bolstered by powerful mnemonic aids; sometimes arguing instead that memory is safe in the present but monuments are needed to transmit it across generations; yet frequently invoking a startling counterargument—that the memory of heroism is undying and will outlast even monuments, which are therefore built simply as proof of memory's reality and strength." I found the same rationales, and additional ones, in African American legislators' arguments for commemoration.

31. House, Rep. Clyburn of South Carolina speaking on Black History Month, 104th Cong., 1st sess., 140 *Cong. Rec.* (22 February 1995): H2044; Senate,

Senator Moseley-Braun, speaking on the King Holiday and Service Act of 1994, 103rd Cong., 2nd sess., 140 *Cong. Rec.* (23 May 1994): S6165; House, Rep. Tucker of California speaking on Black History Month, 103rd Cong., 2nd sess., 140 *Cong. Rec.* (23 February 1994): H656; House, Rep. Watt of North Carolina, "Role of Civil Rights Organizations in History," 105th Cong., 1st sess., 143 *Cong. Rec.* (11 February 1997): H439; House, Rep. Owens of New York, ibid.: H440.

32. House, Rep. Mfume of Maryland, "In Memory of Dr. Martin Luther King, Jr." (extension of remarks), 103rd Cong., 1st sess., 139 *Cong. Rec.* (7 April 1993): E928; House, Rep. Hilliard, speaking on the King Holiday and Service Act of 1994, 103rd Cong., 2nd sess., 140 *Cong. Rec.* (15 March 1994): H1332; House, Rep. Norton of the District of Columbia, "Freedom Summer Remembered," 103rd Cong., 2nd sess., 140 *Cong. Rec.* (21 June 1994): H4759; House, Rep. Lewis, "Tribute to James Farmer, Civil Rights Freedom Fighter," 105th Cong., 1st sess., 143 *Cong. Rec.* (24 April 1997): H1870; House, Rep. Lewis of Georgia, "Commemorating the 30th Anniversary of the Voting Rights Campaign of 1965," 104th Cong., 1st sess., 141 *Cong. Rec.* (7 March 1995): H2795; House, Rep. McKinney of Georgia, "The Real Environmental Extremists," 104th Cong., 1st sess., 141 *Cong. Rec.* (24 May 1995): H5565; House, Rep. Watt of North Carolina, "Commemorating the 30th Anniversary of the Voting Rights Campaign of 1965," 104th Cong., 1st sess., 141 *Cong. Rec.* (7 March 1995): H2801.

33. House, Rep. Johnson of Texas speaking on Black History Month, 105th Cong., 1st sess., 143 *Cong. Rec.* (11 February 1997): H430; House, Rep. Clay of Missouri speaking on Black History Month, 103rd Cong., 2nd sess., 140 *Cong. Rec.* (23 February 1994): H666; Senate, Sen. Mosely-Braun, "The 25th Anniversary of the Assassination of Martin Luther King, Jr.," 103rd Cong., 1st sess., 139 *Cong. Rec.* (3 April 1993): H4499; Rep. Jackson-Lee speaking on the Selma to Montgomery National Historic Trail, 104th Cong., 2nd sess., 142 *Cong. Rec.* (14 May 1996): H4917; House, Rep. Waters of California, "Preventing Teenage Pregnancy," 104th Cong., 2nd sess., 142 *Cong. Rec.* (12 March 1996): H2110.

34. Donald C. Bacon, Roger H. Davidson, and Morton Keller, *The Encyclopedia of the United States Congress* (New York: Simon and Schuster, 1995), 400, 166. On the curbing of committees' autonomy, see ibid., 420.

35. On the Sandinistas and Zapatistas, see Robert S. Jansen, "Resurrection and Reappropriation: Historical Uses of Political Figures in Comparative Perspective," unpublished typescript, University of California at Los Angeles, 2004.

36. For an example of the political costs of giving a speech on the wrong occasion, see the discussion of the Jenninger affair in Jeffrey K. Olick and Daniel Levy, "Collective Memory and Cultural Constraint: Holocaust Myth and Rationality in German Politics," *American Sociological Review* 62 (1997): 921-36.

1. On popular views of love, see Ann Swidler, *Talk of Love: How Culture Matters* (Chicago: University of Chicago Press, 2001); on technology, see William A. Gamson, "Political Discourse and Collective Action," *International Social Movement Research* 1 (1988): 219–44.

2. On AIDS activists' challenge to norms of scientific review, see Steven Epstein, *Impure Science: AIDS, Activism, and the Politics of Knowledge* (Berkeley and Los Angeles: University of California Press, 1996).

3. On narrative's capacity to grasp historical detail, contingency, causal complexity, sequence, and agency, see James Mahoney, "Nominal, Ordinal, and Narrative Appraisal in Macrocausal Analysis," *American Journal of Sociology* 104 (1999): 117; Jill Quadagno, and Stan J. Knapp, "Have Historical Sociologists Forsaken Theory? Thoughts on the History/Theory Relationship," *Sociological Methods and Research* 20 (1992): 481–507. On narrative's contribution to macrocausal explanation, see Robin Stryker, "Beyond History versus Theory: Strategic Narrative and Sociological Explanation," *Sociological Methods and Research* 24 (1996): 304–52; and Larry J. Griffin, "Temporality, Events, and Explanation in Historical Sociology: An Introduction," *Sociological Methods and Research* 20 (1992): 403–27, and "Narrative, Event-Structure Analysis, and Causal Interpretation in Historical Sociology," *American Journal of Sociology* 98 (1993): 1094–1133. Mahoney, "Macrocausal Analysis," 117.

4. Griffin quotes Stone in "Narrative," 1097; Stryker paraphrases him in "Beyond History versus Theory," 305. Andrew Abbott, "From Causes to Events: Notes on Narrative Positivism," *Sociological Methods and Research* 20 (1992): 428; Stryker, "Beyond History versus Theory," 309; Quadagno and Knapp, "Historical Sociologists," 486. The articles I reviewed include Abbott, "Narrative Positivism"; Ronald Aminzade, "Historical Sociology and Time," *Sociological Methods and Research* 20 (1992): 456–80; Kevin Fox Gotham and William G. Staples, "Narrative Analysis and the New Historical Sociology," *Sociological Quarterly* 37 (1996): 481–501; Griffin, "Temporality," and "Narrative"; Mahoney, "Macrocausal Analysis"; Stryker, "Beyond History versus Theory"; and Quadagno and Knapp, "Historical Sociologists." I say that Stone uses *narrative* and *story* interchangeably on the basis of two pieces of evidence. He defines "storytelling" as "the circumstantial *narration* in great detail of one or more 'happenings'" (emphasis added). He also describes the "revival of non-analytical modes of writing history, of which *story-telling* is one" and then writes in the next sentence: "Of course *narrative* is not the only manner of writing the history . . ." (emphasis added). This suggests that narrative and story refer to the same non-analytical mode of writing history. Lawrence Stone, *The Past and the Present* (Boston: Routledge and Kegan Paul, 1981), 16, 17.

5. The distinction between *fabula* and *sjuzhet* is made by, among others, Vladimir Propp, in *The Morphology of the Folktale* (Austin: University of Texas

Press, 1968 [1928]). Griffin, "Narrative," 1099; Stryker, "Beyond History Versus Theory"; Quadagno and Knapp, "Historical Sociologists"; Aminzade, "Historical Sociology," 457–58; Griffin, "Temporality," 419.

6. Stone, *Past and Present*, 4.

7. Stryker ("Beyond History versus Theory"), and Gotham and Staples ("Narrative Analysis"), talk about narrative's capacity to capture agency and structure; Griffin, in "Temporality" (414), discusses its capacity to comprehend the larger significance of events "without vulgarising or losing contact with the experienced lives of the protagonists" (quoting Philip Abrams, *Historical Sociology* [Ithaca, NY: Cornell University Press, 1982], 200); and Mahoney ("Macrocausal Analysis"), Stryker ("Beyond History versus Theory"), Griffin ("Narrative"), and Quadagno and Knapp ("Historical Sociologists"), discuss narrative's capacity to capture temporal sequence and the intersections of multiple causes.

8. Griffin, "Narrative," 1099.

9. On the theoretical underpinnings of historical analysts' concepts, see Stryker, "Beyond History versus Theory."

10. Margaret R. Somers, "Where Is Sociology after the Historic Turn? Knowledge Cultures, Narrativity, and Historical Epistemologies," in *The Historic Turn in the Human Sciences*, ed. Terrence J. McDonald (Ann Arbor: University of Michigan Press, 1996); Lisa Disch, "Impartiality, Storytelling, and the Seductions of Narrative: An Essay at an Impasse," *Alternatives* 28 (2003): 253–66; Joan Wallach Scott, "The Evidence of Experience," in *The Historic Turn*.

11. Griffin, "Narrative"; Peter Bearman, Robert Faris, and James Moody, "Blocking the Future: New Solutions for Old Problems in Historical Social Science," *Social Science History* 23 (1999): 501–33. Abbott discusses optimal sequence matching and what he calls "narrative positivism" more broadly in "Narrative Positivism."

12. On a "disciplined dialogue" between theory and evidence, see E. P. Thompson, *The Poverty of Theory and Other Essays* (New York: Monthly Review Press, 1978), 43. Charles Tilly points out that recounting the same social process, say, a military battle or the racial integration of school, from multiple points of view might lead the researcher to recognize the non-storylike mechanisms that are responsible for the differences and connections among participants' experiences. See his "The Trouble with Stories," chap. 3 of *Stories, Identities, and Political Change* (Lanham, MD: Rowman and Littlefield, 2002).

13. Michael Schudson, "Question Authority: A History of the News Interview in American Journalism, 1860s–1930s," *Media, Culture and Society* 16 (1994): 565–87.

14. "I'm still a reporter . . ." from Isabel Wilkerson, "Interviewing Sources," *Nieman Reports* 56 (2002): 17.

Index

Staples, William G., 180
Starr Report as narrative, x
Stembridge, Jane, 46
stereotypes: as obstacle to justice, 126–28,
167; personal storytelling and rejection
of, 86
Stone, Lawrence, 181
story. *See* narrative; personal stories; storytelling
storytellers: assumptions about, *xi–xii;* authority of, 106, 168; congress members
as, 143–50; credibility of, 2, 26–27; disadvantaged groups as, 83, 86–87, 90,
94, 107–8; scholars as, 179–87; states
(governments) as, 142; women as, 89,
94, 176, 177
storytelling: ambivalence toward, *x–xi,* 1–2,
4–5, 25, 27, 104, 106, 175–76, 181–82;
anecdotal evidence, 82, 119, 139–40; as
collaborative, 88–89, 96–97, 101–2,
107, 108, 132, 197n32; commemorative
function of, 104–5, 144, 149, 156, 159,
160–64, 176–77; common sense and,
21–22, 178; constraints on, 3–4, 7–8,
17, 21–28, 111–12, 117–18, 143, 150,
162–63, 165, 176–77; conventions of
narrative, *xii,* 3–4, 7–8, 17, 21–28, 111–
12, 117–18, 143, 163, 177; as corrective
to privileging of rationality, 82–83; creating new stakes in action, 52; as deceptive, *xi,* 2, 23, 24–25, 183, 204–5, 275;
in deliberation, 82–84, 86–108; disadvantaged groups and, *xii,* 3, 25, 83, 86–
87, 90, 94, 106, 107–8, 139–40, 176;
empathy with the other and, 82, 97–98,
107, 112, 127–28; false universality of
standards revealed by, 83, 107, 108, 167,
183; as "invited" during conversations,
93–94, 96, 97; literary sophistication
and, 129–30, 178, 183; as moral discourse, 2, 10, 12; new issues introduced
to deliberation through, 95–96; 9/11
and impulse toward, 12; as particular,
23–24, 83, 86–87; in policy-oriented
discussions, 102–4, 106, 107–8, 142,
144, 163, 176–77; popular beliefs about,
x, xi, 4, 21–24, 104–6, 178; *vs.* reason-
giving, 89, 176; social conditions and
efficacy of, 167; social status as discursive form, 84; sociology of, 4, 8, 168,
185; as strategic, 4, 34, 51–52, 139–40,

178–79; in strategic choice, 52, 60–62;
as subjective, 105–6; as supporting the
status quo, 15, 26, 87, 140, 163, 166;
vs. testimony, 214n13; verb tense shifts
in, 87, 131–32; as way of knowing, 11,
39, 140. *See also* conventions of narrative's use
strategic choice, 5, 29, 170; constraints on,
54–56, 170, 177; social movement
scholarship on, 53–55
strategic storytelling, 51–52, 177–79; as bid
for support, 34; constraints on, 177;
gender equity and, 139–40
structuralism, 14, 192n9; poststructuralism
and, 14–15
structure: defined, 195n22; *vs.* institution,
195n22; interests and, 5; in relation to
culture, 5, 15
Stryker, Robin, 180
student activists: adult involvement with,
32–33, 34, 36, 201n12; global contexts
for mobilization, 37; as prized social
identity, 36, 38; spontaneity as commitment of, 40–41, 45–47; as "tired," 41–
42, 174. *See also* Student Nonviolent
Coordinating Committee (SNCC)
Student Nonviolent Coordinating Committee (SNCC): Black Power and, 57–58, 74,
77–78; decline and collapse of, 77–78;
formation of, 46; internal debate over
direct action, 46–47; internal debate
over organizational form, 29, 57–58,
64–79, 170–71; interracial tensions in,
70–73; leadership styles and, 79–80;
loose structure linked to white "freedom
highs," 74–75, 79; McDew on sit-in
demonstrations and self-image, 43;
metonymic relations in discourse of,
57–58, 72, 79–81, 171; as model for
white student activism, 47, 78–79;
participatory democracy and, 62–63,
78; sit-in demonstrations and, 39, 52,
57
Students for a Democratic Society, 47, 78
Studies on the Left, 78
survivor stories: child abuse stories told by
adult survivors, 4, 18, 116, 117–18, 138;
domestic abuse and, 115–16, 139–40;
television talk shows and, 118; victims
and, 116
suspense, 39, 50